Regulating the Automobile

Studies in the Regulation of Economic Activity

Studies in the Regulation of Economic Activity

Regulating the Automobile

ROBERT W. CRANDALL

HOWARD K. GRUENSPECHT

THEODORE E. KEELER

LESTER B. LAVE

The Brookings Institution / Washington, D.C.

HD9710
U52
R39
1986

Library of Congress Cataloging in Publication data:

Crandall, Robert W.
  Regulating the automobile.
  Includes bibliographies and index.
    1. Automobiles—Law and legislation—United States.
2. Automobile industry and trade—Law and legislation—
United States.   3. Automobiles—United States.
4. Automobile industry and trade—United States.
I. Title.
KF2209.C73 1986   343.73'078629222   85-48171
ISBN 0-8157-1594-3   347.30378629222
ISBN 0-8157-1593-5 (pbk.)

9 8 7 6 5 4 3 2 1

THE BROOKINGS INSTITUTION is an independent organization devoted to nonpartisan research, education, and publication in economics, government, foreign policy, and the social sciences generally. Its principal purposes are to aid in the development of sound public policies and to promote public understanding of issues of national importance.

The Institution was founded on December 8, 1927, to merge the activities of the Institute for Government Research, founded in 1916, the Institute of Economics, founded in 1922, and the Robert Brookings Graduate School of Economics and Government, founded in 1924.

The Board of Trustees is responsible for the general administration of the Institution, while the immediate direction of the policies, program, and staff is vested in the President, assisted by an advisory committee of the officers and staff. The by-laws of the Institution state: "It is the function of the Trustees to make possible the conduct of scientific research, and publication, under the most favorable conditions, and to safeguard the independence of the research staff in the pursuit of their studies and in the publication of the results of such studies. It is not a part of their function to determine, control, or influence the conduct of particular investigations or the conclusions reached."

The President bears final responsibility for the decision to publish a manuscript as a Brookings book. In reaching his judgment on the competence, accuracy, and objectivity of each study, the President is advised by the director of the appropriate research program and weighs the views of a panel of expert outside readers who report to him in confidence on the quality of the work. Publication of a work signifies that it is deemed a competent treatment worthy of public consideration but does not imply endorsement of conclusions or recommendations.

The Institution maintains its position of neutrality on issues of public policy in order to safeguard the intellectual freedom of the staff. Hence interpretations or conclusions in Brookings publications should be understood to be solely those of the authors and should not be attributed to the Institution, to its trustees, officers, or other staff members, or to the organizations that support its research.

77428

Foreword

THE AUTOMOBILE has become the object of intense government regulation in the past two decades. In the mid-1960s the federal government began to impose safety standards on new automobiles—first on those sold to the federal government and then on all new cars. Federal emissions standards were first imposed on 1968 model automobiles and then tightened by Congress in 1970. In 1975 Congress legislated fuel economy standards for all new cars produced after the 1978 model year.

These three regulatory programs have often been the subject of controversy. In the mid-1970s the emissions control program was blamed for contributing to sharp reductions in vehicle performance. The fuel economy regulations are now being criticized as unduly strict in an era of declining gasoline prices. And the safety program has been continually embroiled in debates over air bags and impact-absorbing bumpers. These controversies often obscure a larger issue: whether these programs are serving their intended purpose at the lowest possible cost. This volume provides an empirical assessment of the costs and benefits of all three programs and analyzes their combined effects and the conflicts among them.

The authors conclude that the substantial costs of the three programs—as much as $2,200 per new automobile for safety and emissions controls alone—are greater than their benefits. All three programs concentrate solely on new automobiles, thereby postponing the replacement of dirty, unsafe, gas-guzzling older cars. Moreover, these regulatory programs have probably contributed to the growing quality gap between Japanese imports and U.S.-produced cars. The authors find that, of the three programs, only safety regulation appears to be generating benefits at least as great as the regulatory costs. They conclude that emissions regulation has become far too stringent and that fuel economy regulation is a seriously flawed approach to energy conservation.

Robert W. Crandall is a senior fellow in the Brookings Economic Studies program. Theodore E. Keeler and Lester B. Lave are former senior fellows at Brookings, and Howard K. Gruenspecht was a Brookings research fellow.

Keeler is now professor of economics at the University of California at Berkeley; Lave is James H. Higgins Professor of Economics and Gruenspecht is assistant professor of economics at the Carnegie-Mellon Graduate School of Industrial Administration.

The authors are indebted to Ann F. Friedlaender, John D. Graham, John E. Kwoka, Jr., Carl E. Nash, William A. Niskanen, Lloyd D. Orr, Sam Peltzman, Paul R. Portney, Leon S. Robertson, Benjamin Ward, and Clifford M. Winston for helpful comments on the manuscript. Research assistance was provided by Eliot L. Birnbaum, Gregory Call, Menzie D. Chinn, James D. Kole, David Parsley, Elizabeth Schneirov, and Val Vaden. Nancy Davidson edited the manuscript, and Carolyn Rutsch and Karen L. Fuller checked its factual accuracy. The index was prepared by Max Franke. The manuscript was typed by Lisa Saunders and Dee Koutris.

This is the twenty-third publication in the Brookings series of Studies in the Regulation of Economic Activity. The series presents the findings of a program of research focused on public policies toward business. The study was supported by grants from the National Science Foundation, the Alfred P. Sloan Foundation, the Ford Foundation, the Alex C. Walker Educational and Charitable Foundation, and the Andrew W. Mellon Foundation.

The views expressed here are those of the authors and should not be ascribed to the persons or foundations whose assistance is acknowledged above, or to the trustees, officers, or other staff members of the Brookings Institution.

BRUCE K. MAC LAURY
President

February 1986
Washington, D.C.

Contents

Tables

Figures

Regulating the Automobile

CHAPTER ONE

Overview

FEDERAL regulation of the automobile began in the mid-1960s when the government began to impose safety and emissions standards upon new vehicles. Throughout the 1970s these standards were either extended or tightened substantially. These standards imposed substantial costs upon the vehicle producers and, presumably, the final consumers of automobile services, but until the 1970s these costs seemed relatively minor compared with the harmful externalities they sought to control.

The economic climate of the 1970s was quite different, both domestically and in the rest of the world, from that of the 1960s. Two oil shocks, declining productivity growth, and accelerating inflation made the public and policymakers more aware of the costs of regulation. Nevertheless, Congress extended the regulatory reach of the federal government even further into automobile product decisions by enacting minimum fleet-average fuel economy standards as part of the Energy Policy and Conservation Act of 1975. Moreover, emissions control requirements continued to be tightened through the 1981 model year.

By the late 1970s the costs of safety, emissions, and fuel economy regulation began to emerge as a major issue because of the troubled state of the auto industry. Japanese imports surged in 1979 after the second oil shock. The U.S. economy plunged into a recession in 1980 and again in 1982, and the automobile industry plunged with it. As a soaring dollar made Japanese import competition even more intense, President Reagan negotiated quotas with the Japanese government. But there was very little relaxation of automobile regulation, either in Congress or in the administration. A few regulations were rescinded, but the most important of these rescissions were in turn reversed by the courts.

Much of the regulatory fervor of the 1960s and 1970s that was directed at the automobile was a reflection of deep public distrust of the industry. The industry was saddled with tight deadlines to meet stringent regulatory requirements in order to "force" technology that some believed would not emerge by any other route. Much of this fervor has subsided. It is now

1

possible to look back over nearly two decades of experience to evaluate this strategy of regulating the undesirable by-products of the automobile and to determine whether some of the regulatory programs should be redesigned. This book is designed to provide a comprehensive examination of the combined effects of all three types of regulatory policies safety, emissions, and fuel economy. We examine the costs and benefits of each policy and provide an integrated assessment of the combined effects of all three policies upon air quality, safety, fuel consumption, and product quality.

The Current Regulatory Framework

Although some may argue that regulatory policies have been designed to discourage automobile use, it is clear that Congress has opted to try to civilize this mode of transportation rather than to encourage wholesale substitution for it. The three major types of social regulation affecting the automobile industry are air pollution standards, safety standards, and fuel economy regulation. The major legislation providing for such regulation is contained in the Clean Air Act Amendments of 1970 and 1977, the National Traffic and Motor Vehicle Safety Act of 1966, the Motor Vehicle Information and Cost Savings Act of 1972, and the Energy Policy and Conservation Act of 1975.[1] The Environmental Protection Agency (EPA) administers the Clean Air Act provisions, the National Highway Traffic Safety Administration (NHTSA) administers the safety standards, and the secretary of transportation is responsible for fuel economy standards.

Air Pollution

Unlike most social regulations, emissions standards for automobiles are set by Congress, not an executive branch agency. The 1970 Clean Air Act Amendments originally set very ambitious goals for the reduction of emissions of hydrocarbons, carbon monoxide, and oxides of nitrogen. Each was to be reduced by 90 or 95 percent of the average levels in 1968 automobiles. The carbon monoxide and hydrocarbon standards were to be 3.4 and 0.41 grams per mile, respectively, by 1975, while the nitrogen

1. 42 U.S.C. 7401; 15 U.S.C. 1392; 15 U.S.C. 2001; and 89 Stat. 871.

oxide standard was to be 0.4 grams per mile by 1976.[2] These deadlines were not achieved, as vehicle manufacturers successfully persuaded first the EPA and then Congress to delay their implementation. In the 1977 Clean Air Act Amendments, Congress modified the emissions standards. The original hydrocarbon and carbon monoxide standards were put off until the 1980 model year, and the nitrogen oxide standard was raised to 2.0 grams per mile through 1980 and 1.0 grams per mile for 1981 and beyond. The 0.4 gram standard was relegated to a "research" goal.

The EPA has the responsibility for making sure that the pollution control systems installed to meet these standards do not degrade rapidly in use. These systems must be certified to work for 50,000 miles. Furthermore, a program for periodic inspection and maintenance is required for areas that failed to attain air quality standards by the end of 1982.

Safety

Unlike the emissions standards, safety standards are set by an executive branch agency—the National Highway Traffic Safety Administration. NHTSA promulgates vehicle safety standards and is empowered to order recalls for vehicle defects that create serious safety problems. Most of NHTSA's standards are performance standards requiring vehicles to meet some minimum safety standard under various operating conditions. Others, such as the bumper standard, are less related to occupant safety than to an attempt to reduce repair bills resulting from collisions. Among the most controversial issues before NHTSA is the passive restraint requirement—requiring the installation of either passive seat belts or air bags—which has been before the agency and the courts for sixteen years. All told, there are more than fifty separate standards for passenger vehicles.

Fuel Economy

Congress included in the 1975 Energy Policy and Conservation Act Amendments a set of corporate average fuel economy (CAFE) standards for new cars produced in the United States. These standards require vehicle manufacturers to achieve a sales-weighted fleet-average fuel economy of 27.5 miles per gallon in the 1985 model year. The secretary of transportation set interim standards of 22 miles per gallon for 1981, 24 mpg for

2. Lawrence J. White, *The Regulation of Air Pollutant Emissions from Motor Vehicles* (Washington, D.C.: American Enterprise Institute, 1982), p. 21.

1982, 26 mpg for 1983, and 27 mpg for 1984.[3] The secretary has the authority to modify the standards for the 1986 model year and beyond, and has reduced the 1986 standard to 26.0 mpg. Only cars manufactured in the United States may be used by domestic companies in computing the corporatewide fuel economy for the purposes of these regulations. They also apply to foreign companies' exports to the United States.

In addition to CAFE standards, the Department of Transportation is ordered to police the requirement that states enforce the speed limit of 55 miles per hour by cutting off federal highway funds to states with lax enforcement programs. This sanction has never been used despite considerable evidence of frequent violations. Finally, Congress enacted "gas-guzzler" taxes to be imposed as manufacturers' excise taxes on automobiles failing to achieve a minimum level of fuel efficiency.

The Effects of Regulation

Obviously, each statute requiring federal regulation of the automobile is designed to force automobile manufacturers to provide some attribute—emissions control, safety, or fuel economy—to a greater degree than the market would dictate. In the case of emissions, individuals might demand very little control on their own cars while wanting other cars controlled. For fuel economy, however, individuals could be expected to demand more fuel-efficient cars as gasoline prices rose even if such cars were more expensive. Safety is an intermediate case: individuals probably have at least a rough assessment of their own exposure to risk from a collision, but they might not guard against exposing others to danger.

An obvious question to ask for each program is whether regulation has succeeded in reducing the undesired by-product or externality that it addresses. Has safety regulation actually reduced highway deaths? Is the air cleaner because of federal vehicle emissions standards? Although fuel consumption is not an externality in the usual sense, one might ask if cars are more fuel efficient due to federal fuel economy standards than they would otherwise have been.

Examining the impact of regulation on each of these by-products of automobile use is not an easy task. Regulations that require cars to be safer could lead drivers to operate their cars less safely, thus offsetting the

3. U.S. Regulatory Council, *The Automobile Calendar: Recent and Pending Federal Activities Affecting Motor Vehicles* (Government Printing Office, 1981), p. 372.

favorable effects of regulation upon occupant safety. Federally mandated speed limits also enhance safety and could be difficult to separate from the effects of direct regulation designed for crash protection.

Similarly, the automobile is only one of many sources of air pollution. Regulating the automobile without similar controls on other sources or even other transportation modes might prove quite ineffectual. Unfortunately, the reduction of emissions does not necessarily create a proportional improvement in air quality. Reducing one of the precursors of photochemical smog—hydrocarbons or nitrogen oxides—might be ineffectual without the appropriate reduction of the other. Finally, an automobile is used for approximately 100,000 miles over a period of more than a decade. The emissions and safety devices can fail long before the automobile is scrapped. Thus simply requiring more sophisticated emissions control devices on new cars may not even reduce emissions over the life of the automobile.

Even if it is possible to demonstrate a positive effect of regulation, it is by no means clear that the current federal approach to regulation is the most efficacious of all options. Forcing technology on automobile manufacturers with accompanying tight deadlines greatly complicates product development decisions. If regulation were targeted more toward results than engineering design, safety and emissions regulation might be more effective and product design changes might be accomplished more smoothly. The recent quality problems experienced by U.S. automobile manufacturers may well have been exacerbated by the piling up of regulatory standards during periods of intense product redesign following the oil shocks.

Fuel economy regulation might work to increase fuel economy when the government is simultaneously suppressing oil prices, but it seems a strangely contradictory and inefficient method of accomplishing conservation. The deregulation (and subsequent increase) of oil and gasoline prices obviously reduced the need for such regulation. However, as new car buyers responded to declining gasoline prices in 1983–85, fuel economy regulation once again became a binding constraint upon product design and pricing decisions.

Finally, each type of regulation is likely to impose some costs upon automobile producers that are reflected in auto prices. These higher prices, in turn, discourage new car purchases, thereby keeping more of the older, gas-guzzling, polluting, and unsafe vehicles on the road. In this respect, a very tight "technology-forcing" schedule of regulations is likely to be counterproductive for a number of years, greatly reducing vehicle sales and thereby delaying the progress toward cleaner, safer, and more fuel-efficient cars. When this effect is combined with the impact of tight deadlines on product quality, the result is high-priced problem cars that consumers reject.

The Costs of Regulation

Clearly, the principal costs of regulation are those of the design and production required to meet the various standards. In principle, these costs should be easy to identify, but they can prove difficult to measure. First, it is difficult to separate the costs of any system designed both to provide automobile services and to meet a given regulatory standard. For example, electronic equipment may improve an ignition system and simultaneously allow manufacturers to meet emissions standards (when combined with other equipment), but allocating the costs between improved ignition systems and emissions control is inherently rather arbitrary.

A second problem in measuring the costs of regulation derives from the technology forcing so prevalent in the regulatory approach required by Congress. New devices can be very costly to design into current models but much less expensive to incorporate into major vehicle redesigns. If headrests cost, say, $30 per car in the mid-1970s, they may now cost only $20 because manufacturers have learned how to incorporate them into new cars more efficiently in the past decade. Since some regulations have been in force since 1968, one cannot simply estimate their initial cost and inflate the estimate by the inflation that has occurred in the interim. Indeed, it is even possible that some regulations add nothing to the cost of current models even through they were initially quite expensive to incorporate into vehicle models of the 1960s.

The cost of one regulation has to include its effect upon other attributes of the automobile that are themselves subject to regulation. Safety regulation increases vehicle weight, which in turn reduces fuel economy. Requiring major reductions in emissions controls may also reduce fuel economy and make it more difficult for the producers to achieve their mandated fleet averages.

Certain costs of regulation are irreversible. Once expenditures have been made to redesign a car to meet a given engineering standard, rescinding this regulation may not allow a very large portion of this cost to be avoided in future models. If dashboards or steering columns have to be redesigned for safety reasons, it is unlikely that they will be redesigned once more if these safety standards are rescinded.

Finally, there is an intangible cost of regulation that is difficult to measure. If automobile performance is reduced along any measurable dimension due to regulation, this reduction in quality can be identified and given a value. But if cumulative regulation reduces product reliability, this reduction may be difficult to measure. Given the recent experience of Detroit with product recalls and other quality problems, one cannot eliminate the possibility that regulation has contributed to declining product quality. This issue deserves much closer attention than it typically receives in the literature on regulation.

A Summary of the Study

The effects of regulation upon the automobile industry cannot be understood without examining the devastating effects of recent economic events upon the industry. Chapter 2 attempts a cursory review of the recent roller-coaster ride of the industry in terms of sales, profits, import penetration, and product offerings. The difficulties of the 1980–82 period and the recent protection afforded by import quotas provide two contrasting environments in which policymakers were asked for regulatory changes.

The costs of safety and emissions regulation are detailed in chapter 3. This chapter places existing engineering information in a somewhat more refined analytical perspective and provides a new econometric approach for estimating the full costs of regulation. It shows that by 1981 safety and emissions regulation was adding between $1,300 and $2,200 to the present value of the costs of owning and operating an automobile. These costs are passed on to automobile consumers, who have reduced their rate of purchase of new automobiles as a result.

The effects of safety regulation upon the highway fatality rate are examined in chapter 4. A rather detailed econometric examination reveals that automobiles have become much safer for their occupants since regulation began in 1966, but there is some evidence of an increase in the risk to pedestrians and bicyclists.

Chapter 5 reviews the results of nearly two decades of emissions controls in automobiles. The rapid pace of technology forcing has forced vehicle manufacturers to design control systems that have proved to degrade in use. As a result, although automobile emissions have been reduced, they have not been reduced as dramatically as the legislative standards would suggest. Moreover, the performance penalties and the high cost of the emissions controls have reduced new car sales, inducing motorists to keep high-emissions vehicles on the road much longer. There is very little evidence that the emissions reductions that have been achieved have actually improved air quality; hence the high costs of this program do not seem to be justified.

Fuel economy regulation is reviewed in chapter 6. It appears that CAFE standards had very little effect upon fuel economy during 1975–81 as U.S. producers reacted to higher gasoline prices. Since 1981, however, CAFE has become a binding constraint distorting vehicle-manufacturing decisions. To the extent that it is thought to be desirable to encourage energy conservation beyond that chosen by motorists at current or future gasoline prices, it would be much more efficient to obtain it through higher gasoline taxes.

Chapter 7 reviews the evidence on the conflicts among the three types of regulation—safety, emissions, and fuel economy. Clearly, safety regulation and emissions controls have penalized fuel efficiency. Similarly, CAFE compromises safety by encouraging the producers to offer smaller cars. The dynamic effects of regulation may be more important. Focusing all emissions, safety, and fuel economy regulation on new cars increases the price of new cars sharply, thereby postponing replacement decisions and keeping gas-guzzling, dirty, and unsafe older cars on the road much longer. In addition, the rapid yet uncertain pace of regulation has apparently had a deleterious effect upon engineering and quality control. The U.S. car producers have suffered large declines in the reliability of their cars relative to Japanese imports, and these declines are correlated with increases in regulatory costs for some companies.

CHAPTER TWO

The Automobile Industry in Transition

IN THE past fifteen years, the automobile industry has been buffeted by enormous changes that industry executives could not have foreseen. In the 1950s and the early 1960s, the industry settled down into a rather comfortable oligopoly of three major firms and one minor producer, with relatively little to fear from foreign competition. Imports were generally less than 10 percent of domestic sales, in large part because U.S. gasoline prices and driving conditions differed markedly from those in Europe (or, later, in Japan). Despite rapidly rising wage costs, the industry's profitability remained substantially above the profit rate for all U.S. manufacturing. In the late 1960s, however, this stable oligopoly began to run into some foul weather. Profits began to fluctuate wildly, imports rose steadily, and government regulation began to play an important role in the industry.

In the 1970s, the climate went from bad to worse. Already feeling the increased competition from imports, the industry was first subjected to price controls and then to extremely unstable energy prices. The 1973–74 Arab oil embargo and the government regulation of energy prices that followed created an unpredictable environment for product planning. Regulation kept gasoline prices below world market levels during a period in which the government simultaneously established fuel economy standards. After the second oil shock of 1978–79, imports soared, particularly those from Japan. By 1980 the industry had discovered that it could not compete with the Japanese in the production of small cars. Not only were the Japanese vehicles increasingly attractive to American buyers because of their performance, fuel efficiency, and general appearance, but studies began to show a shockingly large cost advantage for the Japanese.[1]

1. Harbour and Associates, *Analysis of the Japanese Landed Cost Advantage for the Manufacture of Subcompact Cars* (Berkley, Mich.: Harbour and Associates, 1982), p. 52. See also National Academy of Sciences, *The Competitive Status of the U.S. Auto Industry* (National Academy Press, 1982), pp. 169–88.

In 1980 the Ford Motor Company and the United Auto Workers filed petitions for import relief with the International Trade Commission (ITC).[2] Congress began to consider a domestic content bill that would effectively require large Japanese producers to build their American models in the United States. Even though the ITC rejected Ford's request for protection and Congress failed to pass the domestic content bill, President Reagan imposed "voluntary quotas" on the Japanese in 1981–85. Operating behind a protective shield, the industry's profits soared. But the fear remains that U.S. producers cannot compete with the Japanese in at least the smaller range of vehicle sizes and that the Japanese may be in the process of extending their advantage to the intermediate-size cars.

Market Structure

By 1965 the U.S. automobile industry had settled down into a triopoly with one fringe firm—American Motors. In the previous two decades, a number of smaller firms competed with the Big Three (Chrysler, Ford, and General Motors), but most of these firms either left the industry, encountered bankruptcy, or merged into American Motors. By 1966 the Big Three accounted for 97 percent of domestic automobile production.[3]

Two developments have severely weakened the hold of the Big Three companies since 1966. First, imports began to rise rapidly in the late 1960s (table 2-1), fueled by both lower prices and the improving quality of European and Japanese cars. Second, the oil shocks of the 1970s increased the demand for fuel-efficient cars and led to a second surge in imports. The share of imports was held below 30 percent only by the voluntary export restraint agreement with the Japanese in 1981–85.

The rising volume of imports occurred during a period of rapid change in the world automobile industry. In 1970, 59 percent of U.S. import sales were from Germany and only 24 percent were from Japan. A decade later, 79 percent were from Japan and only 13 percent were from Germany.[4] The Japanese production of motor vehicles actually surpassed U.S. pro-

2. U.S. International Trade Commission, *Certain Motor Vehicles and Certain Chassis and Bodies Therefor, Report to the President on Investigation TA-201-44* (USITC, December 1980).

3. Robert F. Lanzilloti, "The Automobile Industry," in Walter Adams, ed., *The Structure of American Industry,* 4th ed. (Macmillan, 1971), p. 264.

4. Motor Vehicle Manufacturers Association, *MVMA Motor Vehicle Facts and Figures '82* (Detroit: MVMA, 1982), p. 18.

Table 2-1. Import Penetration of U.S. Automobile Market, 1960–84
Hundreds of thousands unless otherwise indicated

Year	Total new car registrations	Imports	Import share (percent)
1960	6.58	0.50	7.60
1961	5.85	0.38	6.50
1962	6.94	0.34	4.90
1963	7.56	0.39	5.16
1964	8.07	0.48	5.95
1965	9.31	0.57	6.12
1966	9.01	0.66	7.33
1967	8.36	0.78	9.33
1968	9.40	0.99	10.53
1969	9.45	1.06	11.22
1970	8.39	1.23	14.66
1971	9.83	1.29	13.12
1972	10.49	1.53	14.59
1973	11.35	1.72	15.15
1974	8.70	1.37	15.75
1975	8.26	1.50	18.16
1976	9.75	1.45	14.87
1977	10.93	1.98	18.28
1978	10.95	1.95	17.81
1979	10.36	2.35	22.68
1980	8.76	2.47	28.20
1981	8.44	2.43	28.79
1982	7.75	2.27	29.29
1983	8.92	2.46	27.58
1984	10.12	2.52	24.90

Source: *Automotive News: Market Data Book, 1985*, p. 26.

duction for the first time in 1980, a remarkable feat given the fact that the Japanese industry barely existed in 1960.[5]

As the German role in world automobile exports waned, a German company—Volkswagen—decided to build a production facility in the United States. Attracted by very favorable terms from the Commonwealth of Pennsylvania, VW began production at its western Pennsylvania plant in 1978. This facility has not lived up to expectations because the public demand for its principal product—the Rabbit—weakened. As a result, VW has never produced more than 180,000 cars a year in the United States.[6]

The Japanese have recently begun to invest in assembly facilities in the

5. *Automotive News: 1982 Market Data Book*, p. 2.
6. MVMA, *MVMA Motor Vehicle Facts and Figures '82*, p. 11.

United States. Toyota has had a small presence in Southern California to assemble truck chassis and bodies. In 1982 Honda began to produce Accords in Marysville, Ohio. Nissan has built a truck plant in Smyrna, Tennessee, and has recently decided to expand its output to include automobiles. Toyota has formed a joint venture with General Motors, using GM's Fremont, California, plant, and will build its own plant in the United States in the late 1980s. Toyo Kogyo (Mazda) has announced its intentions to build a U.S. assembly plant in Flat Rock, Michigan, and Mitsubishi will build a plant with Chrysler in central Illinois.[7]

Other foreign companies have also taken a more active role in the U.S. market. Renault now has almost a 50 percent interest in American Motors. This investment has allowed it to begin producing one of its subcompacts in the United States. Peugeot has been involved in coproduction arrangements with Chrysler; Mitsubishi has supplied Chrysler with subcompact cars; and Isuzu and Suzuki have similar relationships with General Motors.[8]

As recently as 1971, one economist could lament the market power of the Big Three automobile companies in the United States and even argue for antitrust action to improve market performance.[9] Since that time, however, the surge in imports and the decisions of seven major foreign competitors (Renault, Mazda, Toyota, Honda, Nissan, Mitsubishi, and Volkswagen) to enter into production in the United States have served as competitive spurs to the domestic industry. This import penetration and new entry, combined with volatile gasoline prices, changing consumer tastes, and severe product quality problems have so reduced the Big Three's power that one member (Chrysler) had to secure government loan guarantees to stave off bankruptcy and another (Ford) hinted at abandoning U.S. automobile production altogether.

In short, the past fifteen years have been a period of enormous upheaval in Detroit. Even if there had been no change in government policy from the early postwar period, the major automobile companies would have had significant problems of cost, production quality, and consumer acceptance as they adjusted to a world of higher energy prices. But government policy

7. "Another Turn of the Wheel: A Survey of the World's Motor Industry," *The Economist*, vol. 294 (March 2, 1985), pp. 6–7; *Automotive News*, June 10, 1985, p. 3; and *Automotive News*, October 14, 1985, p. 2.

8. "Another Turn of the Wheel."

9. Lawrence J. White, *The Automobile Industry since 1945* (Harvard University Press, 1971), p. 284.

changed dramatically in the late 1960s, and the auto companies were faced with new safety and emissions requirements, compounding the challenge ahead. After 1975 they were also subjected to mandatory fuel-efficiency standards. Had these requirements been imposed upon a healthy industry, they might have been absorbed fairly easily, if not willingly. The other difficulties faced by the industry in the 1970s, however, have made these requirements much more onerous and controversial.

Automobile Sales

By at least one measure, the U.S. motor vehicle industry enjoyed a relatively stable environment in the 1970s. In only two years, 1970 and 1975, were factory sales of motor vehicles below 10 million units. Passenger-car sales averaged nearly 8.5 million units from 1975 through 1979, almost exactly the average rate of sales in 1965–69.[10] After a mild decline in the early 1970s, domestic auto sales returned to about the late 1960s level. Although there was no long-term growth in the sales of U.S.-produced automobiles, at least there was no evidence of secular decline. Underneath this relatively tranquil exterior of factory sales trends, however, more serious problems were lurking. The price of gasoline rose much more rapidly than the general price level in the 1970s, driven initially by the effects of the 1973–74 Arab oil embargo (figure 2-1). This led consumers to begin to shift away from larger, powerful cars to lighter, more fuel-efficient vehicles. This shift was erratic in 1975–78 because U.S. policy suppressed gasoline prices in the face of OPEC oil price increases, but after 1978 and the second oil price shock, it was almost a stampede. For instance, in 1970, 87 percent of all passenger cars produced in the United States had eight-cylinder engines, and the remainder had six-cylinder engines (table 2-2). By 1977, three years after the Arab oil embargo, the share of eight-cylinder cars was still 76 percent, with four-cylinder cars accounting for 6 percent and six-cylinder vehicles the remainder. By 1980 the bottom had fallen out of the eight-cylinder market; fewer than one-third of U.S. passenger cars were so equipped.

Similarly, the average weight of U.S.-produced passenger cars changed dramatically in the late 1970s after two decades of gradual increase. In 1960 the average U.S.-produced car weighed 3,384 pounds (table 2-3). By

10. MVMA, *MVMA Motor Vehicle Facts and Figures '82*, p. 9.

Figure 2-1. Consumer Price Indexes for Motor Fuel and New Automobiles, 1960–84

Price indexes (1967 = 100)

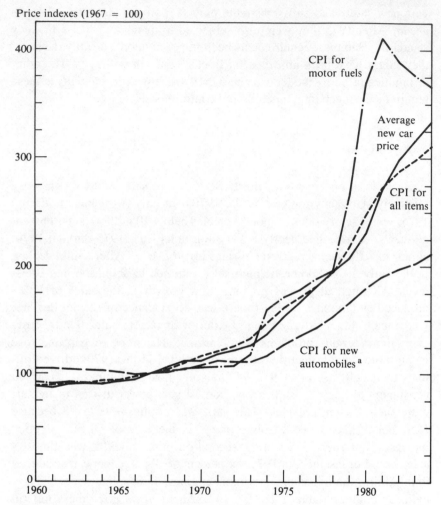

Sources: *Economic Report of the President, February 1985;* and Motor Vehicle Manufacturers Association, *MVMA Motor Vehicle Facts and Figures '84.*
a. Adjusted for changes in quality by the Bureau of Labor Statistics.

1970 it had grown to 3,664 pounds. The average weight continued to rise through 1972. Beginning in 1977, however, the weight began to decline, falling to 2,868 pounds in 1980 as all U.S. producers rushed downsized, front-wheel-drive vehicles onto the market.[11]

11. These estimates are based upon analysis of leading model lines and sales weights from 1947 to 1982. Recent EPA data on new vehicle weight are somewhat higher, but

Table 2-2. U.S. Automobile Production, by Number of Cylinders, Selected Model
Years, 1965–84
Percent

	Cylinders		
Year	4	6	8
1965	0.0	26.6	73.4
1970	0.3	12.8	86.9
1971	7.2	12.3	80.5
1972	9.4	10.8	79.8
1973	8.6	9.9	81.5
1974	12.7	18.7	68.6
1975	8.5	18.9	72.6
1976	10.3	20.9	68.8
1977	6.3	17.9	75.8
1978	10.2	23.9	65.9
1979	17.4	23.6	59.0
1980	31.4	36.5	32.1
1981	39.9	33.2	26.9
1982	41.4	30.3	28.3
1983	38.7	29.1	32.2
1984	45.1	26.8	28.1

Source: *Ward's Automotive Yearbook, 1985*, p. 35.

Further corroboration of this trend may be found in the data on size classes. In 1970 three-fourths of all U.S.-produced passenger cars were intermediate, standard, or luxury models. By 1978 this share had fallen to less than two-thirds, but the wave of new subcompact models in the 1979–81 period reduced the share of the bigger cars to less than one-half. By 1981 compacts and subcompacts accounted for 51 percent of U.S.-produced cars.[12] Thus lighter, smaller cars with four or six cylinders began to dominate the U.S. market as the 1980s dawned.

It was the shift to small cars after 1978 that left the domestic industry gasping. Imports soared as consumers turned to the smaller vehicles. New model introductions by Chrysler (the K car), Ford (the Escort), and GM (the X car and the J car) failed to stem the tide of imports. The shift in the sales mix placed the U.S. industry directly into competition with an array of European and Japanese cars that offered much better performance and reliability than the new U.S. models. Forced to rush these newer lines to

exhibit the same trend. See R. M. Heavenrich and others, "Passenger Car Fuel Economy . . . Trends thru 1984," U.S. Environmental Protection Agency paper 840499 (EPA, 1984), p. 4.

12. *Automotive News: 1982 Market Data Book,* p. 18.

Table 2-3. Estimated Average Weight of U.S. Passenger Cars, Selected Model Years, 1960–82
Pounds

Year	New passenger cars (domestic only)	All passenger cars on the road
1960	3,384	3,363
1965	3,449	3,364
1970	3,664	3,389
1971	3,702	3,394
1972	4,026	3,422
1973	3,933	3,462
1974	3,844	3,492
1975	3,885	3,496
1976	3,908	3,507
1977	3,695	3,516
1978	3,422	3,500
1979	3,306	3,455
1980	2,868	3,400
1981	2,757	3,339
1982	2,817	3,302

Source: Authors' calculations based on the model run output from *Automotive News: Market Data Book,* various years; scrappage rates from Motor Vehicle Manufacturers Association, *MVMA Motor Vehicle Facts and Figures '82,* p. 28; and specifications from *Ward's Automotive Yearbook,* various years, and *Automotive News: Market Data Book,* various years.

market, the U.S. companies were apparently unable to develop the quality control and "fit and finish" of their foreign rivals. As a result, by 1980 Ford was reduced to asking for trade protection from the Japanese, and Chrysler had been led through a government-directed reorganization.

Since 1981 consumers have shifted back once more to the larger, more powerful cars in response to the 21 percent decline in real gasoline prices between 1981 and 1984. Compact and subcompact cars accounted for only 42 percent of the market in 1984, but the larger cars were much lighter and more fuel efficient than their predecessors of the 1970s. The shift back to larger cars placed Ford and GM in the difficult position of producing the cars that consumers desire, but not being able to meet the mandated fuel economy standards if they satisfy this demand.

Profitability

In the 1960s the major automobile companies enjoyed high and relatively stable returns on capital. Despite low rates of U.S. economic growth until the Vietnam era, the industry managed to keep its after-tax return on equity between 11.4 and 19.5 percent (figure 2-2). Beginning in 1970,

Figure 2-2. Regulatory Costs, Import Share, and Profit Rates in the U.S. Automobile Industry, 1960–84

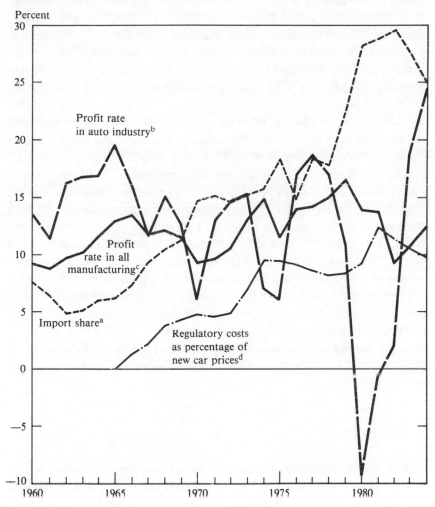

Sources: *Automotive News: Market Data Book,* various years; U.S. Bureau of the Census, *Quarterly Financial Report,* various issues; data provided by the Bureau of Economic Analysis; and authors' calculations based on table 3-5.

a. Imports as a percentage of U.S. new passenger-car registrations.

b. After-tax return on equity for SIC 371, motor vehicles and equipment.

c. After-tax return on equity for all manufacturing.

d. Cost of equipment·only, with 5 percent learning curve (see table 3-5), as a percentage of the average retail price of a new domestic automobile.

however, the industry's profit rate began to fluctuate widely. Moreover, the average profit rate fell from about 15 percent to 10 percent in the early 1970s. But even worse days were ahead.

With the change to smaller cars came far greater import competition and therefore lower profit margins. Despite a relatively strong year in

1979, profits fell dramatically from an average of 17 percent (after tax) on equity to less than 11 percent. At the same time the profitability of manufacturing in general actually rose. In 1980 and 1981, the auto industry found its sales declining by about one-third from the 1977–78 average. Passenger car demand declined because of the 1980 recession, but the demand for U.S.-produced cars fell even further as consumers switched to imported models. The 1982 recession, combined with a sharp rise in the dollar, compounded the producers' problems. As a result, profit rates for the domestic assemblers in 1980–82 were not only volatile, but generally negative. In just twenty years, the industry had been transformed from a model of stable oligopoly to an industry under severe duress.

The combination of high interest rates, recession, and rising import penetration led the Reagan administration to negotiate "voluntary" quotas with the Japanese in 1981. These quotas limited Japanese imports to 1.68 million cars per year through 1984 and 1.85 million cars in 1984–85. The result of these quotas has been to increase U.S. producers' market share and to allow them price increases greater than those that would have been otherwise attainable.[13] Not surprisingly, these quotas combined with the recovery in the U.S. demand for passenger cars to provide the Big Three with record nominal after-tax profits in 1983 and 1984. In fact, real profits per vehicle in 1983 were 50 percent higher than in 1975, a year of similar domestic car sales. These quotas were relaxed in March 1985, however, so the industry's profitability could decline substantially in the next few years.

Regulation

It would be difficult to attribute most of the industry's recent problems and its low profitability in 1980–82 to government regulation, but the timing of the shift in profitability in the late 1960s is at least prima facie grounds for further investigation. The costs of safety regulation appear to have increased steadily in the late 1960s and to have accelerated dramatically in the 1974 model year (see chapter 3). The costs of emissions controls were modest until 1972, but surged in 1972–73 and then receded somewhat in the 1975 model year with the adoption of catalysts (figure 2-3). Meeting the 1980–81 emissions standards provided an even greater

13. See Robert W. Crandall, "Import Quotas and the Automobile Industry: The Costs of Protection," *Brookings Review,* vol. 2 (Summer 1984), pp. 8–16.

Figure 2-3. Equipment Costs of Federal Automobile Safety and Emissions Standards, 1966–84

Cost per car in 1980 dollars

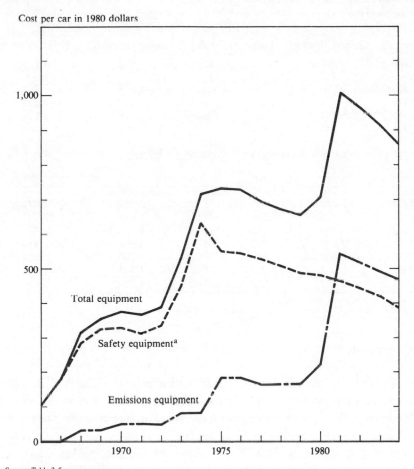

Source: Table 3-5.
a. With 5 percent learning curve.

increase in equipment costs than those occasioned by the 1972–73 standards. The average return on equity in the U.S. automobile industry did not return to its 1965 rate until 1983, when the Japanese quotas began to have a major impact upon vehicle prices. While most of the costs of these regulatory programs have undoubtedly been passed on to consumers, the effect upon demand and therefore upon the profits of the producers may have been substantial (see chapter 7).

Table 2-4. Expenditures on Special Tooling by Three Largest U.S. Automobile Producers, Selected Years, 1960–84
Millions of dollars

Year	General Motors	Ford	Chrysler	Total (current dollars)	Total (1972 dollars)[a]
1960	615	202	85	902	1,136
1965	730	367	157	1,254	1,356
1970	1,149	484	242	1,875	2,012
1971	631	430	136	1,197	1,231
1972	899	463	166	1,528	1,528
1973	941	594	298	1,833	1,801
1974	1,096	619	242	1,957	1,790
1975	1,036	342	220	1,958	1,266
1976	1,308	504	197	2,007	1,499
1977	1,776	673	337	2,786	1,976
1978	1,827	970	333	3,139	2,091
1979	2,015	1,288	342	3,645	2,295
1980	2,600	1,185	395	4,180	2,472
1981	3,178	970	214	4,362	2,430
1982	2,601	1,362	227	4,190	2,288
1983	2,084	975	415	3,473	1,899
1984	2,452	1,223	447	4,123	2,216

Source: Annual reports of the companies.
a. Using GNP implicit nonresidential business equipment deflator. Figures are rounded.

Investment

A very large share of investment in the automobile industry is devoted to special tools designed for a given make and model. Even without the disruptive influences of escalating oil prices, changing consumer tastes, or government regulation, periodic model changes require substantial investment in new special tooling. Expenditures on this tooling are almost as high as all other capital expenditures by the major automobile companies.

The increased competitive pressures from imports and the change in consumer tastes during the late 1970s generated substantial pressure for redesigning the U.S. assemblers' model lines. As a result, expenditures on tooling by the three major U.S. producers rose sharply in the late 1970s (table 2-4). During this period, the number of new front-wheel-drive vehicles offered by these companies expanded rapidly, and even the rear-wheel-drive vehicles were downsized and made lighter for fuel efficiency. Since 1981, however, real expenditures on tooling have declined substantially.

Total investment in the motor vehicle industry demonstrates a similar pattern (table 2-5, columns 2 and 4). In the mid-1960s, as demand

Table 2-5. Investment Expenditures of U.S. Automobile Industry, 1960–84
Millions of dollars

	Gross investment in motor vehicle industry [a]		Gross investment expenditures by U.S. motor vehicle and equipment producers [b]	
	Current dollars	1972 dollars	Current dollars	1972 dollars
Year	(1)	(2)	(3)	(4)
1960	1,000	1,390	1,470	2,040
1961	730	1,012	1,380	1,910
1962	854	1,176	1,450	2,000
1963	1,137	1,546	1,820	2,460
1964	1,496	1,999	2,480	3,330
1965	1,852	2,455	3,000	3,980
1966	1,897	2,406	3,130	4,030
1967	1,589	1,945	2,850	3,530
1968	1,606	1,879	2,670	3,150
1969	1,880	2,123	2,990	3,370
1970	1,854	1,971	3,050	3,260
1971	1,322	1,359	2,420	2,490
1972	1,841	1,841	3,000	3,000
1973	1,521	1,465	3,830	3,710
1974	2,374	2,077	4,290	3,820
1975	1,872	1,389	3,330	2,540
1976	2,076	1,461	3,600	2,610
1977	3,377	2,197	5,820	3,960
1978	4,042	2,437	7,190	4,570
1979	4,345	2,342	8,340	4,810
1980	5,221	2,515	9,020	4,770
1981	7,417	3,245	9,830	4,860
1982	n.a.	n.a.	7,770	3,780
1983	n.a.	n.a.	7,290	3,560
1984	n.a.	n.a.	11,110	5,340

Sources: U.S. Department of Commerce, Office of Business Analysis; capital stock data from U.S. Census establishment data; U.S. Department of Commerce, *Survey of Current Business*, vol. 65 (February 1985), table 7, and vol. 65 (April 1985), p. 22.
n.a. Not available.
a. Includes only those establishments that are in Standard Industrial Classification 371.
b. Includes all companies whose principal activity is automobile production.

strengthened, the industry increased its capital outlays sharply. In 1965 and 1966 real capital expenditures were double the 1960–62 level. Thereafter investment receded somewhat until the recovery from the 1975 recession and the drive to meet the new consumer demands for small cars generated a substantial increase in real investment spending. In 1978–81 the average real capital outlays for the industry were nearly 50 percent above their level in the early part of the decade.

It is difficult to identify surges in investment caused by safety or emissions regulation. The surge in investment in 1965–66 antedates the major regulatory requirements imposed by the National Highway Traffic Safety Administration by more than two years. This rise in investment could have been associated with the development of General Services Administration safety standards in 1965–66 or the 1967 California emissions standards. A major increase in emissions and safety equipment costs occurred in 1973–75. Finally, in 1980–81 emissions equipment costs rose sharply. Real investment spending rose in 1972–74 and then again in 1977–78. Whether these surges were caused by regulatory requirements is not easily ascertained.[14] Certainly the 1977–78 rise is due in large part to downsizing U.S. automobiles and the introduction of a number of new front-wheel-drive models.

From 1981 to 1983 real investment outlays in the industry declined noticeably. The Department of Commerce data on investment by motor vehicle companies show a decline of nearly 27 percent between 1981 and 1983 (table 2-5, column 4). The companies' reported real tooling expenses fell by 22 percent in the same period. In 1984 capital spending rose substantially, but the average real expenditure in 1981–84 was below the average for 1977–80. Thus import restraints can hardly be said to have generated a major surge in investment in modernization.

International Competitiveness

The U.S. industry appears to suffer a substantial cost disadvantage in producing small, fuel-efficient automobiles. Some students of the automobile industry estimate that the Japanese enjoy a landed-cost advantage of more than $1,500 a car over their U.S. competitors for U.S. sales of subcompacts.[15] Others, however, think that this advantage is substantially smaller.[16] Whatever its magnitude, much of this advantage derives from

14. Only GM reported specific figures for investment to meet auto safety and emissions requirements. Comparable figures are available only for 1973–80, and range from a low share of 0.029 of total investment (real estate, plant and equipment, special tools) in 1976 to a high share of 0.20 in 1973. Given the magnitude of these expenditures, it would appear that regulation had an important impact upon investment spending in 1972–74, but a lesser effect in other recent years.

15. Harbour and Associates, *Japanese Landed Cost Advantage,* p. 51; and NAS, *Competitive Status of the U.S. Auto Industry,* p. 93.

16. José A. Gómez-Ibáñez and David Harrison, Jr., "Imports and the Future of the U.S. Automobile Industry," *American Economic Review,* vol. 72 (May 1982, *Papers and Proceedings, 1981*), pp. 319–23.

higher labor productivity, better inventory management, lower wages, and a variety of other management practices, as well as the appreciation of the dollar since 1980. U.S. producers are having difficulty competing with the smaller, fuel-efficient cars from Japan despite importation costs of approximately $400 per automobile.[17]

Part of the industry's competitiveness problem derives from high wages, but a large share is the result of lagging productivity growth. The U.S. automobile companies have granted large wage increases to their workers since the mid-1970s even though these workers were already much more highly paid than the average industrial worker. As table 2-6 demonstrates, U.S. auto worker compensation was nearly 50 percent above the U.S. manufacturing average in 1975, while the German auto worker received only a 24 percent premium and the Japanese worker received only a 17 percent premium. By 1980 the U.S. auto companies had allowed this premium to rise to 65 percent while the Japanese and German premiums remained much lower.

This large wage premium might not have been a problem for domestic automobile producers if it had reflected higher labor productivity than that achieved in Japan or Germany. In fact, recent studies have shown that U.S. firms use more labor per small car than their Japanese competitors.[18] General Motors and Toyota have launched their joint venture in California partly because General Motors wants Toyota to demonstrate how its management-labor practices can raise U.S. productivity to Japanese levels.

Since 1977 productivity in the U.S. auto industry has lagged badly, but recent data show a substantial rebound. Between 1977 and 1981 labor productivity declined by 7 percent. Between 1981 and 1983 it rose by about 18 percent, or approximately 8 percent a year.[19] Over the entire period from 1977 to 1983, however, it rose by less than 2 percent a year, hardly a rate sufficient to close the gap with Japan.

In 1979 Chrysler received a substantial wage concession from the United Auto Workers, and in 1982 Ford and GM negotiated some concessions from the UAW. In 1984, however, both GM and Ford signed new agreements that are likely to raise compensation by about 1 percentage

17. NAS, *Competitive Status of the U.S. Auto Industry,* p. 92.

18. Harbour and Associates, *Japanese Landed Cost Advantage,* p. 51; and NAS, *Competitive Status of the U.S. Auto Industry,* p. 93.

19. Data from Bureau of Labor Statistics, Division of Industry Productivity and Technology Studies, November 1985. Productivity figures are for all employees.

Table 2-6. Average Hourly Compensation for Production Workers in Automobile Industry and Industrial Sector, United States, Japan, and Germany, 1975–84

	United States		Japan		West Germany	
Year	Automobiles ($/hour)	Manufacturing ($/hour)	Automobiles (¥/hour)	Manufacturing (¥/hour)	Automobiles (DM/hour)	Manufacturing (DM/hour)
1975	9.44	6.35	1,056	904	18.85	15.20
1976	10.27	6.93	1,192	979	20.56	16.64
1977	11.45	7.59	1,290	1,078	22.59	18.11
1978	12.67	8.30	1,427	1,155	23.93	19.35
1979	13.68	9.07	1,506	1,199	25.73	20.69
1980	16.29	9.89	1,555	1,266	28.23	22.37
1981	17.28	10.90	1,659	1,361	30.06	23.75
1982	18.66	11.63	1,788	1,419	32.12	25.31
1983	19.04[a]	12.26[a]	1,841[a]	1,459[a]	33.87[a]	26.50[a]
1984	19.94[a]	12.82[a]	1,922[a]	1,525[a]	34.13[a]	27.23[a]

Source: Data from Bureau of Labor Statistics, Office of Productivity and Technology, January 1985.
a. Estimated.

Table 2-7. Exchange Rates, Selected Currencies, 1975–84

Year	Trade-weighted value of dollar (March 1973 = 100)	Dollar/¥ × 100	Dollar/DM × 100
1975	98.5	0.337	40.73
1976	105.6	0.337	39.74
1977	103.3	0.373	43.08
1978	92.4	0.480	49.87
1979	88.1	0.450	51.56
1980	87.4	0.443	55.09
1981	102.9	0.454	44.36
1982	116.6	0.403	41.24
1983	125.3	0.421	39.24
1984	138.2	0.421	35.23

Source: *Economic Report of the President, February 1985*, p. 351.

point more than the cost of living.[20] Chrysler workers negotiated similar increases in 1985. Thus under the protection of trade restraint the industry has failed to reduce its wage costs significantly, and it is now likely that automobile compensation will return to a level between 60 and 65 percent above the industrial average.

Finally, some mention of the dramatic changes in the value of the dollar is necessary. Between 1980 and the end of 1984 the dollar appreciated by more than 60 percent against the currencies of its trading partners. The appreciation against European currencies, such as the German mark, was particularly severe (table 2-7), but the appreciation against the yen was more modest. These exchange rate movements subjected U.S. import-competing industries, such as automobiles, to enormous competitive pressure. In 1984 car prices in Japan were as much as 40 percent less than those in the United States. Some Mercedes models were three times as high in the United States as in Germany (a small part of which is due to regulatory costs).[21] Were truly open borders to exist, U.S. auto prices would have been substantially lower and U.S. companies would have found it difficult to realize any profits, much less record ones. In 1985 the dollar began to fall once more, and by early 1986 it was approaching a

---

20. The 1982 concessions are outlined in "Detroit's New Balance of Power," *Business Week*, March 1, 1982, p. 90. The 1984 agreements are similarly discussed in "The GM Settlement Is a Milestone for Both Sides," *Business Week*, October 8, 1984, pp. 160–62; and *New York Times*, October 15, 1984.

21. *World Cars, 1984* (Pelham, N.Y.: Herald Books for the Automobile Club of Italy, 1984).

trade-weighted average that had returned to its 1970 value (121.1 with March 1973 = 100).

Summary

A snapshot of the industry in 1985 provides a rather misleading image of its health and robustness. Profits returned to 1977–78 levels even if sales of domestically produced vehicles were approximately 2 million units lower. Behind a trade barrier, the U.S. automobile companies appear to have recovered from the worst of their 1980–82 difficulties. But it is far from clear that they can compete with the Japanese in smaller cars unless the value of the dollar depreciates substantially from its value in late 1985. If the Japanese are free to export to the United States without limit, the profits of U.S. companies may fall precipitously.

There can be little doubt that the auto industry has been through an enormously disruptive two decades. Regulation was only one of the many sources of this disruption, but it may have been an important one. In the following chapters, we ask whether the regulatory programs have achieved their objectives and at what cost. Moreover, we attempt to look at the effect of these programs upon the industry's overall performance.

CHAPTER THREE

The Costs of Safety and Emissions Regulation

THERE is strong reason to believe that the federal automobile safety and emissions programs have added substantially to the cost of producing a vehicle. The automobile companies have argued that these programs have imposed a substantial burden on the industry and that regulatory requirements should be eased to allow some relief, particularly during periods of low profitability. Proponents of regulation have argued not only that the requirements are justified, but that the claims of cost savings from relaxation of the rules are exaggerated. Rolling back regulations would not reduce regulatory costs to the same extent that the initial regulations added to these costs. Moreover, many proponents of regulation believe that estimates of regulatory costs are biased upward because they originate from the companies themselves.

In this chapter, we review the engineering estimates of the costs of regulation, providing an analysis and synthesis of their results. In addition, we develop a new statistical method for estimating these costs that takes account of some aspects that the engineering methods are likely to ignore.

An Analytical Framework

To evaluate the costs of auto regulation accurately and to answer related questions, such as who bears those costs, it is necessary to apply economic analysis to some basic facts concerning the automobile industry. The arguments made in intuitive form in this section are made more rigorously in appendix A.

The costs of auto regulation are imposed initially on several different groups. The hardware necessary to meet the regulations is manufactured by the auto industry and by its various suppliers. It is possible that these manufacturers absorb these costs, that they pass them on to car buyers, or

27

that some combination of these effects occurs. But the consumers also pay some of the costs of regulation directly, regardless of whether the manufacturers pass on the hardware costs. Safety and emissions regulations decrease the fuel economy of a car, all other things being equal, both because they make the car heavier and because, in the case of emissions controls, they require the operation of auxiliary devices, such as air pumps, and the retuning of the engine to less than optimal fuel efficiency. Emissions controls can also reduce the reliability and increase the repair costs of the car, and they can reduce product quality in such dimensions as acceleration and drivability, thereby imposing a nonpecuniary (but still very real) cost on the consumer.

In order to analyze the effects of regulation on the cost of owning and operating an automobile, it is helpful to answer two questions. First, given that the market that produces automobiles and their services is divided among several groups, do the manufacturers have an incentive to minimize the overall costs to society of meeting the regulations? (Certainly producers have an incentive to minimize the effect of regulation on the purchase price of a car; but it is less obvious that they have an incentive to minimize the combined production costs and operating costs that result from regulation.) Second, given what is known about the market for automobiles, to what extent will the producers pass on the costs of regulation imposed on the manufacture of cars and to what extent will they absorb those costs?

As appendix A shows, under some relatively unrestrictive assumptions, automobile producers will seek to minimize the overall costs of ownership and operation of a car (including regulatory costs). This conclusion holds for conditions of either monopoly or competition in the market for new cars.

Although competitors and monopolists will behave in the same way in minimizing the costs of regulation, they will not be equally successful in passing on the costs of regulation. The increase in auto costs resulting from regulation can be viewed as being conceptually similar to a specific unit sales tax imposed on an industry. A competitive industry will pass on such a tax in full or in part, depending upon the elasticity of supply. Whether a monopolist absorbs or passes on the tax depends on the elasticity of demand it faces as well as the nature of its cost function. Before imports became such an important factor in the U.S. market for autos, U.S. auto producers undoubtedly enjoyed some market power. Therefore it is appropriate that we should analyze the extent to which these costs are passed on.

Before doing so, however, we turn to the more basic task of estimating what those costs are, using the simplest (engineering) techniques. By way of introduction to all our estimates of regulatory costs, we must clarify what we mean by the "costs of regulation." We define them as the total increase in costs to producers and consumers that have occurred as a result of mandated improvements in emissions and safety over the costs before regulation was imposed. This definition is not completely satisfying because it is possible that in the absence of regulatory constraints the private marketplace would have improved automobiles relative to the benchmarks we consider. Hence not all the changes discussed are necessarily the results of regulation. This is unlikely to be a problem with our cost estimates for emissions regulation because the private marketplace has no incentive to correct for such a pure externality. In the case of safety, however, it is possible that we have overstated the cost of regulation because the private marketplace would have brought about some of these changes in the absence of regulation.

Emissions Standards

Emissions standards have changed dramatically over the past fifteen years, as discussed in chapter 1. The current standards for automobiles are 0.41 grams of hydrocarbons, 3.4 grams of carbon monoxide, and 1.0 grams of nitrogen oxides per mile of operation under a "standard" driving cycle, but waivers have been allowed from these standards for certain vehicles. By 1984, however, these waivers were no longer available, and all passenger cars had to meet the standards.[1]

The progress from "unregulated" automobiles in 1967 to stringent regulations in 1985 has not been constant and predictable. Periodic delays and congressional alterations of the timetable have created a "perils of Pauline" atmosphere in the industry as companies have been faced with tight deadlines and incentives to argue that they cannot meet these deadlines. Because the automobiles cannot be sold until the model is certified to meet the standards, the companies can easily argue that their inability to meet a deadline will force them to abandon production altogether. Such a threat catches the attention of politicians; hence delays were granted in 1973, 1974, and 1977, but such delays have not been granted recently.

1. Lawrence J. White, *The Regulation of Air Pollutant Emissions from Motor Vehicles* (Washington, D.C.: American Enterprise Institute, 1982), p. 15.

Table 3-1. The Costs per Automobile of Emissions Regulation, Model Years 1968–81
Current dollars

Year[a]	Standards[b]	Equipment only	All other costs[c]	Total
1968	5.9/50.8/. . .	14	0	14
1969	5.9/50.8/. . .	15	0	15
1970	4.1/34.0/. . .	24	0	24
1971	4.1/34.0/. . .	25	0	25
1972	3.0/28.2/. . .	25	170	195
1973	3.0/28.2/3.1	44	488	532
1974	3.0/28.2/3.1	49	541	590
1975	1.5/15.0/3.1	119	187	306
1976	1.5/15.0/3.1	126	197	323
1977	1.5/15.0/2.0	123	343	466
1978	1.5/15.0/2.0	133	369	502
1979	1.5/15.0/2.0	148	411	559
1980	0.41/7.0/2.0	222	684	906
1981	0.41/3.4/1.0	600	951	1,551

Sources: Calculated from data in Lawrence J. White, *The Regulation of Air Pollutant Emissions from Motor Vehicles* (Washington, D.C.: American Enterprise Institute, 1982), pp. 60–63; and 40 C.F.R. 86.081–.084 (1984).
    a. Testing procedures for pre-1972 cars differed from those used for 1972 and later model years. Therefore the standards for 1968–71 are not precisely comparable with the later standards.
    b. Grams per mile for hydrocarbons, carbon monoxide, and nitrogen oxides.
    c. Present value of lifetime fuel penalty, maintenance, and unleaded gasoline premium.

The stringent deadlines and political maneuvering cannot have been conducive to efficient pollution control. As Congress has shifted deadlines, the companies have not been able to undertake the most efficient model design and investment plan to achieve the ultimate standards. Thus the estimated costs of proceeding from the unregulated status to the current standards have evidenced an erratic path.

White has reviewed the engineering evidence on the costs of emissions standards.[2] We draw upon his estimates for present purposes since no new information has appeared since the publication of his monograph. These estimates, presented somewhat differently, appear in table 3-1. The costs are divided into two components: emissions equipment costs and all other costs, including fuel penalties and additional maintenance. The costs of equipment rose at a modest rate through 1974, but total costs, including lifetime maintenance and fuel penalty costs, rose sharply in 1972–74 and then receded in 1975–79 with the introduction of catalysts. As the standards were tightened further in the 1980–81 model years, the costs per new automobile doubled in constant dollars.

The Environmental Protection Agency offers a much lower estimate for

2. Ibid., chap. 6.

the 1981 cost of emissions controls than White's. It estimates the cost of the equipment at $265 to $452 in 1981 dollars.[3] This estimate is derived from the sum of the prices of the required components purchased at the repair-parts counters of automobile dealers, multiplied by a factor to correct for the difference between the retail price of a car and all of its components purchased at retail. Unfortunately, there is no reason to believe that such a factor is constant across all repair parts; hence the estimate must be viewed as speculative at best. White's $600 estimate reflects his decision to split the difference between the automobile companies' estimates and those of the EPA.

The EPA questions the fuel economy penalties widely attributed to emissions controls. It claims that the unleaded gasoline premium is largely offset by reduced wear of spark plugs, exhaust equipment, and valves.[4] Moreover, it cites a Canadian study that shows that 1984 U.S. and Canadian cars have similar fuel economy despite the much weaker Canadian emissions standards.[5] From this study, it appears that much of the difference between U.S. and Canadian fuel efficiency has disappeared during 1981–84 as U.S. fuel economy standards have become more binding.

White estimates that the fuel economy penalties due to the tighter 1980 and 1981 standards are 6 and 7 percent, respectively.[6] These estimates are consistent with the results of a simple statistical analysis based upon the fuel economy model we present in chapter 6. We estimate the relationship between fuel economy and weight, engine displacement, and time for each of the Big Three producers for 1970–79, and these results are used to project fuel economy improvements in 1980–84 for new cars tested by Consumers Union.[7] Fuel economy is between 1.4 and 6.7 percent below

3. Environmental Protection Agency, Office of Mobile Source Air Pollution Control, *The Cost of Controlling Emissions of 1981 Model Year Automobiles* (EPA, 1981), p. 18. Reported figures are adjusted by the change in the consumer price index to 1981 dollars.

4. Memorandum, Charles L. Gray, director of EPA Emission Control Technology Division to Bruce Jordan, chief of EPA Ambient Standards Branch, Office of Air Quality Planning and Standards, "Updated Cost Estimates of Controlling HC Emissions from Mobile Sources," November 28, 1983, pp. 13–14.

5. Letter to the author from Richard D. Wilson, director, Office of Mobile Sources, EPA, December 14, 1984; and Jeffrey Dowell and others, "U.S. and Canadian Comparison of Passenger Car Fuel Economy and Technological Trends, 1978 to 1984" (Ottawa: Energy, Mines and Resources Canada, Coal and Alternative Energy Branch, December 1984).

6. White, *Regulation of Air Pollutant Emissions*, pp. 63–64.

7. Specifically, the logarithm of the harmonic average of city and highway estimates of miles per gallon is regressed on the logarithm of vehicle weight, the logarithm of engine displacement, and time for all 1970–79 vehicles tested by Consumers Union. The time trend

predicted values for 1981–84. The weighted average overprediction is
approximately 4 percent for 1981–84. Assuming that 1979 emissions standards were causing at least a modest loss of fuel efficiency, this analysis
would appear to support White's estimate of a 7 percent penalty due to the
1981 standards.

In a 1979 report to Congress, the EPA estimated that additional lifetime
maintenance costs due to the 1981 emissions standards would be $184 (in
1977 dollars) per car.[8] Therefore, if we use the EPA's upper range of
equipment costs plus its own estimate of maintenance costs, the costs of
the 1981 standards are $728 per car. Assuming that the fuel penalty is
about 7 percent, that the price of gasoline remains at $1.31 (1981 dollars)
for ten years, and that the real discount rate is 3 percent, the fuel penalty
for the life of a car is approximately $397.[9] Therefore, even if the higher
price of unleaded gasoline is fully offset by the reduction in maintenance
costs resulting from the elimination of lead, a lower bound of the costs of
the 1981 standards would appear to be about $1,100 per car. If subsequent
research or technological change eliminates the estimated fuel penalty
with no increase in equipment costs, this might decline to as little as $728,
as described above.

Safety Standards

In analyzing the costs of federal safety regulation, two magnitudes are
relevant: the initial cost of meeting regulatory standards and the cost to the
automobile companies of complying with these standards after they have
had sufficient time to redesign their vehicles to accommodate the standards

---

begins with 1970 for General Motors and 1974 for Ford and Chrysler, since GM began to
stress downsizing and fuel efficiency in the early 1970s while Ford and Chrysler did not do
so until later. The estimated trend rate of annual improvement is 2.6 percent for GM (1970–
79); 3.5 percent for Ford (1974–79); and 3.1 percent for Chrysler (1974–79). When the
equations are used to predict 1980–84 fuel economy, they overpredict GM's mileage by 4.1
percent in 1980 and 2.3 percent in 1981–84; Ford's by 10.8 percent in 1980 and 5.2 percent
in 1981–84; and Chrysler's by 3.3 percent in 1980 and 6.7 percent in 1981–84.

8. *The Cost of Clean Air and Clean Water: Annual Report of the Administrator of the
Environmental Protection Agency*, S. Doc. 96-38, 96 Cong. 1 sess. (Government Printing
Office, 1979), p. 42.

9. Assuming that an average 1981 car is driven 10,000 miles per year for ten years and
it realizes 20 miles per gallon, it uses 500 gallons per year. The 7 percent fuel penalty costs
9.2 cents per gallon times 500 gallons per year, or $46. At a 3 percent real discount rate, the
present value of $46 per year for ten years is $397.

at the lowest cost. These two magnitudes differ because today's cost is not the addition of past years' costs plus the additional cost of new regulations, nor is it the cost of achievement last year escalated by an appropriate price index.

Technological change, economies of volume, and changes in the design of the vehicle should change the cost of complying with safety regulations over time. Compliance costs for a given set of regulations will fall somewhat with time since improved technology and product redesign will ease some of the constraints on vehicle companies in meeting the standards. However, some changes in vehicle design may make attainment of the standard more difficult with time—a phenomenon perhaps most graphically illustrated by the problems of meeting crash survivability requirements in a world of smaller, more fuel-efficient cars.

Cumulative Cost Estimates

There are only two major sources of comprehensive cost data for safety standards: a U.S. General Accounting Office (GAO) report that provides data only through 1974, and annual estimates of the incremental cost of new standards provided by the U.S. Bureau of Labor Statistics (BLS) in their adjustment of new car prices for "quality" changes. Data from these two sources are shown in tables 3-2 and 3-3. The GAO data in table 3-2 are based upon information supplied by domestic and foreign assemblers, but the details of the calculations are not explained. Presumably the estimates reflect the estimated current-dollar costs of all regulations in existence for each of the model years.

The BLS data in table 3-3 are annual estimates of new regulatory costs in each year; therefore they do not represent the current-year costs of all applicable regulations for each year's cars. Nevertheless, adding the BLS data results in estimates of each year's costs rather similar to the GAO data for 1968–74, once an adjustment is made for regulations imposed by the General Services Administration in 1966–67 for all cars purchased by the federal government (not included in BLS estimates).

The accumulated costs of safety regulation rose sharply in the late 1960s with the promulgation of a variety of interior crash protection rules. These included seat belts, collapsible steering columns, and headrest requirements. The costs rose once again very sharply with the introduction of bumper standards in 1972–73 and seat belt ignition interlock systems in 1974. In 1975 Congress acted to rescind the 1974 seatbelt interlock sys-

Table 3-2. Estimated Average Compliance Cost per Automobile of Federal Motor Vehicle Safety Standards, Model Years 1966–74
Current dollars

Standard	1966	1967	1968	1969	1970	1971	1972	1973	1974
Accident avoidance	18	31	41	48	55	55	55	55	55
Crash survivability									
Occupant protection on interior impact	7	10	20	19	19	19	19	19	19
Head restraints and seating systems	. . .	3	5	19	19	18	18	19	19
Steering column protection and displacement	. . .	13	17	17	17	17	17	17	17
Glazing materials	3	3	4	4	3	3	3	3	3
Door locks, wheel nuts, discs, etc.	1	1	1	2	2	2	2	2	2
Occupant crash protection, seatbelt assemblies, etc.	11	13	32	32	32	32	45	50	94
Windshield mounting	*	*	*	*	*	*	*	*	*
Side door strength	. . .	. . .	. . .	5	7	9	10	15	15
Exterior protection (bumpers)	. . .	. . .	. . .	. . .	. . .	. . .	5	61	136
Roof crush resistance	. . .	. . .	. . .	. . .	. . .	. . .	. . .	. . .	3
Fuel system integrity and flammability of materials	. . .	. . .	. . .	1	1	1	1	5	5
Total crash survivability[a]	22	43	79	97	99	101	120	191	313
Total, all standards	40	74	120	145	154	156	175	246	368
Yearly increase	. . .	34	46	25	9	2	19	71	122
Crash survivability without bumper standard[b]	22	43	79	97	99	101	116	130	177

Source: General Accounting Office, *Effectiveness, Benefits, and Costs of Federal Safety Standards for Protection of Passenger Car Occupants*, National Highway Traffic Safety Administration, Department of Transportation, CED-76-121 (GAO, 1976), p. 26.
* Less than $1.
a. Figures are rounded.
b. Bumper standard is not designed for human safety, but rather to protect integrity of vehicles.

tem, but BLS did not report separately the cost savings associated with this rescission. The BLS estimate for the 1974 cost of the interlock requirement is $46.80. We subtracted this amount from all post-1974 estimates as a very rough approximation of the cost savings from the rescission.

How Have Costs Changed?

While the evidence on annual costs of compliance might serve to identify the pace of safety regulation, these data are unlikely to be useful for measuring the full cost of safety regulation for a 1980 or 1981 model. The cost of meeting a standard in 1966 might have been $10 (in 1981 dollars), and the cost of meeting a second standard in 1967 might have been $20 (in

Table 3-3. Estimates of Incremental Compliance Costs per Automobile for Federal Automobile Safety and Damageability Standards, Model Years 1968–84

| Year | Annual increase | | Cumulative costs (current dollars)[a] |
	Current dollars[a]	1980 dollars	
1968	29.65	70.23	29.65
1969	14.00	31.47	43.65
1970	26.50	56.24	70.15
1971	10.00	20.35	80.15
1972	2.00	3.94	82.15
1973	85.60	158.72	167.75
1974	107.60	179.79	275.35
1975[b]	−36.10	−55.27	239.25
1976	13.40	19.40	252.65
1977	6.95	9.45	259.60
1978	0.00	0.00	259.60
1979	5.75	6.53	265.35
1980	13.29	13.29	278.64
1981	4.29	3.89	282.93
1982	0.00	0.00	282.93
1983	0.00	0.00	282.93
1984	−12.09	−9.59	270.84

Source: Bureau of Labor Statistics, "Report on Quality Changes for Passenger Cars," *News*, November, various years.

a. Not adjusted for prior years' costs for inflation.

b. 1975 data for annual increase include a negative adjustment of $46.80 for taking out seat belt interlock systems.

1981 dollars), but one cannot expect that the cost of complying with both in 1981 would be $30. Technology and relative prices change. It is likely that the real cost of meeting, say, the 1966–71 standards in 1981 fell substantially for a number of reasons. First, the engineering required to design the automobile to meet a standard after fifteen years of experience should be less than the initial requirements. Second, the cost of designing a car to meet a variety of standards should, with sufficient lead time, be less than the cost of sequentially adjusting to regulations as they emanate from the National Highway Traffic Safety Administration (NHTSA). Finally, the cost of designing something into a completely new vehicle should be less than the cost of fitting it into an existing design. Given the enormous changes in U.S. automobiles since the mid-1970s, simply adding up the annual increases in compliance costs would result in estimates that are biased upward.

There also may be reasons why costs of safety regulations have risen with time. The cost of adequate protection in a smaller car may be much higher than the cost in a larger, inherently safer vehicle. Second, recent models are more tightly designed than earlier models because of the necessity of increasing fuel economy while maintaining performance and satisfying space requirements. Fitting safety devices into these cars may be more expensive than in earlier years. Third, relative price changes might increase the cost of regulatory compliance. For example, higher feedstock costs caused by the OPEC shocks of the 1970s could have raised the price of plastics used in bumpers and padded interior components by more than the general rate of inflation.

The potential for overestimating compliance costs can be determined in a rough manner by comparing recent NHTSA studies of the cost effectiveness of standards with the earlier GAO or BLS estimates of selected standards. To date, NHTSA has completed reevaluations of twelve standards. In general, the NHTSA cost estimates, published between 1979 and 1982, are substantially lower than the earlier BLS or GAO cost estimates. The exceptions are the side door crush-resistance standard and the braking standard. The estimates of improvement range from as little as 1.9 percent a year to as much as 30 percent. Since the rate of decline in costs estimated by NHTSA may be biased, we have chosen 5 percent as the approximate rate of decline in the annual costs of meeting each standard (the "learning curve").

Total Safety Costs

To obtain an estimate of the cost of all safety regulations applicable to each model year's average automobile, we must adjust for both inflation and learning. For example, table 3-3 shows BLS estimates of 1969 regulatory costs as $44 per car: $30 from the applicable 1968 regulations plus $14 for regulations effective for the first time in 1969. The $44 estimate for 1969 regulations that carry over to 1970 and beyond is surely in error. Inflation will increase the cost of variable inputs required to produce padded dashboards or other interior protection devices, but learning should reduce it. To adjust these estimates, therefore, we first increase all costs of prior years' regulations by the rate of increase in the consumer price index.[10] This adjustment is reflected in the first column in table 3-4. Then we adjust the regulatory costs for an assumed 5 percent annual learning curve. This adjustment is reflected in the second column. The

---

10. "CPI-new cars" is not used because it adjusts for quality changes.

Table 3-4. The Total Costs of Safety Regulation, Model Years 1966–84
Current dollars per automobile

	Equipment costs		
Year[a]	Without learning curve[b]	With 5 percent annual learning curve	Fuel penalty[c]
1966	40	40	0
1967	75	73	0
1968	124	119	9
1969	156	144	14
1970	174	154	15
1971	184	155	16
1972	209	172	16
1973	293	245	73
1974	447	381	125
1975	452	361	116
1976	491	377	98
1977	530	390	94
1978	571	400	92
1979	641	431	116
1980	741	481	152
1981	822	512	159
1982	872	517	146
1983	900	508	123
1984	924	491	118

Source: Tables 3-2, 3-3.
a. GAO estimates for 1966–74; 1975–84 based upon BLS estimates in table 3-3.
b. Adjusted for rate of increase in consumer price index.
c. Based upon estimated elasticity of fuel consumption assuming a weight of -0.8, a real discount rate of 3 percent, and ten years of vehicle operation of 10,000 miles per year. Total weight increase due to safety regulation is calculated as the sum of weights reported in NHTSA contractor studies or various safety standards, and NHTSA, *The Cost of Automobile Safety Regulations* (DOT, 1982). The elasticity estimate is from chap. 6 below.

divergence between the two approaches obviously grows over time, becoming very large by the 1980s.

Finally, an important cost of the safety standards is the fuel penalty they exact from motorists because of the weight they add to the car. Much of this cost comes from the bumper standard, which is not a safety standard per se, but is administered by NHTSA. We include this in the cost of safety regulation. The last column of table 3-4 contains an estimate of the lifetime fuel penalty due to safety regulations. This estimated fuel penalty reaches its maximum of $159 in 1981, a year of high gasoline prices, but it declines steadily thereafter due to the declining price of gasoline and the easing of the bumper standard.[11]

11. 47 Fed. Reg. 21820 (1982).

Table 3-5. The Costs of Safety and Emissions Regulation, Model Years 1966–84
Current dollars

| | Safety | | | Emissions | | Total | | | |
| | Equipment only | | | | | Equipment only | | Full costs | |
Year	Without learning curve	With learning curve	Fuel penalty	Equipment only	Full costs	Without learning curve	With learning curve	Without learning curve	With learning curve
1966	40	40	0	0	0	40	40	40	40
1967	75	73	0	0	0	75	73	75	73
1968	124	119	9	14	14	138	133	147	142
1969	156	144	14	15	15	171	159	185	173
1970	174	154	15	24	24	198	178	213	193
1971	184	155	16	25	25	209	180	225	196
1972	209	172	16	25	195	234	197	420	383
1973	293	245	73	44	532	337	289	898	850
1974	447	381	125	49	590	496	430	1,162	1,096
1975	452	361	116	119	306	571	480	874	783
1976	491	377	98	126	323	617	503	912	798
1977	530	390	94	123	466	653	513	1,090	950
1978	571	400	92	133	502	704	533	1,165	994
1979	641	431	116	148	559	789	579	1,316	1,106
1980	741	481	152	222	906	963	703	1,799	1,539
1981	822	512	159	600	1,551	1,422	1,112	2,532	2,222
1982	872	517	146	607[a]	1,582[b]	1,479	1,124	2,600	2,245
1983	900	508	123	596[a]	1,607[b]	1,496	1,104	2,630	2,238
1984	924	491	118	592[a]	1,601[b]	1,516	1,083	2,643	2,210

a. Extrapolated from table 3-1, using a 5 percent learning curve and the annual change in the consumer price index.
b. Extrapolated using CPI for automobile maintenance and actual price of gasoline.

The Total Costs of Safety and Emissions Regulation

Total estimates of safety and emissions costs are shown in table 3-5: the costs of safety equipment are added to emissions equipment costs and to total emissions control costs per vehicle. The safety equipment costs are displayed with and without the effects of learning.

The estimated full costs of *equipment* installed on new automobiles in model years 1966 through 1981 rise from $40 per car (current dollars) to between $1,112 and $1,422 per automobile.[12] When the fuel and maintenance penalties are added, the 1981 costs of emissions and safety regulation rise to a range of $2,222 and $2,532, with safety costs accounting for between 30 and 39 percent of the total. An extrapolation based upon changes in the consumer price index and 5 percent learning results in estimates for the 1984 model year that are virtually identical to the 1981 estimates.

Reduced Drivability

The costs of regulation include not only the increased capital and operating costs of an automobile, but the reduction in the value of services from the car caused by the installation of regulatory devices. When tight regulatory deadlines are imposed to force technology, the automobile companies may be forced to compromise the driving quality of the cars in order to meet the standards. The emissions standards of the early 1970s are an obvious example. In 1973 and 1974, before the installation of catalysts, cars often operated poorly due to the severe detuning of the engines and the reduction of axle ratios. Had the manufacturers been given more time, these suboptimal control strategies might have been avoided.

Safety regulation has not been plagued with the severe technology forcing of emissions control. Except for the decision to require interlocks in 1974 models, NHTSA has not mandated standards that have had direct effects upon drivability. Increases in vehicle weight resulting from safety equipment may have reduced fuel economy, but they apparently have not reduced the service quality of the car.

12. The emissions equipment costs for 1966–81 do not include an explicit adjustment for learning because these costs are based upon nearly contemporaneous estimates of the equipment requirements for meeting the successively tighter standards. For instance, the cost of the 1981 standards is estimated circa 1980. It is not a cumulative estimate of incremental standards from the 1968–81 model years.

Langenfeld has attempted to estimate the increase in indirect costs of vehicle operation resulting from regulation through the 1977 model year. His results show that emissions regulation reduced the value of automobiles by an estimated 3.3 to 19.4 percent.[13] These estimates include all maintenance, fuel economy, and drivability penalties. Our estimates of fuel and maintenance penalties are approximately 6 percent of the average price of a new 1977 model car; hence Langenfeld's estimates add as much as 13 percent to this cost in the form of reductions in drivability.

More recently, Bresnahan and Yao have estimated the changes in the relative user costs of cars due to changes in emissions standards.[14] They find that drivability costs of emissions standards in the mid-1970s were slightly less than $500 per automobile (in 1981 dollars), or about 6 percent of the value of the average 1977 car. The shift to closed-loop control systems and fuel injection in the 1981 model year in order to meet the 1981 standards has more than eliminated this drivability penalty.

Are the Costs Passed on to Consumers?

Given the magnitude of the costs of safety and emissions regulation, how these costs are borne by consumers and the automobile producers is of more than passing interest. In appendix B, we describe a simple two-equation recursive model of prices and profits that has been estimated for 1960–80 data. This model relates the price of new cars to unit labor costs, unit capital costs, material costs, and the engineering estimates of the cost of safety and emissions equipment, in addition to a measure of capacity utilization. Profits per vehicle are, in turn, a function of the price of automobiles and the various cost variables.

The results of estimating this simple model are found in table B-1. Roughly two-thirds of regulatory costs appear to be passed on to consumers with a one-year lag, but these costs are absorbed immediately by the companies. Therefore it would appear that the net cost of regulation is borne partly by firms and partly by consumers. One cannot reject the

---

13. James Langenfeld, "The Costs and Benefits of Automobile Emissions Controls and Safety Regulation," Working Paper 83, rev. (Washington University, St. Louis, Center for the Study of American Business, 1984), p. 14.

14. Timothy F. Bresnahan and Dennis A. Yao, "The Nonpecuniary Costs of Automobile Emissions Standards," Technical Report 33 (Stanford University, Center for Economic Policy Research, June 1984), p. 27.

hypothesis that eventually the price of cars reflects the full estimated cost of regulation.

An Integrated Statistical Approach

The evidence provided so far on the costs of auto regulation has been found by adding up cumulatively the costs of individual safety and emissions costs, with learning effects incorporated. This approach has many advantages, including the likely accuracy of the underlying engineering estimates of regulatory costs. But these estimates also leave some important questions unanswered. Most important, it is quite possible that safety and emissions regulations have interactive effects on auto costs that are not captured: together, they tend to make the car heavier and less fuel efficient than it would otherwise be, requiring reengineering of the car and the power train. Additional costs of regulation occur, not only through a fuel penalty from weight and emissions controls, but also from increased repair and maintenance costs to the consumer stemming from tighter emissions controls.

To resolve some of these issues, we have estimated the costs of auto regulation to the consumer from a rather different perspective from the previous sections. This model is fully developed in appendix A; we describe its main elements and conclusions in this section.

First, we develop a model of ownership and operating costs for the private automobile, taking account of the trade-offs just mentioned. This model is based on the economic theory of production. Second, we show that under conditions of either competition or monopoly or plausible models of oligopoly, auto manufacturers will generally produce cars that minimize not only the costs of regulation in the manufacture of the cars, but the total ownership and operating costs to the consumer, given regulatory policies, fuel prices, and repair costs. Third, using this theoretical model specifying the effects of regulation, we develop an econometric model to estimate the full effects of regulation on consumers' costs of owning and operating an auto. This model, based on a translog cost function, was estimated jointly with a set of factor share equations, using Zellner's method of seemingly unrelated coefficients.

The results of estimating this model, shown in table 3-6, give estimates of the cost of safety and emissions regulation for various model years, taking account of the interactions just discussed. These results indicate

Table 3-6. Estimates of the Cost of Regulation, Selected Model Years, 1969–81
Costs in current cents per mile

Year	Auto body type	Total operating cost	Cost attributable to regulation
1969	Full	10.26	0.13
1971	Full	11.53	0.21
1973	Full	12.33	0.50
1974	Full	14.87	0.65
1975	Full	16.20	0.63
1977	Full	16.61	0.72
1978	Full	17.37	0.77
1979	Full	20.95	0.97
1980	Full	24.11	1.24
1981	Full	27.22	1.53
1981	Intermediate	22.98	1.29
1981	Compact	21.96	1.23
1981	Subcompact	17.87	1.01

Source: Based on regression results, as described in appendix A, with use of Runzheimer data series.

that regulation has had a strong impact on the costs of owning and operating a car. They indicate that for 1981, regulation added about 1.3 cents per mile to the operating costs of a typical compact or intermediate American car. Over a car's lifetime of roughly 100,000 miles, this amounts to a present value of costs of roughly $1,100. The costs of unleaded gasoline, which we have excluded from the dependent variable of our regressions, will add about $200 to the cost of operating the car over its lifetime, for a total cost of $1,300. Comparable cost figures based on engineering data from an earlier section of this chapter would suggest a higher cost due to regulation, approximately $2,200. Thus the econometric estimates of the cost of regulation to consumers are slightly lower than the engineering-based ones developed earlier. This could be the result of errors in measurement or the possibility that the auto manufacturers have absorbed a portion of these costs themselves. As was pointed out earlier in this chapter, it is possible that manufacturers have absorbed at least a small portion of these costs.

Summary

In this chapter we have analyzed the costs of automobile regulation using two rather different empirical approaches. The first is based on engineering estimates. The second (reported in appendix A) is an econometric model based on a translog cost function and a detailed theoretical analysis of the extent to which a competitive or monopolistic producer will pass on the costs of regulation, and the extent to which that producer will alter the product in the face of regulation to assure that the auto provides transportation at least cost.

The results of both approaches are quite similar: they indicate that the cost of emissions and safety regulation was between $1,300 and $2,200 (in 1981 prices) for a 1981 vehicle, though the cost is likely to vary considerably depending upon such factors as the model, the engine used, or the transmission. Given that safety and emissions regulations have changed little since 1981, the cost for 1985 models should be little different except for prospective learning economies.

The results are also consistent with the hypothesis that the auto producers pass on most of the costs of regulation to consumers, although there is mild evidence that the producers absorb at least a small portion of these costs, and it is somewhat ambiguous just how long a lag there is between the imposition of regulatory costs and the passing of those costs on to consumers.

CHAPTER FOUR

The Effects of Regulation on Automobile Safety

THE rapid growth of automotive travel in the first half of the twentieth century was inevitably accompanied by an increase in traffic fatalities. Between 1921 and 1941, for example, the number of miles traveled by all motor vehicles in the United States increased sixfold from 55 billion to 334 billion a year. During this period, the number of traffic deaths tripled from 13,900 in 1921 to 39,969 in 1941.[1] By themselves, these data suggest that highway travel was becoming safer, for the fatality rate per mile of travel actually fell by 50 percent from 25.3 to 12.0 deaths per 100 million vehicle miles.

Since 1950 the number of traffic deaths has continued to climb, but generally at a slower rate than vehicle miles driven. Fatalities exceeded 50,000 for the first time in 1966 and did not recede to fewer than 50,000 until 1974, the year of the Arab oil embargo.[2] More important, the mid-1960s marked the first time in the post–World War II era that the fatality rate per vehicle mile of travel showed a sustained increase. Between 1947 and 1961 the total traffic death rate declined from 8.8 to 5.2 fatalities per 100 million vehicle miles. In the next four years the rate rose to 5.5 fatalities per 100 million miles.[3] Thus an annual improvement of 3.8 percent a year was reversed as the fatality rate actually rose by 1.7 percent a year for four years (table 4-1).

The natural political result of the sudden reversal of decades of progress in reducing the highway death rate was the National Traffic and Motor Vehicle Safety Act of 1966, empowering the federal government to set

1. Bureau of the Census, *Historical Statistics of the United States, Colonial Times to 1970*, vol. 2 (Government Printing Office, 1975), pp. 718, 720.
2. U.S. Department of Transportation, Federal Highway Administration, *Highway Statistics Summary*, various years, table HA-202.
3. Bureau of the Census, *Historical Statistics*, pp. 718–19.

Table 4-1. Highway Fatalities and Some Probable Causes, Selected Years, 1947–83

Year	Highway deaths per 100 million vehicle miles	Passenger-car-occupant deaths per 100 million passenger-car miles	Alcohol consumption per adult (gallons per year)	Average speed on main rural roads (mph)	Ratio of youthful drivers to total drivers	Share of miles driven on limited-access highways
1947	8.82	5.75	1.94	46.90	0.20	0.01
1949	7.42	5.22	1.76	47.60	0.19	0.01
1951	7.60	5.66	1.97	49.00	0.19	0.01
1953	7.04	5.49	1.94	49.80	0.18	0.01
1955	6.32	5.10	1.95	50.50	0.18	0.02
1957	5.95	4.84	2.03	51.40	0.19	0.03
1959	5.40	4.33	2.12	52.00	0.18	0.05
1961	5.15	4.09	2.21	52.60	0.18	0.07
1963	5.41	4.48	2.32	55.60	0.20	0.10
1965	5.52	4.58	2.58	56.40	0.20	0.12
1967	5.52	4.54	2.79	58.00	0.21	0.17
1969	5.27	4.33	3.01	60.00	0.21	0.18
1971	4.61	3.64	3.06	60.60	0.22	0.19
1973	4.26	3.31	3.01	60.30	0.22	0.19
1975	3.46	2.65	3.02	55.80	0.22	0.20
1977	3.35	2.53	2.98	56.40	0.22	0.18
1979	3.40	2.55	2.99	56.00	0.22	0.19
1981	3.27	2.49	2.85	56.00	0.22	0.20
1983	2.70	1.92	n.a.	57.00	0.21	0.20

Sources: U.S. Department of Transportation, Federal Highway Administration, *Highway Statistics*, various years, table VM-2, and *Traffic Speed Trends Report*, various years; National Safety Council, *Accident Facts, 1970*, and *Accident Facts, 1979; The Liquor Handbook, 1983* (New York: Jobson Publishing, 1983); U.S. Bureau of the Census, *Current Population Reports*, series P-25, nos. 310, 311, 519, 917, "Population Estimates" (Government Printing Office, various years); and unpublished data on highway completion from the Federal Highway Administration, Interstate Management Branch.
n.a. Not available.

national safety standards for motor vehicles, and the Highway Safety Act of 1966, designed to provide federal guidance to the states for highway construction, driver education, traffic law enforcement, and other highway safety programs. In the next few years, a number of motor vehicle standards were promulgated by the National Highway Safety Bureau (NHSB) (which later became the National Highway Traffic Safety Administration [NHTSA]), and a resumption of the decline in the highway death rate followed. Beginning in 1967, the rate fell continually for twelve years at an annual rate of 4.0 percent.[4] But can one attribute this revival of the

4. Department of Transportation, *Highway Statistics*, table HA-202.

improvement in highway safety to regulation? Or are there other factors that affect the fatality rate?

Highway Safety Regulation

The National Traffic and Motor Vehicle Safety Act was signed by President Lyndon B. Johnson on September 9, 1966. It required the federal government to set initial standards for all new vehicles sold in the United States by January 31, 1967. In 1964 Congress had authorized the General Services Administration to set standards on cars purchased by the federal government. By the 1967 model year, there had been seventeen GSA standards issued. Because of the short lead time, most of the initial NHSB standards were adopted from the prevailing GSA standards. Thus the automobile manufacturers were not required at first to develop major new systems to comply with federal standards. They had, for the most part, complied with GSA standards on all cars produced in the United States by the 1966 model year. In addition, more than thirty states required the installation of front seat belts on new cars by the 1966 model year. The GSA standards and, subsequently, the NHSB (later NHTSA) standards extended this front seat belt requirement to all states.

The new federal safety standards became effective on January 1, 1968, but they were generally met in the 1968 model year. Nineteen standards were promulgated involving accident avoidance, crash protection, and postcrash survivability. These standards and the subsequent NHTSA standards are itemized in table 4-2.

The federal standards are relatively few in number, and the number of major, costly standards is even smaller. Accident-avoidance standards are largely directed toward braking systems, tires, windshield systems, lamps, and transmission controls. Most of these standards for new automobiles were in place by 1970.

The more costly regulations are the crash-protection standards. These may be divided into occupant-protection requirements and exterior-protection standards. Occupant-protection standards include requirements for seat belts, energy-absorbing steering columns, head restraints, high-penetration-resistant windshield glass, padded instrument panels, and side door strength. The exterior-protection standards specify the energy absorption capacity of front and rear bumpers, but these requirements are

Table 4-2. Federal Motor Vehicle Safety Standards for Passenger Cars

Standard number	Standard title	Effective date
	Accident avoidance	
101	Control location, identification, and illumination	1-1-68
102	Transmission shift lever sequence, starter interlock, and transmission braking effect	1-1-68
103	Windshield defrosting and defogging systems	1-1-68
104	Windshield wiping and washing systems	1-1-68
105	Hydraulic brake—passenger cars	1-1-68
106	Hydraulic brake hoses	9-1-74
107	Reflecting surfaces	1-1-68
108	Lamps, reflective devices, and associated equipment	1-1-68
109	New pneumatic tires	1-1-68
110	Tire selection and rims	4-1-68
111	Rearview mirrors	1-1-68
112	Headlamp concealment devices	1-1-69
113	Hood latch systems	1-1-69
114	Theft protection	1-1-70
115	Vehicle identification number	1-1-69
116	Hydraulic brake fluids	3-1-72
117	Retreaded pneumatic tires	1-1-72
118	Power-operated window systems	2-1-71
119	Tires for vehicles other than passenger cars	9-1-74
121	Air brake systems—trucks, buses, and trailers	9-1-74
122	Motorcycle brake systems	1-1-74
123	Motorcycle controls and displays	9-1-74
124	Accelerator control systems	9-1-73
125	Warning devices	1-1-74
126	Truck-camper loading	1-1-73
	Crash protection and survivability	
201	Occupant protection in interior impact	1-1-68
202	Head restraints	1-1-69
203	Impact protection for driver from steering control system	1-1-68
204	Steering control rearward displacement	1-1-68
205	Glazing materials	1-1-68
206	Door locks and door retention components	1-1-68
207	Seating systems	1-1-68
208	Occupant crash protection—passenger cars	1-1-68
209	Seatbelt assemblies	3-1-67
210	Seatbelt assembly anchorages	1-1-68
211	Wheel nuts, wheel discs, and hub caps	1-1-68
212	Windshield mounting	1-1-70
213	Child seating systems	4-1-71
214	Side door strength	1-1-73
215	Exterior protection	9-1-72
216	Roof crush resistance	8-15-73
217	Bus window retention and release	9-1-73
218	Motorcycle helmets	3-1-74
301	Fuel system integrity	1-1-68
302	Flammability of interior materials	9-1-72

Source: General Accounting Office, *Effectiveness, Benefits, and Costs of Federal Safety Standards for Protection of Passenger Car Occupants, National Highway Traffic Safety Administration, Department of Transportation*, CED-76-121 (GAO, 1976).

meant to reduce vehicle body damage, not to increase occupant safety. Finally, the postcrash-survivability standards include requirements for fuel system integrity and for flammability of interior materials.

What Determines the Highway Death Rate?

Estimating the effect of federal government regulation of motor vehicle safety upon the highway death and injury rates is far from an easy task, given the complex forces that interact to produce highway injuries and deaths. Among the most important of these are vehicle design, highway design, the demographic characteristics of highway users, driver behavior, and regulation of vehicle use.

VEHICLE DESIGN. The NHTSA standards and the GSA standards that preceded them are intended to improve the design of vehicles so that drivers may more readily avoid accidents or survive crashes if they occur. These safety standards may have a substantial effect upon vehicle design, but there are other reasons why manufacturers may be eager to produce safe cars. As per capita income rises, car buyers may demand increased safety. This may help explain the shift to larger cars during periods of rising incomes. Adverse public relations from alleged design defects, such as those that plagued General Motors during the years it produced the Corvair, can make vehicle producers sensitive to safety concerns. In addition, the fear of costly tort suits may cause manufacturers to be very cautious in designing safety into their cars.

HIGHWAY DESIGN. Over the years, the states and federal government have worked steadily at improving highway design.[5] Highway markings, dividers, signals, and road surfaces have been improved substantially. Most important, a large network of divided, limited-access highways has been built, substantially reducing the risk of head-on collisions or collisions involving cross traffic. In the past twenty-five years the share of vehicle miles accumulated on limited-access highways has nearly quadrupled (table 4-1).

DRIVER DEMOGRAPHICS. It is well established that the age, sex, and sobriety of motor vehicle operators are important in explaining the number and severity of accidents. The increase in youthful drivers and the sharp rise in alcohol consumption between the early 1950s and the late 1970s (table 4-1) undoubtedly had a major effect upon the highway fatality rate.

5. For a summary of these activities, see U.S. Department of Transportation, National Highway Traffic Safety Administration, *An Evaluation of the Highway Safety Program*, DOT HS-802-481 (GPO, 1977).

In the analysis that follows, we include these variables along with other variables, such as per capita income and the cost of a collision, in attempting to explain the highway fatality rate.

DRIVER BEHAVIOR. There can be little doubt that highway safety is a reflection of driver behavior. Speed, carelessness, or outright recklessness can contribute importantly to the accident and death rates. More controversial, however, is the question of whether drivers adjust their behavior in response to their perceptions of the prospective risks they face. Specifically, do drivers respond to improvements in highways or vehicle safety by increasing their willingness to assume risks? In the past ten years, a considerable literature has developed on this theory of "risk compensation."[6] Spurred by the research of Peltzman, this literature has focused upon the theory that consumers calibrate their risk taking to perceptions of the dangers they face.[7] Much of the empirical research on risk compensation has been focused upon highway safety. The results of this research are often extremely controversial, particularly those that find that drivers respond to increased highway and vehicle safety by driving less cautiously.[8]

REGULATION OF VEHICLE USE. Obviously, the enforcement of traffic laws should have a major impact upon highway fatalities. Severe penalties for reckless operation, driving while intoxicated, or simply speeding may reduce the collision and fatality rates substantially. In addition, reduced speed limits, such as the 55 mph limit brought about by the 1973–74 oil crisis, may have major effects upon highway safety if they are enforced. More recently, the federal government has induced the states to increase the minimum drinking age to twenty-one years and to require seat belt usage. These regulations apply to vehicle use, rather than vehicle design, but they may be just as important as the NHTSA vehicle safety standards in reducing the highway death rate.

In the remainder of this chapter, we shall try to incorporate all of the above factors into an empirical model of the highway death rate. The

6. For a comprehensive discussion of this theory, see Gerald J. S. Wilde, "The Theory of Risk Homeostasis: Implications for Safety and Health," *Risk Analysis,* vol. 2, no. 4 (1982), pp. 209–25.

7. Sam Peltzman, "The Effects of Automobile Safety Regulation," *Journal of Political Economy,* vol. 83 (August–December 1975), pp. 677–725.

8. See, for example, Leon S. Robertson, "Automobile Safety Regulation: Rebuttal and New Data" (Yale University, Department of Epidemiology, 1984).

purpose of this model is to deduce the effectiveness of federal regulation of automobile safety, or at least of the changes in automobile design that have occurred during a period of increased federal regulation.

Engineering Estimates of the Effectiveness of Safety Standards

Considerable work has been done on the effectiveness of the more important safety standards and on the prospective effectiveness of additional crash-protection requirements for passive restraint systems. This work is useful in providing some estimate of the potential benefits of safety regulation.

Six major occupant-protection categories account for roughly two-thirds of the costs of safety regulation (excluding the bumper standard). The six regulations are: interior protection (no. 201); head restraints (no. 202); steering column (nos. 203 and 204); windshield and other glass (nos. 205 and 212); seat belts (nos. 208, 209, and 210); and side door strength (no. 214). In addition, dual braking systems account for most of the costs of the accident-prevention standards. An analysis of just these seven categories of standards covers more than three-fourths of the entire cost of safety regulation imposed by NHTSA (again excluding the bumper standard). A brief review of the literature on the effectiveness of each of these standards is therefore likely to be quite useful.

INTERIOR PROTECTION. Studies by Gates and Goldmuntz and by Lave and Weber have concluded that padded interior dashboards have only a limited effect upon injuries in automobile accidents. They conclude that instrument panel padding reduces the risk of minor injuries by 1.5 to 4.3 percent, but it has no effect upon more serious injuries or fatalities.[9]

HEAD RESTRAINTS. There is fairly widespread agreement that head restraints have had a beneficial effect upon occupant injuries. General Motors and Ford have estimated that neck injuries have been reduced by 20 percent by head restraints. NHTSA has concurred with a study by States and Balcerak that the number of neck injuries has been reduced by

9. Howard Gates and Lawrence Goldmuntz, *Automotive Safety* (Washington, D.C.: Economics and Science Planning, 1978), p. 30; and Lester B. Lave and W. E. Weber, "A Benefit-Cost Analysis of Auto Safety Features," *Applied Economics*, vol. 2 (October 1970), pp. 265–75.

14 percent by the restraints.[10] In NHTSA's most recent evaluation, integral head restraints, which reduce injuries by 17 percent, are distinguished from adjustable restraints, which reduce injuries by only 10 percent because an estimated 75 percent of them are not in an extended position.[11] O'Neill and others concluded that the effectiveness was between the GM-Ford and NHTSA estimates—17.2 percent.[12] Huelke and O'Day, however, have been more cautious, recommending further laboratory and field studies before concluding that the high-back seat as a head restraint actually reduces whiplash injuries.[13]

STEERING COLUMN. Energy-absorbing steering columns are thought to reduce the probability of fatalities and serious injuries to the driver. A large share of fatal accidents are front-end crashes in which drivers have a significant probability of coming in contact with the steering column, particularly if they are not using seat belts. Based on research including Levine and Campbell's 1971 study, Ford found that an energy-absorbing steering column reduces fatal and dangerous injuries in frontal crashes by 22.2 percent.[14] Gates and Goldmuntz calculate that the effect of energy-absorbing steering columns is to reduce serious and fatal injury rates by 8.4 to 10 percent and to cut less serious injuries by 2.6 to 6.2 percent.[15] Levine and Campbell's estimate for serious and fatal injury reduction is 14 percent.[16] A. J. McLean concluded in his 1974 research that the presence of energy-absorbing steering columns results in a 20 percent reduction in fatal and serious injuries from frontal crashes.[17]

In 1973 the New York State Department of Motor Vehicles published a study based on 1968–69 reports of head-on car-to-car collisions. They found a 24 percent reduction in fatal and serious injury rates for drivers of cars in compliance with the energy-absorbing steering column regulations.[18] Another study attributes a 45 percent reduction in severe (not life-

10. General Accounting Office, *Effectiveness, Benefits, and Costs of Federal Safety Standards for Protection of Passenger Car Occupants, National Highway Traffic Safety Administration, Department of Transportation,* CED-76-121 (GAO, 1976), p. 42.

11. Department of Transportation, NHTSA, *An Evaluation of Head Restraints: Federal Motor Vehicle Standard 202,* DOT HS-806-108 (DOT, 1982), p. 10.

12. Gates and Goldmuntz, *Automotive Safety,* p. 27.

13. GAO, *Effectiveness, Benefits, and Costs,* p. 48.

14. Ibid., p. 50.

15. Gates and Goldmuntz, *Automotive Safety,* p. 27.

16. GAO, *Effectiveness, Benefits, and Costs,* p. 50.

17. Gates and Goldmuntz, *Automotive Safety,* p. 26.

18. Department of Transportation, NHTSA, *An Evaluation of Federal Motor Vehicle*

threatening) to fatal accidents to the steering column regulation.[19] This study was limited to crashes with impact speed of at least 25 mph known to involve chest contact with the steering assembly. More recently, NHTSA has estimated that the steering column regulations have reduced the risk of fatalities in a frontal crash by 12 percent.[20]

WINDSHIELD AND OTHER GLASS. Gates and Goldmuntz calculate that serious and fatal injuries have been reduced by high-penetration-resistant windshield glass by between 0.4 and 2.7 percent.[21] Neither the 1976 GAO report nor NHTSA provides independent estimates of the effectiveness of the two standards dealing with glass. Thus Gates and Goldmuntz's estimate, based in part upon Griffin's review, is the only available measure of the effectiveness of these standards.

SEAT BELTS. The seat belt is undoubtedly the most important and effective safety device installed in the automobile pursuant to federal standards. The GSA standard and more than thirty state laws required seat belts even before NHTSA was formed. Since that time, NHTSA has added a few details involving seat belt assembly anchorages and has required the front outboard positions to have lap-shoulder belts. The remaining positions must have only lap belts. Finally, NHTSA has gone through several years of rulemaking on a passive restraint standard. In 1976 Secretary of Transportation William T. Coleman decided to delay the introduction of a passive restraint standard, substituting a voluntary test of passive restraint systems (air bags) by the automobile manufacturers. In 1977 NHTSA promulgated a standard, scuttling Coleman's decision and requiring that passive restraints be phased in by automobile manufacturers beginning in 1982.[22] The manufacturers were allowed to choose the technology as long as the systems met a performance standard.

In 1981, as part of the Reagan administration's "regulatory relief" program, the passive restraint requirement was rescinded by NHTSA Administrator Raymond Peck, leaving the old (lap-shoulder) active belt standard as NHTSA standard 208.[23] In 1982 the D.C. Court of Appeals

---

Safety Standards for Passenger Car Steering Assemblies: Standard 203, Impact Protection for the Driver: Standard 204, Rearward Column Displacement, DOT HS-805-705 (DOT, 1981), p. 33.

19. Ibid.
20. Ibid., p. 16.
21. Gates and Goldmuntz, *Automotive Safety,* p. 25.
22. 42 Fed. Reg. 34289 (1977).
23. 46 Fed. Reg. 53419 (1981).

reversed this rescission, instructing NHTSA to reevaluate its decision. The Appeals Court's decision was upheld by the Supreme Court in 1983.[24]

The existing lap-shoulder belt system is extremely effective in reducing fatalities and serious injuries from front-end and roll-over crashes. According to studies by Huelke and his collaborators, lap-shoulder belts reduce the probability of serious injury by 64 percent and fatalities by 32 percent for front-seat occupants. In 1973 a General Motors study concluded that these lap-shoulder belts reduce front-seat-occupant fatalities by 31 percent.[25]

Despite the substantial benefits from active seat belts, usage rates have declined since 1974. NHTSA estimates that 26 percent of occupants used seat belts in 1974, but in 1983 usage had fallen to only 14 percent.[26] Part of the decline might be attributed to the 55 mph speed limit and the subsequent sharp decline in the highway death rate. Vehicle occupants may be less concerned about serious injury or death when the death rate is falling.

SIDE DOOR STRENGTH. Early studies of the effects of NHTSA's standard 214, requiring beams in side doors to reduce intrusion into the occupant compartment during crashes, were quite disparate. Ford estimated in May 1974 that 12,400 minor injuries would be avoided, while NHTSA's 1972 report estimated a reduction in injuries of 26,800; both reports concurred that strengthened side doors would have very little effect upon fatalities.[27] More recent analyses by NHTSA conclude that the side door regulation reduces severe injuries or fatalities from side-door-impact single-vehicle crashes by 25 percent and from multiple-car collisions by 8 percent.[28]

DUAL BRAKING SYSTEMS. Lave and Weber have found that 1 percent of accidents involve cars with defective braking systems. Gates and Gold-

24. *State Farm Mutual Automobile Insurance Co.* v. *Department of Transportation,* 680 F. 2d 206 (D.C. Cir. 1982); and *Motor Vehicle Manufacturers Association* v. *State Farm Mutual Automobile Insurance Co.,* 463 U.S. 29 (1983).

25. Donald F. Huelke and James O'Day, "Passive Restraints: A Scientist's Views," in Robert W. Crandall and Lester B. Lave, eds., *The Scientific Basis of Health and Safety Regulation* (Brookings, 1981), pp. 26–27.

26. Department of Transportation, NHTSA, *Traffic Safety Trends and Forecasts,* DOT HS-805-998 (DOT, 1981), p. 31; and NHTSA, *Final Regulatory Impact Analysis: Amendments to Federal Motor Vehicle Safety Standard 208, Passenger Car Front Seat Occupant Protection* (DOT, 1984), p. V-3.

27. GAO, *Effectiveness, Benefits, and Costs,* p. 53.

28. Department of Transportation, NHTSA, *An Evaluation of Side Structure Improvements in Response to Federal Motor Vehicle Safety Standard 214,* DOT HS-806-314 (DOT, 1982), p. xxiii.

muntz argue that since an average of 1.7 vehicles are involved in each accident, the upper bound to the effectiveness of a standard that obtained perfectly safe braking systems would be 1.7 percent.[29] A recent NHTSA study concluded that dual braking systems have reduced accident rates by 0.7 percent.[30]

Although it is difficult to combine the above estimates and to calculate the theoretical effectiveness of the other safety standards, engineering estimates of the effectiveness of all NHTSA safety standards generally fall in the range of 15 to 35 percent,[31] depending upon the assumed level of seat belt usage. In the next section, we use a statistical model in an attempt to estimate the actual effects upon safety of changes in vehicle design since 1966. If risk compensation is important, we should expect to find that improved vehicle design has reduced passenger-car-occupant fatalities by less than the 15–35 percent suggested by engineering estimates. On the other hand, engineering estimates may prove to be conservative, and automobiles may in fact have become much more safe than even these estimates suggest.

A Statistical Analysis of the Highway Death Rate

The demand for safety cannot be assumed to be unaffected by other forces in the economy. Rising income or the increased costs of accidents may well affect driver behavior. Moreover, an increase in the safety of new automobiles may induce offsetting behavior. Cyclists, pedestrians, and occupants of unregulated vehicles may be more endangered by drivers who feel that they have a lower risk of injury or death because of required improvements in crash protection.

A Simple Test

Casual empiricism provides at least some indication that the offsetting behavior theory has some validity. The rate of improvement in passenger-

---

29. Gates and Goldmuntz, *Automotive Safety,* p. 32.

30. Department of Transportation, NHTSA, *A Preliminary Evaluation of Two Braking Improvements for Passenger Cars: Dual Master Cylinders and Front Disk Brakes,* DOT HS-806-359 (DOT, 1983), p. 43.

31. John D. Graham, "Automobile Safety: An Investigation of Occupant Protection Policies" (Ph.D dissertation, Carnegie-Mellon University, 1983), p. 136. Sam Peltzman has pointed out to us that the estimates of the average effectiveness of individual standards cannot simply be added together to obtain an estimate of the total effect of the standards.

car-occupant deaths since 1965 has been accompanied by a deterioration in the rate of improvement for the other victims of highway accidents. To see this, one can simply estimate loglinear relationships of the following form:

(1) $LXXD_t = a_0 + a_1 TREND4765_t + a_2 TREND6681_t + a_3 LVM_t,$

where $LXXD_t$ is the logarithm of the XX category of highway deaths in year t, $TREND4765_t$ and $TREND6681_t$ are trend terms for 1947–65 and 1966–81, respectively, and LVM_t is the logarithm of the number of vehicle miles amassed in year t. The results of such an estimation for total deaths, passenger-car-occupant deaths, nonoccupant deaths, and pedestrian and bicyclist deaths are shown here.

	Trend rates of improvement (t-statistics in parentheses)	
	1947–65 (a_1)	1966–81 (a_2)
Total deaths	−0.0381 (2.00)	−0.0395 (2.75)
Passenger-car-occupant deaths	−0.0195 (1.00)	−0.0422 (3.39)
Nonoccupant deaths	−0.0381 (1.80)	−0.0057 (0.35)
Pedestrian and bicyclist deaths	−0.0449 (2.06)	−0.0217 (1.31)

The projected values of each category of highway deaths for 1965–81, assuming that the 1947–65 rate of improvement continued, are shown with the actual 1965–81 experience in table 4-3. From these results, one could conclude that actual highway deaths were as much as 10,000 fewer per year by the mid-1970s than might have been expected from a simple extrapolation of the 1947–65 experience, but that nonoccupant deaths were as much as 4,000 higher. The very large improvement, therefore, is concentrated in the passenger-car-occupant category—the focus of most NHTSA regulation. Safety regulation may have been working for occupants, but part of their gain may have been at the apparent expense of nonoccupants. Whether such crude results can stand the test of more rigorous analysis is a question to which we now turn.

A More Detailed Statistical Analysis

If safety regulation has reduced highway fatalities, we should be able to identify this reduction in a statistical investigation of the determinants of

Table 4-3. Actual and Predicted Highway Fatalities, 1965–81, Assuming 1947–65 Trend Rate

Year	Total deaths		Passenger-car-occupant deaths		Nonoccupant deaths		Pedestrian and bicyclist deaths	
	Actual	Pre-dicted	Actual	Pre-dicted[a]	Actual	Pre-dicted	Actual	Pre-dicted
1965	49,000	47,922	32,500	32,580	16,500	15,337	9,480	9,105
1966	53,000	48,922	34,800	33,755	18,200	15,379	10,050	9,058
1967	53,100	49,067	34,800	34,185	18,300	15,232	10,100	8,904
1968	55,200	50,580	36,200	35,459	19,000	15,378	10,600	8,916
1969	56,400	52,006	36,800	36,913	19,600	15,496	10,620	8,912
1970	54,800	53,012	34,800	38,179	20,000	15,522	11,220	8,857
1971	54,700	54,793	34,200	39,729	20,500	15,699	11,450	8,885
1972	56,600	57,348	35,200	41,174	21,400	16,016	11,800	8,989
1973	55,800	57,403	33,700	41,782	22,100	15,842	11,650	8,824
1974	46,200	54,049	26,800	39,793	19,400	15,017	9,700	8,312
1975	46,000	54,287	27,200	40,684	18,800	14,889	9,600	8,178
1976	46,700	56,310	27,650	41,982	19,050	15,095	9,200	8,224
1977	49,500	57,329	28,250	43,020	21,250	15,108	9,800	8,166
1978	51,500	58,556	28,450	44,418	23,050	15,154	10,300	8,126
1979	51,900	55,499	29,100	42,284	22,800	14,432	10,400	7,688
1980	52,600	53,062	29,050	40,299	23,550	13,827	10,800	7,317
1981	50,800	52,315	27,730	39,618	23,070	13,533	10,200	7,110

Source: National Safety Council, *Accident Facts*, various years.
a. Uses an estimate of equation 1 substituting passenger-car miles for total vehicle miles.

highway deaths. Peltzman has attempted such an analysis based upon data through 1972, but his results have been quite controversial.[32] The availability of at least nine more years of data, more than doubling the period for estimating the effect of federal safety regulation, should allow us to test and improve upon Peltzman's results.

Peltzman's model of automobile accidents predicts that fatalities or injuries are related to income, the price of accidents (repair and hospitalization costs), alcohol consumption, the age distribution of drivers, the

32. Peltzman, "The Effects of Automobile Safety Regulation." For critiques of his study, see H. C. Joksch, "Critique of Sam Peltzman's Study," *Accident Analysis and Prevention*, vol. 8 (June 1976), p. 131; and Leon S. Robertson, "A Critical Analysis of Peltzman's 'The Effects of Automobile Safety Regulation,'" *Journal of Economic Issues*, vol. 11 (September 1977), pp. 587–600. Peltzman's replies may be found in "The Effects of Automobile Safety Regulation: A Reply," *Accident Analysis and Prevention*, vol. 8 (June 1976), pp. 138–42; and "A Reply," *Journal of Economic Issues*, vol. 11 (September 1977), pp. 672–78. Also see Oscar R. Cantu, "An Updated Regression Analysis on the Effects of the Regulation of Auto Safety," Working Paper 15 (Yale School of Management, 1980).

share of limited-access roads and rural driving in total vehicle miles, and speed. In addition, he includes a time trend, which he interprets as reflecting, in part, the influence of increases in permanent income. He estimates a loglinear relationship between these variables and the highway death rates for 1947 through 1965 and uses the results to predict the fatality rates for 1966 through 1972, the period of regulation. He finds that his model overpredicts the occupant death rate but underpredicts the nonoccupant death rate (pedestrian, motorcyclist, and bicyclist deaths). This leads him to conclude that safety regulation has increased occupant safety but has created offsetting driving behavior that has placed nonoccupants at greater risk. These effects cancel each other, and it is Peltzman's conclusion that the total death rate has been unaffected by regulation—a conclusion that he buttresses with additional cross-sectional results.

There are a number of potential problems with Peltzman's time-series estimates. In the first place, virtually all of the improvement in death rates since 1960 is attributable to his simple loglinear trend term. While he attributes much of the trend to increases in permanent income, he does not make any attempt to provide empirical justification for this attribution. If this underlying trend were changing throughout the 1947–72 period for reasons other than federal safety regulation, it would be invalid to use the estimated 1947–65 value to predict 1966–72 death rates.

Second, Peltzman adjusts his dependent variable for changes in the composition of driving on regular and limited-access highways. This is done in order to preserve degrees of freedom, but it is done in such a complex fashion that no one has been able to replicate his variables.[33] Finally, we show in appendix C that results based upon pre-1966 experience are quite sensitive to choice of period of estimation.

Peltzman's time-series equation is of the form:

$$(2) \qquad ADR = a_0 + a_1 COST + a_2 INCOME + a_3 YOUTH$$
$$+ \, a_4 ALCOHOL + a_5 SPEED + a_6 TREND,$$

where *ADR* is an adjusted death rate, *COST* is the "price" of an accident (medical and accident-repair costs), *INCOME* is earned per capita income, *YOUTH* is the ratio of drivers aged 15–25 years to all other drivers, *ALCOHOL* is alcohol consumption per person (15 years and older),

---

33. Cantu, "An Updated Regression Analysis."

SPEED is the average speed of vehicles on noninterstate rural roads during off-peak hours, and *TREND* is a time trend. All variables, other than *TREND*, are in logarithmic form. The death rate is defined as deaths per vehicle mile adjusted for changes in urban-rural driving and the share of miles driven on limited-access highways.

Because of the difficulty in replicating Peltzman's dependent variables, we perform all estimation with unadjusted highway deaths, including separate independent variables for total miles and the proportion of mileage on limited-access highways.

To estimate the effect of safety regulation on passenger-car occupants, we estimate an equation relating only the passenger-car-occupant fatalities to the relevant demographic and safety variables. Peltzman includes truck- and bus-occupant deaths in his occupant series even though NHTSA regulations for passenger cars do not affect trucks and buses. A separate equation is estimated for nonoccupants—truck occupants, bus occupants, pedestrians, bicyclists, and motorcyclists. In addition, separate results are reported for pedestrian and bicyclists' deaths.

Time-Series Evidence

The analysis that follows utilizes time-series data for 1947–81 as well as cross-sectional data developed by NHTSA and the National Safety Council. We begin with the time-series analysis.

To model highway safety, we follow suggestions advanced by MacAvoy and developed by Graham.[34] If safety regulation induces offsetting driver behavior and if risk taking is therefore a function of the observed highway death rate, a simultaneous-equation model of highway deaths and risk taking is required. Risky driving behavior can be characterized by a number of different measures—such as speed, driving while intoxicated, and driving in marginal weather conditions. Of these, only speed is directly measurable; hence, we use average highway speed as a proxy for driver risk taking. The model of highway deaths and risk is then:

$$(3) \quad DX = f(SPEED, INCOME, YOUTH, ALCOHOL, COST,$$

$$WEIGHT, TRUCK, LIMITED ACCESS, MILES,$$

$$SAFETY, VINTAGE);$$

34. Paul W. MacAvoy, "Comment," in Henry G. Manne and Roger LeRoy Miller, eds., *Auto Safety Regulation. The Cure or the Problem?* (Glen Ridge, N.J.; Thomas Morton, 1976); and Graham, "Automobile Safety."

(4) $SPEED = g(DX, INCOME, YOUTH, ALCOHOL, COST,$

$SAFETY, PFUEL, EMBARGO),$

where *DX* is the number of annual highway deaths in the *X* category. *SPEED*, *INCOME*, *YOUTH*, *ALCOHOL*, and *COST* are the same as Peltzman's formulation of these variables. *WEIGHT* is an estimate of the average weight of cars on the road, derived from Polk data on vintages and manufacturers' data on curb weight. Smaller, lighter cars should increase motor vehicle fatalities. *TRUCK* is a measure of the share of vehicle miles accounted for by trucks since passenger cars and pedestrians obviously fare poorly in collisions with larger vehicles. *LIMITED ACCESS* is the share of total vehicle miles accumulated on limited-access highways. We use this variable as an independent regressor, rather than adjusting the dependent variable for its effect as Peltzman did. *MILES* is the total number of vehicle miles accumulated each year. Annual variations in vehicle miles need not necessarily lead to proportional variations in each type of traffic fatality. *PFUEL* and *EMBARGO* are used to capture the effects of higher fuel prices and the federal speed limit. *PFUEL* is the real price of motor fuel, and *EMBARGO* is a dummy variable equal to 1 before 1974 and $e^{2.78}$ from 1974 through 1981 because equation 3 is estimated in logarithmic form.

Unlike Peltzman, we utilize a direct measure of the apparent improvement in the crashworthiness of new passenger vehicles, *SAFETY*. This index is constructed in two ways, but only the results using the second method are reported in the text. The first method weights each model year's cars according to the results reported by the General Accounting Office in its analysis of North Carolina crashes. These results suggest that since 1965 cars have become safer for occupants at the following rates: 1966–68 models: 13 percent; 1969–70: 22 percent; 1971 and later: 23 percent.[35] The results using this method appear in appendix C. The second weighting is based upon recent research by Graham. He finds that the rate of improvement is greater and has continued through 1974. From his analysis of NHTSA's Fatal Accident Reporting System (FARS) data, he concludes that the improvements are: 1966–67: 4 percent; 1968–69: 19 percent; 1970–71: 24 percent; 1972–73: 28 percent; and 1974 and later: 34 percent.[36] *SAFETY* is constructed by applying these weights to the

35. GAO, *Effectiveness, Benefits, and Costs*, p. 32.
36. Graham, "Automobile Safety," table 3-11.

distribution of automobile vintages in each year's stock of automobiles on the road.

Because older cars accumulate fewer annual miles than new cars, these weights are adjusted by a multiplicative factor reflecting the ratio of estimated miles driven by a car of that age to the average miles driven by a new car.[37] Thus, *SAFETY* is an estimate of the average crashworthiness of an average passenger-car mile in each of our sample years—1947–81. It is set equal to unity in the years 1947–65 and approaches 0.66 as the stock of cars tends toward all post-1974 models.

SAFETY assumes a value of 1.0 for all preregulation years, but this does not necessarily imply that automobiles underwent no improvements in safety before 1966. One way of capturing pre-1966 safety improvements is to use a crude time trend for the preregulatory years. Peltzman argues that a time trend captures the increasing demand for safety that arises from higher permanent income levels. In appendix C, our analysis includes both a separate measure of permanent per capita income and a time trend to capture this effect, but the results are not particularly encouraging. Finally, to estimate the effect of vehicle age upon safety, we include the weighted average age of passenger cars on the road, *VINTAGE*, where the weights are the share of vehicle miles accumulated by each vintage. If *SAFETY* were simply capturing the effect of changing vehicle age, it would be collinear with *VINTAGE*.

If *SPEED* is endogenous, direct ordinary least squares estimates of equation 3 will be biased. Instead, the reduced form of *DX* must be estimated:

(5) $DX = f(SAFETY, WEIGHT, VINTAGE, INCOME, YOUTH,$

$ALCOHOL, COST, EMBARGO, PFUEL,$

$LIMITED\ ACCESS, TRUCK, MILES).$

The mean, standard deviation, and definition of all variables appear in table 4-4. Because most of the effects of the important variables upon the death rate are likely to be multiplicative, we estimate a loglinear form of equation 5 by ordinary least squares. In addition, we estimate equation 3 directly, allowing for the possibility that *SPEED* is not jointly determined with the death rate. The results are reported in tables 4-5 and 4-6 for four

37. Department of Transportation, NHTSA, *Automotive Fuel Economy Program: Fifth Annual Report to the Congress, January 1981* (DOT HS-805-692).

Table 4-4. Variables Used in the Time-Series Analysis, 1947-81

Variable	Mean	Standard deviation	Definition
SAFETY	0.924	0.109	Safety index (see text)
WEIGHT	3,350	1,090	Average weight of cars in use (pounds)
VINTAGE	5.89	0.730	Weighted average of age of cars in use (years)
INCOME	3.305	0.464	Earned per capita income for those aged 15 and older (thousands of 1977 dollars)
YOUTH	0.200	0.015	Ratio of youthful drivers (aged 15–25) to total drivers
ALCOHOL	2.32	0.326	Alcohol consumption per person of drinking age (gallons per year)
COST	185.8	19.45	Weighted average of CPI indexes for hospital care, doctors' services, and auto repair (1967 = 100; weights = 0.22, 0.18, and 0.06, respectively) deflated by CPI
EMBARGO	1.39	0.722	Dummy variable for post-1974 period (EM = 2.78 for years 1974-81 since e^{EM} = 1)
SPEED	54.1	4.1	Average speed on main rural roads during off-peak hours
PFUEL	103.0	13.3	Price of motor fuel (CPI index 1967 = 100) deflated by CPI
LIMITED ACCESS	0.108	0.078	Share of vehicle miles amassed on limited-access highways
TRUCK	0.197	0.022	Share of total vehicle miles amassed by trucks
MILES	9,226	3,754	Total vehicle miles (100 million miles)

classes of fatalities: total highway deaths, passenger-car-occupant fatalities, nonoccupant deaths, and pedestrian-bicyclist deaths. All equations are estimated in logarithmic form; hence coefficient estimates may be read as the elasticities of the relevant death rate with respect to each variable.

The results for total highway deaths reveal a strong influence of

Table 4-5. Estimates of the Determinants of Highway Fatalities, 1947-81, with Speed as Endogenous[a]

Independent variable	Total deaths	Passenger-car-occupant deaths	Nonoccupant deaths	Pedestrian and bicyclist deaths
SAFETY	0.932*	1.96*	−0.854*	−0.714*
	(3.28)	(4.34)	(3.53)	(2.95)
WEIGHT	2.38*	−0.110	−2.46*	−1.48
	(2.40)	(0.56)	(2.84)	(1.77)
VINTAGE	−0.034	−0.774	−0.001	−0.035
	(0.27)	(0.63)	(0.01)	(0.33)
INCOME	1.12*	0.762*	1.43*	0.933*
	(4.93)	(2.30)	(7.38)	(4.83)
YOUTH	0.098	0.166	−0.078	0.707*
	(0.38)	(0.42)	(0.36)	(3.25)
ALCOHOL	−0.046	0.149	0.592*	0.672*
	(0.15)	(0.39)	(2.23)	(2.61)
COST	0.078	0.083	0.054	−0.066
	(1.73)	(1.34)	(1.40)	(1.72)
EMBARGO	−0.049	−0.105	−0.036	−0.183*
	(1.20)	(1.88)	(1.02)	(5.31)
PFUEL	−0.059	0.133	−0.258*	−0.056
	(0.72)	(1.14)	(3.67)	(0.81)
LIMITED ACCESS	−0.029	−0.086	0.080*	0.007
	(1.09)	(1.88)	(3.43)	(0.30)
TRUCK	0.531*	0.485*	0.630*	0.082
	(5.11)	(2.94)	(7.07)	(0.92)
MILES	0.431*	0.768*	−0.538*	−0.475*
	(2.24)	(2.58)	(3.26)	(2.91)
Summary statistics				
$\bar{R}^2$	0.984	0.014	0.990	0.969
Rho	−0.681	0.982	−0.781	−0.622

* Statistically significant at the 95 percent confidence level.
a. All variables except EMBARGO are in natural logarithms; numbers in parentheses are t-statistics.

SAFETY, INCOME, and *TRUCK.* The coefficient of *SAFETY* is both large and highly significant. Most of the attention of safety regulators has been focused upon crash protection; therefore, one would expect the effects of the improvements in vehicle design to be reflected principally in reductions in occupant death rates. Since occupant deaths are only 55 percent of total highway deaths, the coefficient of *SAFETY* should be about 0.55 if the estimates of design improvements incorporated in the *SAFETY* index are correct and if there is no offsetting behavior. In fact, the coefficient of

Table 4-6. Estimates of the Determinants of Highway Fatalities, 1947-81, with Speed as Exogenous[a]

Independent variable	Total deaths	Passenger-car-occupant deaths	Nonoccupant deaths	Pedestrian and bicyclist deaths
SAFETY	0.852*	1.51*	−0.790*	−0.973*
	(2.90)	(2.99)	(2.25)	(3.34)
WEIGHT	−1.87*	−0.873	0.045	−1.116*
	(3.47)	(0.84)	(0.07)	(2.17)
VINTAGE	0.004	−0.206	0.175	0.030
	(0.04)	(0.91)	(1.31)	(0.27)
INCOME	1.13*	0.553	1.478*	0.989*
	(5.26)	(1.67)	(5.73)	(4.64)
YOUTH	−0.107	−0.495	−0.409	0.004
	(0.48)	(1.21)	(1.55)	(0.02)
ALCOHOL	0.074	0.509	1.24*	0.893*
	(0.31)	(1.40)	(4.40)	(3.82)
COST	0.066	0.062	0.028	−0.118*
	(1.61)	(1.02)	(0.57)	(2.90)
SPEED	0.745*	1.17*	1.23*	2.06*
	(2.36)	(2.42)	(3.24)	(6.58)
LIMITED ACCESS	−0.037	−0.056	0.049	−0.003
	(1.51)	(1.12)	(1.68)	(0.12)
TRUCK	0.521*	0.414*	0.653*	−0.017
	(5.84)	(2.15)	(6.11)	(0.20)
MILES	0.240	0.396	−0.993*	−0.939*
	(1.22)	(1.09)	(4.21)	(4.81)
Summary statistics				
$\bar{R}^2$	0.984	0.980	0.981	0.954
Rho	−0.815	0.497	−0.814	−0.820

* Statistically significant at the 95 percent confidence level.
a. All variables are in natural logarithms; numbers in parentheses are *t*-statistics.

SAFETY is consistently close to 0.9 regardless of specification of the empirical model.

The remarkable effects of *SAFETY* are more apparent in the occupant-death equations. The coefficient of *SAFETY* is consistently around 2 when *SPEED* is treated as an endogenous variable and between 1.5 and 2.4 when *SPEED* is entered exogenously. Once again, this result is not materially affected by the deletion or inclusion of the other variables in the equation.

In both the total death and occupant-death equations, earned income proves to have a large and significant estimated effect, as does the share of truck miles in total travel. Higher incomes increase the value of time and therefore may contribute to speed and risk taking. The effect of truck miles on the safety of other highway users is obvious.

It is surprising that *ALCOHOL* and *YOUTH* do not emerge as significant variables in most specifications. *ALCOHOL* is significant in the occupant-death equation when insignificant regressors are dropped from the equation in the specification in which *SPEED* is endogenous. Similarly, the post-embargo years and their 55 mph speed limit do not seem to have a large effect upon total deaths, but *EMBARGO* does have a larger and significant effect on passenger-car-occupant and pedestrian deaths. For some reason, the price of motor fuel is directly associated with the occupant death rate despite theoretical reasons to believe the contrary. Finally, the share of miles driven on limited-access highways is important in explaining reductions in the passenger-car-occupant death rate when insignificant regressors are dropped from the equation.

The results for the nonoccupant and pedestrian-bicyclist equations provide some evidence for the risk compensation hypothesis. The number of deaths in these categories is inversely related to the *SAFETY* index, and this inverse relationship is highly significant. However, the absolute magnitude of these coefficients is considerably smaller than the positive coefficients in the occupant equation. As the total death equation shows, this means that the offsetting effect does not negate the favorable effects of *SAFETY* on total highway deaths.

INCOME, EMBARGO, WEIGHT, and *TRUCK* contribute to the explanation of nonoccupant deaths in a manner similar to that observed in the total and occupant-death equations. But alcohol and youthful drivers appear to be much more devastating to pedestrians and bicyclists than to the occupants. This suggests that youth or alcohol consumption may lead to more reckless operation or greater speed, and that these results imperil helpless pedestrians and bicyclists more than passenger-car occupants.

A comparison of the results in tables 4-5 and 4-6 reveals that there is little to choose between a model that treats speed as endogenous and one that assumes that speed and highway deaths are not jointly determined by a simultaneous system. *SPEED* generally has a significantly positive coefficient despite the measurement problems associated with such a variable. The effects of *YOUTH* are reduced when *SPEED* is entered as a separate regressor, suggesting that *YOUTH* might be a determinant of average highway speed.

These results suggest a very large effect of the improved safety design of automobiles since 1966 upon occupant death rates, an effect that cannot be attributed simply to changes in the average age of automobiles because the separate variable, *VINTAGE*, never adds to the explanatory value of any of the equations.

One might ask if *SAFETY* is not simply picking up the effects of other trend-driven variables. To test for this possibility, two trend terms were employed in addition to *SAFETY*, one for 1947–65 and one for 1966–81. Neither was statistically significant. The value of the coefficient of *SAFETY* falls very slightly in this specification, and its statistical significance is reduced somewhat, but it performs much better than the simple trend terms.[38]

Cross-Sectional Evidence

While the time-series results are very robust against changes in specification, it is possible that the interaction of numerous trend-related variables could lead to spurious inferences. It would be more convincing if the time-series estimates were corroborated by evidence from cross sections at various time intervals since the federal safety program began. For this purpose, we utilize FARS data collected and reported by NHTSA and data reported in the Census Bureau's *Vital Statistics of the United States*. To perform analyses similar to those reported above for the time-series data, we have collected automobile vintage stock data from R. L. Polk for fifty states and calculated safety-weighted vintage automobile stock indexes for each state in 1972, 1975, and 1977. The cross-sectional equations differ from the time-series estimates marginally. With all variables in logarithmic form, each estimated equation is of the form:

$$(6) \qquad DXX = b_0 + b_1 INCOME + b_2 YOUTH + b_3 ALCOHOL$$

$$+ \, b_4 SPEED + b_5 URBAN + b_6 SAFETY + b_7 MILES.$$

38. Specifying the regression in terms of a death rate, annual deaths per 100 million vehicle miles, does not alter the qualitative nature of these results, but it raises the estimated coefficient of *SAFETY*. Moreover, an additive model yields very similar elasticity estimates for the important variables. Finally, a two-stage least squares estimation of equation 3 provides very similar estimates of the coefficient of *SAFETY*. Given the similarity of the results and the impossibility of estimating the cross-sectional model below with two-stage least squares, we report only ordinary least squares estimates.

The dependent variable, *DXX*, is highway deaths of a given type (total, occupants, pedestrians) as in the time-series analysis. *URBAN* is a measure of the ratio of urban to total vehicle miles driven in the state during the year. *YOUTH* is the share of persons aged 25 or under (rather than drivers 25 and under) in the state. Data on youthful drivers are not available for many states, nor are truck miles.

Because the state data are likely to be less precise than the national data, the results of the cross-sectional analysis are less clear than those of the time-series regressions (tables 4-7, 4-8, 4-9, and 4-10). Both the FARS and *Vital Statistics* regressions evidence a strong inverse relationship between *URBAN* and total highway deaths. In addition, the coefficients of *SAFETY* are consistently positive and generally significant in the total highway death equations, suggesting a significant beneficial impact of regulation. The magnitude of the coefficients are implausibly large, perhaps because of omitted variables. *YOUTH* and *ALCOHOL* provide much less consistent contributions to the explanatory power of the total highway death equations, although *YOUTH* seems to provide a statistically significant contribution in the equations that do not include *SPEED*. The equations including *SPEED* are estimated only for a subset of states because speed data are not universally available.

When the data are disaggregated into separate death rates for passenger-car occupants and pedestrians or bicyclists, the results are less clear. For the FARS data, the results for 1977 suggest a positive effect of *SAFETY* on occupant safety, but the 1975 results do not. The 1977 *Vital Statistics* results for occupants are more precise than for earlier years, and the effect of *SAFETY* is correspondingly clearer in 1977 than in 1972 or 1975. Throughout, *URBAN* and occupant deaths are inversely related, surely a sensible result. *SPEED* appears to contribute little to explaining the occupant death rate. *YOUTH* and *ALCOHOL* are related to the occupant death rate in the *Vital Statistics* regressions, but not in those using FARS data.

Once again, the effects of *YOUTH* and *ALCOHOL* are most pronounced in the pedestrian equations. It appears that drinking and youthful drivers are more hazardous to pedestrians and bicyclists than to passenger-car occupants. Pedestrians are more likely to be killed in states with high values of *URBAN*, reflecting the vulnerability of pedestrians in urbanized areas. Finally, while the coefficients of *SAFETY* are consistently negative in the pedestrian-bicyclist equations, they are never statistically significant. This may be due to imprecise data for the dependent variable, but it

Table 4-7. Estimates of the Determinants of Highway Deaths, Using FARS Data, including Speed, 1975 and 1977[a]

Independent variable	Total deaths		Passenger-car-occupant deaths		Pedestrian and bicyclist deaths	
	1975	*1977*	*1975*	*1977*	*1975*	*1977*
SAFETY	3.915*	2.760	1.166	2.184	−2.582	−0.633
	(2.48)	(1.36)	(0.62)	(1.11)	(0.89)	(0.17)
INCOME	−0.543*	−0.276	−0.166	−0.365	−1.688*	−1.265*
	(2.24)	(0.86)	(0.58)	(1.17)	(3.78)	(2.14)
YOUTH	0.373	0.507	0.354	0.120	1.279	1.882*
	(0.98)	(1.20)	(0.78)	(0.29)	(1.83)	(2.43)
ALCOHOL	0.225*	0.067	0.083	0.011	0.629*	0.363
	(2.15)	(0.49)	(0.67)	(0.08)	(3.26)	(1.46)
SPEED	0.015	1.498	−0.010	0.981	0.092	−1.725
	(0.08)	(1.79)	(0.05)	(1.21)	(0.27)	(1.12)
URBAN	−0.149*	−0.072	−0.182*	−0.089	0.336*	0.342*
	(2.66)	(0.98)	(2.74)	(1.24)	(3.26)	(2.53)
MILES	1.008*	0.963*	1.018*	0.990*	1.029*	0.986*
	(26.97)	(19.32)	(22.92)	(20.43)	(14.92)	(10.77)
Summary statistic						
$\bar{R}^2$	0.973	0.956	0.964	0.962	0.940	0.903

Source: Authors' calculations based on data from Department of Transportation, NHTSA, Fatal Accident Reporting System (FARS). Data are state cross sections. Observations are for forty-four states.
* Statistically significant at the 95 percent confidence level.
a. All variables are in natural logarithms; numbers in parentheses are *t*-statistics.

is difficult to identify a clear pattern of offsetting driving behavior from these data.

The cross-sectional results confirm the general impact of safety regulation uncovered in the time-series regressions. The overall highway death rate appears to be lower because of safer post-1965 cars, but one cannot dismiss the possibility of offsetting driver behavior that increases the risks to pedestrians and bicyclists. The time-series results identify such a result even if it cannot be confirmed in the state data.

Further Reflections and Comparisons with Other Studies

The results of our statistical analysis show a surprisingly large improvement in vehicle safety for automobile occupants over 1968–74. This estimate exceeds, by far, the improvements in occupant safety found by Graham or estimated by engineers.[39] It appears that some of this improve-

39. Graham, "Automobile Safety," p. 136.

Table 4-8. Estimates of the Determinants of Highway Deaths, Using FARS Data, excluding Speed, 1975 and 1977[a]

Independent variable	Total deaths		Passenger-car-occupant deaths		Pedestrian and bicyclist deaths	
	1975	1977	1975	1977	1975	1977
SAFETY	2.424	4.998*	0.336	3.645	−3.932	−0.661
	(1.59)	(2.69)	(0.20)	(1.98)	(1.41)	(0.21)
INCOME	−0.233	−0.184	−0.048	−0.154	−1.284*	−1.229*
	(1.11)	(0.59)	(0.21)	(0.50)	(3.36)	(2.33)
YOUTH	0.552	0.851*	0.417	0.420	1.585*	2.205*
	(1.62)	(2.12)	(1.12)	(1.06)	(2.54)	(3.23)
ALCOHOL	0.202	0.103	0.078	0.009	0.622*	0.367
	(1.94)	(0.78)	(0.68)	(0.07)	(3.25)	(1.63)
URBAN	−0.195*	−0.160*	−0.207*	−0.174*	0.196*	0.298*
	(4.44)	(2.85)	(4.31)	(3.14)	(2.44)	(3.13)
MILES	1.029*	1.036*	1.040*	1.048*	1.110*	1.54*
	(33.66)	(26.80)	(31.07)	(27.40)	(19.82)	(16.04)
Summary statistic						
$\bar{R}^2$	0.972	0.960	0.968	0.963	0.936	0.918

Source: Authors' calculations based on data from Department of Transportation, NHTSA, Fatal Accident Reporting System (FARS). Observations are for each of fifty states.
* Statistically significant at the 95 percent confidence level.
a. All variables are in natural logarithms; numbers in parentheses are *t*-statistics.

ment may have been offset by deleterious effects upon the safety of nonoccupants, but this deterioration has not been sufficient to offset the large gains in occupant safety.

Had automobiles been as unsafe in 1981 as in 1965, the estimates in table 4-5 and 4-6 suggest that total fatalities would have been 18,000 to 22,000 above their actual 1981 level. The estimate of lives saved per year is about 30 percent of the total deaths that would have been predicted without safer automobiles. This estimate seems rather high in light of engineering estimates of the increase in *occupant* safety of 10 to 35 percent and our identification of some offsetting behavior.

Why the estimate is so high frankly remains somewhat of a puzzle. But it is interesting that a 30 percent reduction is modest when compared with the reduction in the overall highway death rate in other developed countries. Table 4-11 provides estimates of the reduction in these rates for nine other countries between 1968 and 1979. Only the United States, Canada, and the United Kingdom evidence a decline of less than 40 percent between 1968 and 1979. Of course, these declines are the result of many forces, including seat belt laws and tightened speed limits. But a net

Table 4-9. Estimates of the Determinants of Highway Deaths, Using *Vital Statistics* Data, including Speed, 1972, 1975, and 1977[a]

Independent variable	Total deaths			Passenger-car-occupant deaths			Pedestrian and bicyclist deaths		
	1972	1975	1977	1972	1975	1977	1972	1975	1977
SAFETY	5.223	4.991*	3.191	9.024	7.136	11.276*	2.584	0.299	−0.133
	(1.64)	(4.05)	(1.88)	(0.87)	(1.40)	(2.34)	(0.53)	(0.11)	(0.04)
INCOME	−0.260	−0.622*	−0.335	0.746	0.821	−0.860	−0.706	−1.772*	−1.211*
	(0.75)	(3.29)	(1.25)	(0.66)	(1.05)	(1.13)	(1.33)	(4.41)	(2.47)
YOUTH	0.240	0.289	0.503	3.260*	2.440	1.545	0.585	1.363*	1.568*
	(0.51)	(0.97)	(1.43)	(2.09)	(1.99)	(1.54)	(0.80)	(2.17)	(2.43)
ALCOHOL	−0.031	0.116	0.033	0.128	0.537	0.558	0.250	0.395*	0.343
	(0.23)	(1.42)	(0.29)	(0.28)	(1.59)	(1.74)	(1.18)	(2.27)	(1.66)
SPEED	0.218	−0.076	1.071	−0.206	0.288	2.205	−1.569*	−0.109	−0.820
	(0.51)	(0.52)	(1.54)	(0.15)	(0.48)	(1.11)	(2.37)	(0.35)	(0.64)
URBAN	−0.202*	−0.109*	−0.071	−0.388	−0.219	−0.091	−0.014	0.347*	−0.274*
	(3.13)	(2.49)	(1.15)	(1.83)	(1.22)	(0.52)	(0.14)	(3.74)	(2.44)
MILES	1.073*	1.024*	0.997*	1.222*	1.069*	1.198*	1.222*	1.024*	0.975*
	(25.52)	(35.08)	(24.00)	(8.85)	(8.88)	(10.12)	(18.83)	(16.51)	(12.83)
Summary statistic									
$\bar{R}^2$	0.972	0.985	0.971	0.775	0.780	0.834	0.952	0.951	0.926

Source: Authors' calculations based on data from Bureau of the Census, *Vital Statistics of the United States*, vol. 2: *Mortality*, various years. Observations for 1972 are for thirty-five states, and for 1975 and 1977, forty-four states.
* Statistically significant at the 95 percent confidence level.
a. All variables are in natural logarithms; numbers in parentheses are *t*-statistics.

Table 4-10. Estimates of the Determinants of Highway Deaths, Using *Vital Statistics* Data, excluding Speed, 1972, 1975, and 1977[a]

Independent variable	Total deaths			Passenger-car-occupant deaths			Pedestrian and bicyclist deaths		
	1972	1975	1977	1972	1975	1977	1972	1975	1977
SAFETY	5.668*	2.924*	5.433*	10.703	7.894	13.017*	-3.927	-2.473	-0.089
	(2.51)	(2.23)	(3.34)	(1.63)	(1.78)	(3.18)	(0.93)	(0.93)	(0.03)
INCOME	-0.151	-0.221	-0.283	0.116	0.373	-0.702	-0.519	-1.125*	-1.204*
	(0.54)	(1.23)	(1.04)	(0.14)	(0.62)	(1.03)	(0.98)	(3.10)	(2.81)
YOUTH	0.483	0.605*	0.837*	3.003*	1.935	1.292	0.996	1.941*	1.790*
	(1.10)	(2.06)	(2.38)	(2.36)	(1.95)	(1.46)	(1.21)	(3.28)	(3.24)
ALCOHOL	-0.036	0.065	0.051	0.252	0.604	0.476	0.100	0.324	0.360
	(0.30)	(0.72)	(0.44)	(0.73)	(1.98)	(1.63)	(0.45)	(1.78)	(1.97)
URBAN	-0.168*	-0.132*	-0.114*	-0.248	-0.140	-0.035	0.112	0.241*	0.241*
	(3.15)	(3.48)	(2.31)	(1.60)	(1.09)	(0.28)	(1.12)	(3.16)	(3.12)
MILES	1.069*	1.021*	1.050*	1.252*	1.075*	1.129*	1.145*	1.063*	1.021*
	(32.35)	(38.73)	(31.01)	(13.06)	(12.06)	(13.24)	(18.49)	(20.00)	(19.16)
Summary statistic									
$\bar{R}^2$	0.971	0.980	0.971	0.823	0.801	0.854	0.927	0.941	0.940

Source: Authors' calculations based on data from Bureau of the Census, *Vital Statistics of the United States*, vol. 2: *Mortality*, various years. Data are for each of fifty states.
* Statistically significant at the 95 percent-confidence level.
a. All variables are in natural logarithms; numbers in parentheses are *t*-statistics.

Table 4-11. International Comparisons of the Decrease in the Highway Death Rate per 100 Million Vehicle Miles, 1968–79

Country	1968	1979	Decrease (percent)
Australia	8.9	5.3	40.4
Belgium	19.8	10.4	47.5
Canada	7.6	4.7	38.2
France	16.8	7.4	56.0
Germany	12.4	6.9	44.4
Italy	15.9	5.7	64.2
Japan	20.9	4.2	79.9
Netherlands	13.2	5.2	60.6
United Kingdom	6.1	3.9	36.1
United States	5.4	3.5	35.2

Source: Motor Vehicle Manufacturers Association, *Automobile Facts and Figures '75*, p. 43; and *MVMA Motor Vehicle Facts and Figures '82*, p. 88.

lifesaving effect of 30 percent due to safer automobiles is certainly not outside the range of possibility.

What else might explain the apparent improvement in U.S. automobile safety? One possibility is the vehicle manufacturers' fear of tort suits.[40] In the 1960s General Motors experienced a number of suits because of apparent problems with its Corvair. In the 1970s Ford's placement of the gasoline tank on the Pinto generated a number of highly publicized tort suits against the company. These and a number of other suits could have induced the manufacturers to increase automobile safety even more than regulation would have required. Because manufacturers' expectations of potential tort suits cannot be measured, and there is a lack of data on the actual cost of such suits over time, it is difficult to provide much more than speculation on this issue. A survey published in 1980 revealed that the average cost of all liability risks in 1977 and 1978 for companies in the transportation industry was only 0.29 and 0.20 percent of revenues, respectively.[41] The highest value reported by any responding firm was 2.02 percent, which is far from trivial. There are no continuous time-series data on liability risk or product liability risk that would allow one to estimate whether this risk was becoming more severe over time.

There is some evidence that product liability awards in general increased rapidly in the 1970s. A study of civil settlements in Cook County, Illinois, reported that product liability awards rose by 890 percent

40. We are indebted to George Eads for this suggestion.
41. Risk Insurance and Management Society, *Cost of Risk Survey* (Darien, Conn.: Risk Planning Group, 1980), p. 34.

between 1960–64 and 1975–79 in constant dollars.[42] This fragmentary information from one county for all types of product liability cannot be said to be evidence that automakers were experiencing a rising trend of tort settlements, but more precise data are simply not available.

Nor are our results of offsetting behavior or "risk compensation" consistent with the studies that have been performed since Peltzman. Graham did not find evidence of any increased risk to pedestrians or bicyclists from safety regulation, nor did Graham and Garber.[43] However, no one has used as refined an estimate of the safety of the stock of vehicles on the road as our *SAFETY* variable. Graham and Garber use a measure that assigns the same value to all cars produced after 1966 or 1968. In other research Graham demonstrates the improved safety characteristics of cars of more recent vintage, but he does not attempt to account for this improvement in a separate analysis of pedestrian-bicyclist deaths.[44] His results for total highway deaths are consistent with engineering estimates of safety improvements, but he does not allow for the possibility that occupant deaths may have been reduced more than these engineering estimates suggest and that this greater than expected reduction in occupant deaths has been offset in part by greater pedestrian-bicyclist deaths.

Some students of highway safety vehemently reject even the notion of risk compensation. Robertson associates this theory with the "demon and miasma theories of infectious diseases."[45] His analysis of the FARS data suggests that regulation has even reduced pedestrian and bicycle deaths, but he fails to control for a variety of other causes of vehicle fatalities. Moreover, he assumes that vehicle safety increases linearly with each model year throughout 1966–82. In addition, a study of the mandatory seat belt law in Newfoundland suggests that drivers do not increase the riskiness of their driving along at least a few dimensions when they

42. Mark A. Peterson and George L. Priest, *The Civil Jury: Trends in Trials and Verdicts, Cook County, Ill., 1960–1979*, R-2881-ICJ (Santa Monica, Calif.: Rand Corp., 1982), p. 31.

43. Graham, "Automobile Safety"; and John D. Graham and Steven Garber, "Evaluating the Effects of Automobile Safety Regulations," *Journal of Policy Analysis and Management*, vol. 3 (Winter 1984), pp. 206–24. In a recent paper, Christopher Garbacz finds that safety regulation reduces both occupant and pedestrian deaths, but his safety variable is less precise than our *SAFETY* measure. See Christopher Garbacz, "A Note on Peltzman's Theory of Offsetting Consumer Behavior," *Economics Letters*, vol. 19, no. 2 (1985), pp. 183–87.

44. John D. Graham, "Technology, Behavior, and Safety: An Empirical Study of Automobile Occupant-Protection Regulation," *Policy Sciences*, vol. 17 (October 1984), pp. 141–51.

45. Robertson, "Automobile Safety Regulation."

buckle their seat belts.[46] The spread of state seat belt laws in the United States may provide the opportunity to test the risk compensation theory more directly with disaggregated data.

We are therefore left with a puzzle. It is clear that automobile safety has improved in the past fifteen years by even more than the engineering estimates would suggest. Our results and those of Graham are rather strong evidence of this improvement. Capturing the precise effect of regulation, however, remains a difficult and elusive problem.

A Cost-Benefit Analysis of the Highway Safety Program

Our analysis suggests that automobiles have become substantially safer for occupants, although this improvement may have induced some offsetting behavior and thus increased nonoccupant deaths. We cannot be sure that regulation is the sole contributor to the increased safety of new passenger cars, but the timing of the improvements provides strong evidence that regulation has been responsible for a large part of this improvement.

Undertaking a cost-benefit analysis of the NHTSA auto safety program is obviously difficult without more precise information linking specific safety-related expenditures to improved safety. Nevertheless, a preliminary attempt can be made. In chapter 3, we attempted to calculate the cost per new automobile for all NHTSA safety regulations. These estimates can be used to calculate the annual cost of the program. Similarly, the estimates of fatality reductions in this chapter can be used to calculate the benefits of the safety program. Once we have an estimate for the value of fatalities and injuries avoided, we may compare the magnitudes. Rather than calculating the present value of all past expenditures and the present value of fatalities and injuries avoided since 1968, we simply compare the annual, steady-state magnitudes of both costs and benefits for a world in which all cars have been built with post-1974 standards of safety.

To estimate the effects of safety improvements in automobiles since 1966, we use the first equation in table 4-5 to predict total highway deaths. If all cars are equipped with post-1974 safety equipment, *SAFETY* assumes a value of 0.66. Were all cars of pre-1966 vintage, *SAFETY* would equal 1.0, and the equation from table 4-5 would predict that total

46. Adrian K. Lund and Paul Zador, *Mandatory Belt Use and Driver Risk Taking* (Washington, D.C.: Insurance Institute for Highway Safety, 1983).

fatalities in 1981 would have been 72,800. If all cars were of 1974 vintage or newer, total highway deaths would have been 49,400. Thus the safer automobiles are estimated to result in 23,400 fewer deaths in 1981, as shown here.[47]

Assumed SAFETY coefficient	Actual deaths in 1981	Predicted deaths without regulation	Predicted 1981 deaths with full regulation	Annual reduction in deaths
0.932	50,800	72,800	49,400	23,400
0.550	50,800	63,300	50,300	13,000

If the coefficient of *SAFETY* in the first equation of table 4-5 were to conform to expectations based upon engineering analysis, it should be equal to 0.55, assuming no offsetting behavior, because passenger-car-occupant deaths account for about 55 percent of annual highway deaths. Of course, if crash-avoidance standards reduce nonoccupant deaths as well, the coefficient might be expected to be somewhat greater. Even if the coefficient of *SAFETY* in the total highway deaths equation were only 0.55, the predicted number of deaths with pre-1966 cars would be 63,300, or 13,000 more than with all vehicles subject to post-1974 design.[48]

Since increased auto safety should reduce nonfatal injuries as well as fatalities, it is important to include these reductions in a cost-benefit analysis. Unfortunately, we have no comparable estimate of the determinants of the highway injury rate for the period from 1947 to 1981. In table 4-12, we reproduce NHTSA's estimates of the number of motor vehicle-related injuries for 1979–80, ranked by the Abbreviated Injury Scale (AIS). In addition, we provide estimates of the value of the relative severity of each class of injury, drawn from the work of Hartunian and associ-

47. The first equation in table 4-5 predicts total fatalities of 51,800 for 1981. With a coefficient of 0.932 for the *SAFETY* variable, a reduction in the safety index from its 1981 value of 0.692 to 0.66 would generate a prediction of 49,400 fatalities for 1981. Similarly, if the coefficient of *SAFETY* were only 0.55, the reduction in deaths caused by a movement from 0.692 to 0.66 in the safety index would be to 50,300. To generate predictions for total fatalities with no safety regulation, we simply use a value of 1.0 for *SAFETY* and the two assumed elasticities, 0.932 and 0.55, to obtain estimates of 72,800 and 63,300, respectively.

48. If we were to use the coefficients from the occupant and nonoccupant equations in tables 4-5 and 4-6, we would obtain higher estimates of the lifesaving consequences of post-1965 automobiles. Use of the total death equation seems more reasonable and provides a more conservative estimate of the benefits.

Table 4-12. Injuries and Fatal Accidents, 1979–80 Average

Injury level[a]	Annual number	Relative value
AIS1	3,273,000	0.002
AIS2	452,000	0.009
AIS3	200,000	0.023
AIS4	34,900	0.063
AIS5	11,600	0.662
Fatalities	51,091	1.000

Sources: Department of Transportation, NHTSA, *The Economic Cost to Society of Motor Vehicle Accidents*, DOT HS-806-342 (DOT, 1983), p. VII-47; and Nelson S. Hartunian, Charles N. Smart, and Mark S. Thompson, *The Incidence and Economic Costs of Major Health Impairments: A Comparative Analysis of Cancer, Motor Vehicle Injuries, Coronary Heart Disease, and Stroke* (Lexington Books, 1981), tables 6-1, 6-5, 6-30.

a. The scale ranges according to the severity of the injury from minor (AIS1) to critical (AIS5).

ates. Given these data, one may calculate that each year there are injuries caused by motor vehicle accidents whose combined value in proportion to their number is equal to about half the loss due to the year's fatalities. This, of course, assumes that one is comfortable with the Hartunian estimates of the loss due to serious traffic injuries.

It is difficult to estimate the effect of auto safety regulation upon traffic injuries. On the one hand, one might suspect that crash-protection regulation reduces fatalities by increasing the number of severe injuries. On the other hand, it may be that regulation has reduced the severity of accidents in such a way that injuries and fatalities are reduced proportionately. The latter assumption seems most realistic; hence we use it in the analysis that follows.[49] This means that we multiply the life-saving effects of regulation by 1.5 to include an estimate of the equivalent reduction in the value of injuries.

Placing a value on the reduction in premature deaths is always difficult and controversial. There is no doubt that the loss of life caused by automobile accidents is a tragic component of modern life. A large proportion of the deaths occurs among teenagers and young adults, making the shortening of life even more acute. It is difficult to know just how much people would pay to reduce their risk of an early death, and conceptual experiments are not of much use in providing an answer. Why, for instance, do people resist buckling their seat belts? Hard data drawn from occupational experiences are not very helpful, both because the riskier occupations are likely to draw the least risk-averse workers and because recent analyses

49. This is the conclusion reached in GAO, *Effectiveness, Benefits, and Costs.* When injuries are substituted for total highway deaths in the first equation, the estimate of the *SAFETY* coefficient is virtually unchanged.

Table 4-13. Estimates of the Benefits and Costs of Automobile Safety Regulation

	Assumption	
Benefit and cost	Optimistic[a]	Pessimistic[b]
Benefits[c]		
Reduction in premature deaths	23,400	13,000
Reduction in deaths and injuries (fatality equivalents)	35,100	19,500
Value at $1 million per fatality avoided (billions of 1981 dollars)	35.10	19.50
Value at $300,000 per fatality avoided (billions of 1981 dollars)	10.53	5.85
Costs		
Cost per car (1981 dollars)	671	981
Annual cost (billions of 1981 dollars)[d]	7.0	10.3
Annual cost without bumper standard (billions of 1981 dollars)[d]	4.9	6.9

a. For benefits, assumes a coefficient of 0.932 for *SAFETY;* for costs, assumes a 5 percent learning curve.
b. For benefits, assumes a coefficient of 0.550 for *SAFETY;* for costs, assumes no learning curve.
c. Injury and fatality reductions only.
d. Assumes 10.5 million cars.

find such estimates very sensitive to specification and union-nonunion categorization.[50]

We are thus left with the usual problem of assigning value to the reduction in early fatalities. Since most such estimates are in the range of $300,000 to $1,000,000, we use this range (in 1981 dollars) to bracket the benefit estimates.[51] The cost estimates are based upon steady-state new car sales of 10.5 million per year. In the 1970s new car registrations averaged 9.9 million per year. Given the slow economic growth and energy shocks since 1973, it is reasonable to assume that new car sales should increase in the 1980s in order to accommodate new and repressed replacement demands.

The detailed cost and benefit estimates appear in table 4-13. The optimistic benefit calculations use our econometric estimate of the *SAFETY* coefficient. Even at only a $300,000 value of reducing premature death,

50. There are numerous empirical studies estimating the value of saving lives. See, for example, Robert S. Smith, "Compensating Wage Differentials and Public Policy: A Review," *Industrial and Labor Relations Review,* vol. 32 (October 1978–July 1979), pp. 339–52; Martin J. Bailey, *Reducing Risks to Life: Measurement of the Benefits* (Washington, D.C.: American Enterprise Institute, 1980); John D. Graham and James W. Vaupel, "Value of a Life: What Difference Does it Make?" *Risk Analysis,* vol. 1, no. 1 (1981), pp. 89–95; and William Dickens, "Differences Between Risk Premiums in Union and Nonunion Wages and the Case for Occupational Safety Regulation," *American Economic Review,* vol. 74 (May 1984, *Papers and Proceedings, 1983*), pp. 320–23.
51. Graham, "Automobile Safety," pp. 260–61.

Table 4-14. Societal Costs of Motor Vehicle Accidents
Billions of 1980 dollars

Category	Fatal accidents	Accidents involving AIS 1–5 injuries	Accidents with property damage only	Motorists uninvolved in accidents[a]	Total
Medical	0.07	3.26	. . .	. . .	3.33
Productivity	12.10	2.14	. . .	. . .	14.24
Property	0.17	3.83	16.98	. . .	20.98
Other	1.38	6.16	4.73	6.38	18.65
Total	13.72	15.39	21.71	6.38	57.20

Source: NHTSA, *The Economic Cost to Society of Motor Vehicle Accidents*, table I-1, p. I-4.
a. Insurance costs.

these estimates produce annual benefits of $10.53 billion per year. This is far more than the cost of all safety regulation by NHTSA. Assuming a 5 percent annual learning rate, the 1981 cost of safety regulations is $671 per automobile (table 3-5). With no learning, it is $981 per car. Thus the annual cost of safety regulation for 10.5 million cars per year is between $7.0 billion and $10.3 billion, but without the bumper standard this total is only $4.9 billion to $6.9 billion. Only the pessimistic assumptions concerning the effect of safety regulation (a coefficient of 0.55 for *SAFETY*) and the value of reducing premature death will provide an unfavorable ratio of benefits to costs. But there are other potential benefits, and some of the costs should not properly be attributed to saving lives or reducing injuries.

In table 4-14 we reproduce NHTSA's recent estimates of the societal costs of motor vehicle accidents. Note that $40 billion of the $57 billion in annual costs are not associated with life and limb. Medical costs are only $3.3 billion of the $57 billion, while property damage is $21 billion. Moreover, other costs, such as insurance administration, legal and court costs, and public-sector emergency-service costs, add $18.7 billion to the total costs of vehicle accidents. It is difficult to know how a reduction in the fatality-injury rate affects these various cost components, but it clearly must reduce many of them. For instance, the $18.7 billion in insurance administration and public-sector costs must certainly be affected by the extent and severity of accidents. Even if these have been reduced by only 10 percent as a result of improved crashworthiness of passenger cars, the annual savings would be enough to make even the pessimistic estimate of benefits greater than the gross costs of safety regulation. In short, there is considerable evidence that the benefits from safer passenger cars are at least as great as the costs and perhaps substantially greater.[52] Whether these improvements in safety are solely the result of regulation or not, they appear to have been worth it on average. This is not to say that the marginal benefits of each and every regulation are greater than the incremental costs, but only that the total benefits appear to be greater than the costs of safety improvement in cars.

Alternative Approaches to Improving Highway Safety

Even though our results are consistent with the theory of offsetting behavior, we find that safety regulation probably has improved economic welfare through its effect on passenger-car-occupant fatalities. This conclusion is based upon our econometric results, which obtain unexpectedly large effects of changes in automobile characteristics on fatality rates during the period in which automobile safety requirements were being introduced. Therefore it is possible that our estimates of the value of safety regulation are too large.

Is it possible that alternative approaches to highway safety might offer greater possibilities for enhancing economic welfare? In this concluding section, we consider two options: an incentive-based insurance system and compulsory seat belt laws. In addition, we comment on the continuing regulatory saga of passive restraints.

Insurance

It is often possible to achieve many of the benefits of prescriptive or proscriptive regulation by a system of prices or fees that reward desirable behavior or punish undesirable behavior. In the case of automobile safety, one could employ a system of insurance rates that induce safe driving and the purchase of demonstrated life-saving safety options on new automobiles. Orr has suggested that a carefully structured program of no-fault insurance be substituted for the current federal safety regulation program.[53] Each individual's insurance premium would be determined by his demographic characteristics, his accident experience, and the actual

52. Of course, equality of *total* benefits and *total* costs may indicate that marginal benefits are less than marginal costs.
53. Lloyd D. Orr, "Incentives and Efficiency in Automobile Safety Regulation," *Quarterly Review of Economics and Business*, vol. 22 (Autumn 1982), pp. 43–65.

crashworthiness experience of the automobile he drives. The last of these factors would reflect, ex post, the effect of offsetting behavior on the safety of the vehicle since cars would be rated in terms of their actual experience, not theoretical engineering measures of their crashworthiness.

Orr suggests that this no-fault system would allow a much more finely tuned approach and preserve incentives for improving safety. Moreover, it would require less information than the current system. Of course, separating the actuarial effects of demographics from those of the vehicle may not be easy. For instance, can one determine the crashworthiness of a Corvette from that of a Lincoln Continental without adjusting for the difference in drivers of these two types of cars? It might not be easy to separate the risk-averse from the more risk-assuming drivers simply on the basis of standard demographic variables.

Given the evidence that offsetting behavior actually occurs and the difficulty in knowing which safety regulations actually contribute to it, it might be better to move toward a sophisticated no-fault system such as that proposed by Orr than to attempt to increase the regulation of driver behavior or require passive restraints. Unfortunately, such an approach seems to have little political appeal, perhaps because many people believe that the current system's regulatory compliance costs are borne largely by the automobile producers. We have shown that consumers do bear the cost of safety regulation; hence they might eventually be persuaded that other approaches could be more efficient or effective.

Mandatory Seat Belt Laws

In 1984 Secretary of Transportation Elizabeth Dole attempted to extricate herself from the dilemma confronting her after the court reversal of the 1981 decision not to require passive belts. She effectively postponed requiring passive restraints by announcing a campaign to persuade the states to pass mandatory seat belt usage laws. If states with two-thirds of automobile registrations pass such laws, she will not impose passive restraints.[54]

Mandating the use of active lap-shoulder belts has been tried by a number of countries, including most European countries, Australia, and Canada. Evidence on the success of such laws is mixed. Adams claims that there is no improvement in fatality rates after implementation of these

54. 49 Fed. Reg. 28962 (1984).

laws, but Jonsson finds a substantial improvement for Sweden.[55] Part of the controversy derives from the apparent difficulty in enforcing such laws. If the most cautious drivers buckle up, but the least cautious ones are less likely to respond, there may be no noticeable improvement in fatality rates. Moreover, if offsetting behavior is important, the beneficial effects may be offset by riskier driving. Adams appears to accept the risk compensation hypothesis, but he does not test the theory directly.

Several states have passed compulsory seat belt laws. At the same time, a major federal media program of encouraging seat belt use is being developed. How much these attempts to increase seat belt usage will reduce fatalities remains to be seen.

Passive Restraints

As of late 1985, the passive restraint issue was going through yet another round of rulemaking. As mentioned above, the attempt by the Reagan administration to rescind the Carter administration's passive restraint standard for new passenger cars was overturned in the U.S. Court of Appeals and the Supreme Court. The latter decision criticized the Reagan NHTSA both for failing to consider requiring air bags (given its dismissal of passive belts as cost ineffective) and for not providing sufficient grounds for rescinding a rule that had passed through the entire administrative process.[56] This issue has been before NHTSA and the courts for fifteen years, and it is unlikely to be resolved soon.

The principal issues in mandating passive restraints involve the usage rate and the cost of alternative systems. Detractors of such a regulation argue: occupants currently do not use belts, thus revealing their limited demand for passive restraints; if passive belts were mandated, many people would simply disconnect or disarm them; and air bags are untested and expensive.

The case for passive restraints derives from the fact that 27,000 front-seat passenger-car occupants die per year at current rates. If all front-seat occupants were to use their three-point belts, between 30 and 60 percent of

55. John Adams, "The Efficacy of Seat Belt Legislation," Working Paper 38 (University College, London, Department of Geography, 1981); and Ernst Jonsson, "The Social Profitability of the Swedish Seat-Belt Law," *Journal of Traffic Medicine*, vol. 6 (September 1978), pp. 40–43.
56. For a detailed review of the history of the passive restraint issue, see John D. Graham and Patricia Gorham, "NHTSA and Passive Restraints: A Case of Arbitrary and Capricious Deregulation," *Administrative Law Review*, vol. 35 (Spring 1983), pp. 193–252.

these fatalities could be avoided.[57] Of course, some offsetting behavior could occur, reducing the effectiveness of the belts. But given usage rates in the 10–15 percent range, the three-point belt is not having its intended effect. If a restraint system could be devised that embraces front-seat occupants without their conscious effort, it might be possible to achieve the potential life-saving effects of the manual belts despite people's apparent resistance to these devices.

There are essentially two alternatives to manual seat belts: air bags and passive belts that automatically embrace the occupant with the closing of the front door. In 1974 NHTSA tried a third option—an ignition interlock system for manual belts—but the public rebelled so strongly that Congress rescinded the requirement.[58]

The choice between passive belts and air bags is a difficult one for regulators. Passive belts are likely to be substantially cheaper than air bags and less susceptible to failure. They do not need to be rearmed after a crash; they do not offer problems for passengers, particularly children, who are not in normal seating positions. The problem with passive belts is that they can be disabled by car owners. Given the experience with the interlock system in 1974, manufacturers will be very reluctant to offer passive belts that cannot be detached by front-seat occupants. The necessity for quick egress during a fire or after an accident makes such detachability essential. But if these "automatic" belts are readily detachable, they become manual belts since occupants will have the opportunity to disconnect them at any time and not reconnect them. Indeed, it was this issue over which NHTSA and antagonists battled when NHTSA rescinded the requirement.[59]

The problem facing NHTSA is thus quite clear. Motorists have strongly signaled their distaste for seat belts by not using them. There is considerable doubt that detachable passive belts would have very high usage rates, and nondetachable belts would probably create a political uproar. Air bags would be the most effective system, but they would be by far the most costly.

The details of NHTSA's dilemma are very simply presented in the table

57. Graham, "Automobile Safety"; and Huelke and O'Day, "Passive Restraints: A Scientist's View," pp. 21–35.

58. See Graham and Gorham, "NHTSA and Passive Restraints," pp. 198–99.

59. Comments of William Nordhaus on Notice at Proposal Rulemaking on Federal Motor Vehicle Safety Standards: Occupant Crash Protection, NHTSA Docket 74-14, May 26, 1981, pp. 7–9.

below.[60] The annual benefits from either restraint system would be equal to the product of the effectiveness ratio, the usage ratio, the number of annual front-seat fatalities (currently about 27,000), and the value of each equivalent automobile fatality. The annual costs would be equal to 10.5 million cars times the estimated cost of the system per car. Air bags would generate a reduction in occupant fatalities of between 27 and 40 percent, or between 7,300 and 10,800 per year, assuming no offsetting behavior. If the value of reducing fatalities is between $300,000 and $1,000,000 and each fatality averted is accompanied by reduced injuries equal in value to 0.5 fatalities, the benefits from air bags in terms of potential occupant protection would range between $3.3 billion and $16.2 billion.[61] The costs of the air bags would be between $2.1 billion and $4.2 billion per year. Thus a value of life in the vicinity of $500,000 would generate a positive cost-benefit ratio, ignoring the feedback effects upon new car demand and offsetting behavior.

	Cost per car (1981 dollars)	Lifesaving effectiveness rate	Usage rate
Air bags	200–400	0.30 to 0.40	0.90 to 1.00
Passive belts	50–150	0.40 to 0.55	0.15 to 0.50

Requiring air bags would be an extremely costly option, raising the regulatory costs from NHTSA regulation from the range of $700–$1,000 per car (in 1981 dollars) to perhaps as much as $900–$1,400. If this induces a substantial postponement of the decision to replace the pre-1974 cars in the automobile stock, the net benefits from air bags would be reduced substantially. Moreover, if offsetting behavior exists, as our earlier estimates suggest, the net benefits could be reduced further.

Passive belts would reduce between 6 percent and 27.5 percent of fatalities at an annual cost of $525 million to $1.6 billion. Using the above methodology, this translates into benefits of between $0.7 billion to $11.1 billion. The wide range reflects the uncertainty over usage rates. It is possible to argue against passive belts if detachability so reduces their

---

60. Adapted from Graham, "Automobile Safety," chap. 5.

61. Assume the reduction in injuries is proportional to the reduction in fatalities. Using table 4-12, one can calculate $(\sum_{j=1}^{5} v_j/i_j)/v_f f$ = value of all injuries relative to the value of deaths, where v is the relative value of injuries of level j, i is the annual number of injuries of level j, v is the relative value of fatalities, and f is the annual number of fatalities.

usage rate that they are little better than the manual belt system at current usage rates.

In short, there is a substantial probability that air bags are an inferior passive restraint option, but motorists do not view belts very kindly either. One's view of the appropriate course of action on this matter is therefore likely to depend heavily upon his philosophical view. If one views with equanimity motorists' decisions to risk their lives without a belt or other restraint system, the decision can be left to the market. In contrast, a more paternalistic view, accompanied by a high valuation of fatalities averted, makes the air bag attractive. This same paternalism, plus a belief that motorists will not disconnect the belts, is required to make the passive belt the preferred solution.

Summary

There can be little doubt that passenger cars are safer today than they were twenty years ago. Most of this improvement occurred in the 1966–74 model years, precisely the period in which federal safety regulation was applied. Time-series evidence shows that these safer cars decreased the fatality rate for passenger-car occupants substantially, but they may have had some deleterious effects upon pedestrians, bicyclists, and motorcyclists due to offsetting behavior by passenger-car drivers.

The total benefits from the lifesaving effects of safety regulation are substantially greater than the costs of the required safety features on passenger cars under most reasonable assumptions. Proposals for passive restraints for car occupants have been debated for twenty years without a resolution. These passive restraints could reduce occupant deaths substantially, but at potentially large costs. The dilemma facing safety regulators is that the lower-cost option—the passive belt—may be disarmed by the automobile owner, but the higher-cost option—the air bag—may not generate sufficient benefits to justify its installation. Declining costs of air bags may make this the more attractive option to regulators, but they fear the potential backlash from motorists who may be afraid that the air bags will be activated inadvertently.

CHAPTER FIVE

Automotive Emissions Control

FEDERAL REGULATION of automobile emissions began at approximately the same time as federal automobile safety regulation, in 1968. The Department of Health, Education, and Welfare set light-duty vehicle standards for carbon monoxide and hydrocarbons for the 1968 model year. These standards were supplanted by legislated standards in the Clean Air Act Amendments of 1970, which also set nitrogen oxide emissions standards for automobiles beginning in the 1973 model year.

Because emissions controls have had serious effects upon fuel economy and operating performance in some model years and have been quite expensive in recent years, they have been much more controversial than most safety standards. In this chapter, we review their effect upon emissions and their somewhat less successful effect upon ambient air quality. In addition, we take a critical look at the new programs of inspection and maintenance upon which Congress has placed much of the burden for future reductions in automobile emissions.

The Problem

By the mid-1950s it was quite clear that automobile emissions were linked to photochemical smog in major metropolitan areas, particularly those prone to atmospheric inversion layers. By the early 1960s California began to consider requiring emissions control devices on new cars.[1] Despite the automobile manufacturers' decision to reduce some hydrocarbon emissions voluntarily, the California Motor Vehicle Pollution Control Act was enacted in 1963.

As late as the mid-1960s evidence on the health and welfare effects of air pollution created by automobiles remained unclear.[2] Photochemical

1. Lawrence J. White, *The Regulation of Air Pollutant Emissions from Motor Vehicles* (Washington, D.C.: American Enterprise Institute, 1982), p. 14.
2. Ibid., chap. 1.

smog, or its components, were believed to be an important source of reduced pulmonary (lung) function and to contribute to asthma, chronic bronchitis, and emphysema.[3] In addition, there was evidence that carbon monoxide, another automotive emission, might cause increases in cardio-vascular problems by reducing the ability of the blood to carry oxygen.

Surprisingly, there are no satisfactory data on the extent of the smog problem before the 1960s. Indeed, the more recent evidence on ambient air quality trends since the mid-1970s is also very sketchy. The situation is somewhat better with respect to emissions data since reasonable ex post estimates can be made based on performance characteristics of vehicles and the composition of the vehicle fleet.

The public became increasingly concerned about air pollution problems in the 1960s and 1970s. This concern was based upon more than the health evidence relating photochemical oxidants and carbon monoxide to respira-tory and cardiovascular problems. Visibility and other aesthetic values provided additional motivation for the original clean air movement. Fol-lowing the inception of emissions controls, evidence that photochemical oxidants damaged ornamental shrubbery and reduced agricultural yields helped sustain backing for the program. Finally, the problem of acid rain heightened concern over nitrogen oxide emissions from both mobile and stationary sources, since these emissions are precursors of the nitric acid component of acid rain.[4]

Clearly, automobile emissions affect the quality of life in many ways. Whether the auto emissions control program has improved these aspects of the quality of life by an amount sufficient to offset its substantial costs is a question to which we return later in this chapter.

The Federal Emissions Control Program

The 1970 Clean Air Act Amendments provide the foundation for all federally imposed air pollution controls. While standards for stationary pollution sources have been left largely to the administrative judgment of the Environmental Protection Agency, Congress chose to legislate auto

3. Charles E. Schoettlin and Emanuel Landau, "Air Pollution and Asthmatic Attacks in the Los Angeles Area," *Public Health Reports*, vol. 76 (June 1961), pp. 545–49.
4. Acid rain is predominantly sulfuric acid, which is not formed from automotive emissions. The composition of acid rain varies by location, with nitric acid playing a relatively larger role in the western half of the country.

emissions standards directly. Several factors motivated this approach. First, automobiles are the largest single source of pollution in terms of aggregate emissions weight.[5] Second, auto emissions had already been identified as the main cause of smog in the Los Angeles air basin, the country's most visible and publicized air pollution problem. Finally, automobile executives displayed little willingness to respond voluntarily to congressional desires for major emissions reductions.

The confrontation with the automobile manufacturers led Congress to adopt a set of standards designed to force the development of emissions control technology by imposing stringent requirements according to a rigid timetable. Emissions of hydrocarbons and carbon monoxide were to be reduced by 95 percent from the pre-1968 level by the 1975 model year, while nitrogen oxide emissions were to be reduced by 90 percent from the 1970 level by the 1976 model year. This "technology-forcing" strategy was motivated in part by a congressional view that the auto industry was implacably opposed to emissions abatement.

The specific goals and deadlines proved to be much too ambitious, leading manufacturers to use jury-rigged systems to demonstrate compliance. The costs of these extreme measures were particularly evident in the 1974 cars, which were severely "detuned" at the expense of fuel economy and drivability to meet standards easily attainable using the oxidation catalyst technology that became available in 1975.

The manufacturers' opposition and the energy crisis led to a series of administrative and legislative modifications of the standards and deadlines specified in the 1970 act.[6] Research into the health effects of individual pollutants also favored a reduced emphasis on auto emissions. Photochem-

5. The share of auto emissions was actually lower in 1970 than was thought at the time. A 1970 study by the Department of Health, Education, and Welfare credited motor vehicles with 48 percent of total hydrocarbon emissions, 32 percent of total nitrogen oxide emissions, and 59 percent of total carbon monoxide emissions. U.S. Department of Health, Education, and Welfare, National Air Pollution Control Administration, *Control Techniques for Carbon Monoxide, Nitrogen Oxide, and Hydrocarbon Emissions from Mobile Sources*, AP-66 (HEW, 1970), p. 2-15. However, the EPA's most recent emissions inventory report puts the automobile share of overall 1970 emissions at 32 percent for hydrocarbons, 21 percent for nitrogen oxides, and 48 percent for carbon monoxide. Environmental Protection Agency, Office of Air, Noise and Radiation, *National Air Pollutant Emission Estimates, 1940–1983*, EPA-450/4-84-028 (Research Triangle Park, N.C.: EPA, 1984), tables 9, 10, 11, 14, 15, 16.

6. In 1973 the EPA granted a year's delay in the standards on the grounds that the requisite technology was unavailable. The Energy Supply and Environmental Coordination Act of 1974 and the Clean Air Act Amendments of 1977 included additional changes in the emissions timetable.

Regulating the Automobile

Table 5-1. Federal and California Emissions Standards for Passenger Cars, Model Years 1970–84
Grams per mile

Year[a]	Federal			California		
	Hydro-carbons	Carbon monoxide	Nitrogen oxides	Hydro-carbons	Carbon monoxide	Nitrogen oxides
1970	4.1	34	. . .	4.1	34	. . .
1971	4.1	34	. . .	4.1	34	6.2
1972	3.0	28.2	. . .	2.85	28.2	4.65
1973	3.0	28.2	3.1	2.85	28.2	3.1
1974	3.0	28.2	3.1	2.85	28.2	2.07
1975–76	1.5	15.0	3.1	0.9	9.0	2.0
1977–79	1.5	15.0	3.1	0.9	9.0	1.5
1980	0.41	7.0	2.0	0.41	9.0	1.0[b]
1981	0.41	3.4[c]	1.0[d]	0.41[e] / 0.41[e]	3.4[e] / 7.0[e]	1.0[b,e] / 0.7[e]
1982	0.41	3.4[c]	1.0[d]	0.41[e] / 0.41[e]	7.0[e] / 7.0[e]	0.4[b,e] / 0.7[e]
1983–84	0.41	3.4	1.0[d]	0.41	7.0	0.4[f]

Sources: 40 C.F.R. 86.081-.084 (1984); and California Administrative Code, title 13 R.1960 (1984).
a. Test cycle in 1970 and 1971 differed from cycle for 1972–84.
b. 1.5 grams per mile allowed with 100,000-mile durability.
c. Waiver to 7.0 grams per mile possible.
d. Waiver to 1.5 grams per mile for diesel.
e. California allowed manufacturers to select either option for 1981–82. Nearly all have chosen the first option.
f. 1.0 grams per mile allowed with 100,000-mile durability; 0.7 grams per mile allowed with seven-year 75,000-mile emissions warranty.

ical smog and carbon monoxide resulting from auto emissions were found to pose a lesser threat to health and the environment than the sulfur oxides and particulates emitted from stationary sources, such as coal-burning boilers. As the early focus on total emission weight gave way to an increased understanding of the health effects of each pollutant, automobile standards were deemphasized and controls on new stationary pollution sources were tightened.

Table 5-1 shows the actual standards imposed through the 1984 model year. Since California already had a more stringent program than the federal program that was established, it was allowed to continue setting its own standards. California standards have typically led the federal standards by several years, providing a natural laboratory for testing emissions control innovations. The 1973–74 standards were met by severe detuning of the engines produced during those years, resulting in a significant fuel penalty. Oxidation catalysts became the standard approach to pollution control on the 1976–79 models, reducing the fuel penalty substantially but requiring more expensive unleaded gasoline. Unfortunately, leaded gasoline could "poison" these catalysts, thereby reducing their effectiveness and greatly increasing emissions.

To meet the 1980 California and 1981 federal nitrogen oxide standards, the automobile companies had to install catalysts capable of nitrogen oxide reduction. Complex closed-loop control systems for continuously monitoring and varying the fuel-air mixture are used in conjunction with these catalysts in order to maintain the composition of the engine exhaust stream within the narrow range required for their effective operation. As pointed out in chapter 3, this sharply increased the cost of emissions control.

For both political and technical reasons, the use of stringent emissions standards for new equipment, with less strict standards for existing equipment, has been the standard method for implementing pollution control. It is usually cheaper to build pollution controls into new equipment than it is to add them to existing equipment. Even where the costs are similar, the added cost of pollution controls for new equipment is perceived as a small surcharge on the cost of the equipment itself, while the cost of controls for existing equipment tends to be viewed in isolation. Owners of existing equipment can organize to fight regulation that adversely affects their interests. For instance, California automobile owners successfully fought retrofit requirements in the 1960s. In contrast, future purchasers of new equipment do not constitute as cohesive an interest group; therefore regulation tends to be focused upon new vehicles.[7]

Potential Problems with the Regulatory Strategy

Regulation by means of performance standards for new sources has several generic defects, all of which apply to the auto emissions standards.[8] First, by increasing the cost of new vehicles, new-source standards encourage the retention of old, relatively dirty cars in the vehicle fleet. This effect can partially or fully offset the direct emissions-reducing impact of tighter standards for a considerable period. Second, new-source regulation links success in achieving emissions reductions directly to fleet turnover. When new car sales fall below trend, as they did in 1980–82,

7. See Robert W. Crandall, *Controlling Industrial Pollution: The Economics and Politics of Clean Air* (Brookings, 1983), chap. 7, for discussion of the new-source bias in environmental policy.
8. Howard K. Gruenspecht, "Differentiated Regulation: A Theory with Applications to Automobile Emissions Control" (Ph.D. dissertation, Yale University, 1982).

progress in emissions reduction can be severely compromised. Third, new-source performance standards provide no incentive for individual car owners to maintain emissions control systems, except where compulsory inspection and maintenance programs have been instituted. In fact, emissions control systems may be intentionally degraded by adjustments to improve vehicle performance or by the use of leaded gasoline in catalyst-equipped vehicles.[9]

The concentration upon new sources also allows manufacturers to subvert the program. Under current federal law, vehicles not certified to meet emissions standards cannot be sold. This penalty is too severe to be credible or desirable. Individual manufacturers have found they can obtain waivers, postponements, or changes to avoid the plant closings that would follow a sales ban on an entire year's production. Announcements by the major domestic manufacturers that they could not comply have at times forced changes in the law, most recently in the 1977 Clean Air Act Amendments.

The program also lacks effective mechanisms for enforcement of the standards beyond the certification stage, which takes place before each model's initial production. Certification can be revoked if selective enforcement audits of production line vehicles indicate a likely failure rate above 40 percent for the entire production run.[10] The leniency of this criterion, the infrequency of audits, and the manufacturers' ability to produce alternative configurations in the unlikely event that certification is suspended severely limit the enforcement value of the audit system. The EPA also has recall authority, but this has been used only where a design or manufacturing flaw affecting a well-defined set of cars has resulted in extremely poor emissions performance. The "ordinary" poor performance reflected in the EPA's own emissions tests of in-use vehicles has gone largely unpenalized.

In principle, the requirement that manufacturers provide a five-year, 50,000-mile warranty on all emissions control systems should induce manufacturers to develop durable systems in order to avoid the expense of warranty repairs. In practice, manufacturers know that consumers have no incentive to exercise their warranty rights unless they are made liable for poor emissions performance through compulsory inspection and maintenance programs.

9. Since the 1981 model year, manufacturers have been required to deter adjustments by sealing the idle mixture adjustment mechanism at the factory.
10. 40 C.F.R. 86.602–.608 (1980).

During the 1970s, when compulsory inspection and maintenance programs were not in widespread use, manufacturers faced no penalties for poor in-use performance of emissions controls. In this environment, development efforts and technology selection were focused on the certification process rather than the social objective of reducing on-the-road emissions. In view of these built in defects, it is hardly surprising that the program has not fully achieved its emissions-reduction objectives.

The Results of the Program

As White points out, reducing auto emissions is only the proximate goal of the program.[11] Its ultimate intent is to reduce the damage to health, vegetation, and aesthetic values from air pollution by improving ambient air quality. Ideally, an evaluation of the auto emissions program would entail three stages. First, the reduction in emissions would be estimated. Second, the emissions reduction would be translated into an estimated improvement in air quality. Finally, the implications of improved air quality for health and welfare would be estimated. Because knowledge of the key relationships at the second and third stages is limited, we focus most of our attention on the effect of the program on emissions.

Emissions

The emissions standards applied to newly produced cars are only one of the many factors that determine the aggregate level of automotive emissions. The rate at which emissions performance deteriorates as mileage is accumulated, the distribution of registrations across model years, total vehicle miles traveled, and the distribution of mileage accumulation across vintages in the fleet all play key roles in determining total emissions. The EPA has developed computer models to project aggregate emissions levels taking all of the above factors into account.

Aggregate automotive emissions estimates for 1970–82 are reported in table 5-2. They show that the program has already had a major impact on hydrocarbon and carbon monoxide emissions levels. Despite a 26 percent increase in vehicle miles traveled over 1970–82, estimated annual emissions of these two pollutants from passenger cars fell by 58 and 42 per-

11. White, *Regulation of Air Pollutant Emissions,* p. 54.

Regulating the Automobile

Table 5-2. Automobile Emissions and Vehicle Miles Traveled, 1970–82[a]

Year	Emissions (teragrams)			Vehicle miles traveled (billions of miles)
	Hydro-carbons	Carbon monoxide	Nitrogen oxides	
1970	8.53	47.61	3.89	910.0
1971	8.34	46.99	4.19	954.2
1972	8.04	45.99	4.51	1,003.5
1973	7.56	43.87	4.71	1,036.5
1974	6.76	40.17	4.37	1,013.1
1975	6.52	39.39	4.37	1,050.5
1976	6.40	39.66	4.41	1,098.2
1977	6.02	36.92	4.41	1,141.2
1978	5.77	35.79	4.36	1,194.0
1979	5.01	32.00	3.97	1,162.5
1980	4.44	29.21	3.67	1,129.8
1981	4.08	27.29	3.51	1,124.8
1982	3.94	26.37	3.50	1,191.6
1983	3.87	25.54	3.41	1,233.8[b]

Sources: Environmental Protection Agency, Office of Air, Noise and Radiation, *National Air Pollutant Emission Estimates, 1940–1983*, EPA 450/4-84-028 (Research Triangle Park, N.C.: EPA, 1984), tables 14, 15, 16; and Federal Highway Administration estimates.
a. Passenger cars only.
b. Estimated.

cent, respectively, over the same period. In contrast, nitrogen oxide emissions, which were not controlled until 1973, fell by only 10 percent from their 1970 level.

A major share of total 1982 vehicle miles was accumulated by cars not subject to stringent emissions standards. As the phaseout of precontrol and early control model years continues, further emissions reductions will occur. By the year 2000, emissions of hydrocarbons, carbon monoxide, and nitrogen oxides from passenger cars are projected to decline to 20, 40, and 78 percent of their respective 1970 levels despite a projected 58 percent increase in aggregate vehicle miles traveled over the 1970 level.[12]

There is little evidence to support the view that emissions rates would have fallen significantly without the emissions standards program.[13] White found that changes in vehicle characteristics, such as engine displacement, have no power in explaining time-series data on emissions rates, while the

12. Calculated from the EPA mobile-source emissions model (MOBILE 2).
13. Paul W. MacAvoy, *The Regulated Industries and the Economy* (Norton, 1979), pp. 101–02.

standards themselves have significant power.[14] Moreover, the higher emissions rates observed where standards are more lenient, as in Canada and the Western European countries, belie the notion that emissions reductions are driven by factors other than the emissions standards. Thus emissions would have risen from their 1970 levels had controls not been implemented.

The emissions estimates presented in table 5-2 show that the program is having a large impact on emissions. Is it, however, achieving its objectives? In-use performance of emissions controls is perhaps the most important determinant of the level of aggregate automotive emissions. For this reason, the EPA has made a major effort to track in-use performance by conducting emissions tests on randomly selected vehicles. More than 13,000 tests have been conducted since the inception of this program in 1971. Using these data, the EPA estimates zero-mileage emission rates and deterioration factors for each model year before 1981 by fitting the following equation for each pollutant.[15]

$$E = ZML + (b)M + c,$$

where

E = emission rate (grams per mile);
ZML = zero mile level;
b = deterioration rate per 10,000 miles;
M = odometer mileage (in 10,000s);
c = error.

For 1981 and later model years, separate factors for vehicles with closed-loop system failures, misfueled vehicles, and normal emissions control system operations are combined into aggregate emissions factors based on estimated migration patterns from one category to another.[16] The EPA uses the coefficients of the equation and the composite factors for

---

14. White, *Regulation of Air Pollutant Emissions*, p. 47.

15. The EPA actually uses an analysis of covariance procedure that is operationally equivalent to this linear regression. See Environmental Protection Agency, Office of Mobile Source Air Pollution Control, "Derivation of the Highway Mobile Source Emission Factors" (EPA, 1980), p. 3.

16. See Environmental Protection Agency, Office of Mobile Source Air Pollution Control, "Derivation of 1981 and Later Light Vehicle Emissions Factors for Low Altitude Non-California Areas," EPA-AA-IMS/80-B (EPA, 1980).

Table 5-3. Actual Performance versus Emissions Standards, by Pollutant and Model Year

Pollutant and year	Estimated by EPA	Standard	Ratio of estimate to standard
Hydrocarbons			
Pre-1968	8.13	...	...
1968–69	5.69	5.9	0.96
1970–71	4.85	3.9	1.24
1972–74	4.22	3.0	1.41
1975–79	2.75	1.5	1.83
1980	1.28	0.41	3.12
1981	1.14	0.41	2.78
1982	1.10	0.41	2.68
1983	1.10	0.41	2.68
Carbon monoxide			
Pre-1968	89.41	...	...
1968–69	69.12	50.8	1.36
1970–71	57.98	33.3	1.74
1972–74	54.00	28.0	1.93
1975–79	34.96	15.0	2.33
1980	14.10	7.0	2.01
1981	14.79	3.4[a]	4.35
1982	13.63	3.4[a]	4.01
1983	13.47	3.4	3.96
Nitrogen oxides			
Pre-1968	3.44	...	...
1968–72	4.35	...	...
1973–74	3.18	3.1	1.03
1975–76	2.90	3.1	0.94
1977–79	2.49	2.0	1.25
1980	2.21	2.0	1.11
1981	1.27	1.0	1.27
1982	1.30	1.0	1.30
1983	1.24	1.0	1.24

Emission rate at 50,000 miles (grams per mile)

Sources: EPA estimates of actual emissions performance from Environmental Protection Agency, Office of Mobile Sources, Test and Evaluation Branch, *Compilation of Air Pollutant Emission Factors*, vol. 2: *Mobile Sources*, 4th ed. (Ann Arbor, Mich.: EPA, forthcoming), p. H–4. Federal emissions standards from Lawrence J. White, *The Regulation of Air Pollutant Emissions from Motor Vehicles* (Washington, D.C.: American Enterprise Institute, 1982), p. 15.
a. Waivers to 7.0 grams per mile allowed in 1981 and 1982.

recent model years to capture the in-use performance of emissions controls in its aggregate emissions model.

The results of the EPA's testing program show that in-use performance for all three pollutants falls significantly short of that required by the Clean Air Act. Table 5-3 compares, for each model year and pollutant, the EPA's estimate of in-use emissions at 50,000 accumulated miles with those required by the standards.[17] While the program has greatly reduced emissions rates, as can be seen by comparing the pre-1968 emissions rates with those for newer vintages, hydrocarbon and carbon monoxide emission rates two to four times greater than those required by Congress are the rule rather than the exception.

The impact of this performance shortfall on the total emissions level can be assessed by comparing aggregate emissions estimates based on observed in-use performance with alternative emissions estimates calculated using statutory emissions rates. The two scenarios show similar aggregate emissions estimates in the early 1970s, when uncontrolled (pre-1968) vehicles contributed the lion's share of emissions and the gap between the standards and observed performance was relatively small. However, the difference between aggregate emissions estimates based on actual and statutory emissions rates grows as pre-1968 vehicles are retired, and the gap between the mandated and actual performance grows with the imposition of more stringent standards (see table 5-3).

By 1982 levels of hydrocarbons, carbon monoxide, and nitrogen oxides were respectively 30, 76, and 5 percent above those that would have prevailed had emissions rates met the standards of the Clean Air Act. By the end of the century, when the entire fleet will consist of vehicles subject to the stringent 1981 standards, the levels are projected to be 191, 486, and 49 percent above those that would prevail if the rates specified by the Clean Air Act were achieved.[18] The disparity between observed and statutory emissions rates is growing and may become more serious if recent (post-1980) models begin to experience catastrophic failures of their sophisticated emissions control systems. From this perspective the program is not nearly as successful as the earlier comparisons with a "no-program" baseline suggest.

The turnover rate is another important determinant of aggregate emis-

---

17. The Clean Air Act specifies that the standards be met at 50,000 miles, the approximate half-life of the typical car.

18. These estimates were calculated by the authors using version 2 of the EPA mobile-source emissions model (MOBILE 2), with parameters set at the EPA-supplied default values. These estimates were based upon federal standards without credit for inspection and maintenance. The inclusion of California standards and inspection and maintenance credits would result in somewhat lower projections of actual emissions. A newer version of the model, MOBILE 3, has recently been released by the EPA. The intertemporal pattern of emissions and the divergence between actual and mandated performance are insignificantly different between MOBILE 2 and MOBILE 3; hence we have used MOBILE 2 throughout this chapter.

Table 5-4. Composition of the Vehicle Fleet by Age, Selected Years, 1967–82
Percent

Age (years)	1967–78 average	1978	1981	1982
Less than 1	7.45	7.21	4.86	4.12
1–2	10.76	10.09	8.33	7.75
2–3	10.49	9.21	9.68	8.26
3–4	10.18	7.08	9.72	9.04
4–5	9.95	9.16	9.22	9.50
5–6	9.38	10.26	8.25	9.04
6–7	8.48	8.88	6.11	7.93
7–8	7.59	7.12	7.61	5.79
8–9	6.55	6.59	7.99	7.02
9–10	5.18	5.91	6.42	7.14
10–11	3.93	4.78	4.66	5.60
11–12	2.87	3.49	4.00	3.97
12–13	2.10	3.00	3.18	3.35
13–14	1.44	2.30	2.49	2.64
14–15	0.99	1.50	1.80	2.07
15–16	0.66	0.99	1.56	1.51
More than 16	2.05	2.43	4.11	4.88
Total registrations (thousands)	. . .	102,956	105,829	106,855

Source: Motor Vehicle Manufacturers Association, *MVMA Motor Vehicle Facts and Figures*, various years.

sions from the automobile fleet. Table 5-4 summarizes the composition of the vehicle fleet in several recent years, as well as its average composition over 1967–78.[19] The aging of the fleet in recent years has tended to elevate aggregate emissions levels. Holding the level of aggregate vehicle miles traveled constant, actual 1982 emissions of hydrocarbons, carbon monoxide, and nitrogen oxide were, respectively 26, 23, and 11 percent higher than they would have been had the 1982 fleet composition matched the 1967–78 average.[20] In effect, the shift in fleet composition is equivalent to a setback of three to four years in the timetable for reducing emissions.

Most of the change in fleet composition is due to macroeconomic developments, not emissions regulation itself. However, regulation does affect fleet composition through its impact on the prices and performance of new cars, which in turn affect new car purchases and scrapping decisions. For example, the 1981 emissions standards necessitated the use of

19. The 1978 registration distribution is used as the default in the MOBILE 2 model. The data in table 5-4 show that it is not representative of current experience.

20. Calculated from MOBILE 2 model runs using 1982 and 1967–78 average fleet composition in place of the default.

Table 5-5. Effects upon Emissions and Sales, Using 1980 Standards for Post-1980 Automobiles, 1981-90[a]
Percentage change

| | | Emissions | | |
Year	Hydrocarbons	Carbon monoxide	Nitrogen oxides	Sales
1981	-0.83	0.70	0.86	4.09
1982	-1.86	-1.01	5.47	3.35
1983	-2.29	-1.60	9.76	2.72
1984	-1.64	-1.15	14.35	2.20
1985	-0.52	0.81	18.39	1.84
1986	2.63	0.79	23.00	-0.66
1987	5.81	2.27	26.95	-0.32
1988	9.54	3.57	29.87	0.09
1989	12.93	4.46	32.10	0.56
1990	16.19	5.31	33.33	0.93

Source: Howard K. Gruenspecht, "Differentiated Regulation: The Case of Auto Emissions Standards," *American Economic Review*, vol. 72 (May 1982, *Papers and Proceedings*, 1981), p. 330.

a. Projected percentage difference between standards in effect in 1980 and standards in effect since 1981 when applied to post-1980 automobiles.

an expensive three-way catalyst technology with closed-loop control of the fuel-air mixture on most vehicles—with a total cost penalty of approximately $500 (see table 3-5). This added cost reduced new vehicle sales and postponed decisions to scrap older cars. Given the wide disparity in emissions rates across vintages (see table 5-3), even a small change in scrapping rates can exert a significant effect on short-run emissions outcomes.

The EPA's MOBILE 2 model, which in its standard form assumes a fixed composition of the vehicle fleet, was modified to account for the impact of regulation-induced price increases on new car sales and scrappage rates. (Appendix D summarizes the model.) Table 5-5 compares emissions and sales outcomes under the current (1981) standards with an alternative regime that freezes emissions standards at 1980 levels. Hydrocarbons and carbon monoxide emissions are lower for the less stringent alternative regime through 1984 because of the effect of tighter emissions standards on vehicle prices and therefore new car sales. This result suggests that further reliance on new-source performance standards is an unattractive means for attaining emissions objectives in the short run. It also highlights the economic interaction of different regulatory programs affecting the automobile, since any regulation that results in higher new car prices will raise aggregate emissions through the mechanism outlined above.

Air Quality

Although the desire for improved air quality was undoubtedly the driving force behind the decision to regulate auto emissions, the relationship between emissions levels and air quality measures is tenuous at best.

Air quality measures reflect the combined impact of all pollution controls, not just those for mobile sources. In 1970, when the Clean Air Act was amended, passenger cars accounted for 48 percent of all estimated carbon monoxide emissions, but only 32 percent of estimated hydrocarbon emissions and 21 percent of nitrogen oxide emissions.[21] The small share of passenger car emissions in the latter two estimates is only one cause of the difficulty in identifying a direct relationship between these emissions and ambient concentrations of nitrogen dioxide and ozone, which is generated from hydrocarbons and nitrogen oxides in the atmosphere. A more serious difficulty lies in the photochemical reaction process through which ozone is formed.

Meteorological factors that vary from location to location and time to time, such as solar intensity, mixing height, temperature, and windspeed, play a crucial role in ozone-forming reactions. Moreover, the response of ozone output to changes in the supply of its hydrocarbon and nitrogen oxide precursors is extremely complicated. Depending on the initial ratio in which these two precursors are present, a simultaneous reduction in them can have less impact on ozone levels than an identical reduction in hydrocarbons with no reduction in nitrogen oxides. Since the relative amounts of these two pollutants emitted from stationary sources vary with each location, the impact of automotive emissions reduction on ozone levels would vary from place to place even if there were no meteorological differences to consider. Finally, the degree to which smog is dispersed depends very much upon local topographical and climatological conditions. In areas with inversion layers and mountains that limit the movement of air masses (such as Los Angeles), smog problems can be very severe.

These location-specific factors preclude any translation of the effect of national emissions reductions upon air quality. At best, there are only crude estimates of emissions of the relevant pollutants over the past four decades, since the EPA and the states have never engaged in intensive monitoring of emissions from industrial, utility, or mobile sources. It is

21. EPA, *National Air Pollutant Emission Estimates, 1940–1983,* tables 9, 10, 11, 14, 15, 16.

impossible to model the effects of emissions controls in most areas of the country because the required local air quality and emissions data are not available.

Nor is it possible to draw inferences from measures of actual air quality over time. Surprisingly, and even shockingly, Congress has legislated emissions controls on mobile, industrial, and utility sources without insisting upon careful measurement of the effects of these programs. Expenditures on air pollution controls have exceeded $20 billion a year in recent years, but there appears to be little interest in spending even as much as 1 percent of that amount to measure the effect of these expenditures upon air quality. Repeated warnings by the General Accounting Office that air quality is not being accurately measured have only recently been met with a response from the EPA in the form of additional monitoring sites.[22] But even when the national and state monitoring systems are fully in place, it will be impossible to gauge the effects of emissions reduction achieved during the past fifteen years because there are no historical data of comparable quality. Finally, it is unlikely that even the full implementation of the monitoring network planned by the EPA will be sufficient to capture the effects of mobile-source controls across the many air sheds with air pollution problems. Congress must show some interest in gauging the effects of automobile emissions controls before the EPA will develop a monitoring system and an analytical framework that is capable of measuring the impact of exhaust controls upon local air quality.

Very limited insight into the impact of *all* pollution control programs on ambient air quality can be obtained from direct measurement of trends in ambient air quality. Figure 5-1 shows that the average maximum daily ozone concentration remained almost constant through 1975–78 and declined by only 8 percent during 1978–83 despite the significant reduction in automotive hydrocarbon emissions over that period.[23] These measurements are drawn from only sixty-four sites, which may not represent an average profile for the United States. It is also interesting to note that despite the fact federal emissions standards began in 1968, there was little attempt to collect systematic information on air quality until the mid-1970s.

More detailed air quality results are available for Southern California,

22. General Accounting Office, *Air Quality: Do We Really Know What It Is?* (GPO, 1979).
23. Environmental Protection Agency, *National Air Quality and Emissions Trends Report, 1983*, EPA-450/4-84-029 (EPA, 1985), p. 3-35.

Figure 5-1. Ambient Concentrations of Ozone at National Air Monitoring Stations, 1975–83[a]

Ozone concentration (parts per million)

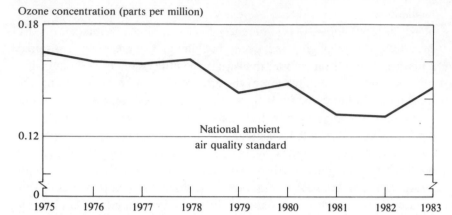

Source: Environmental Protection Agency, *National Air Quality and Emissions Trends Report, 1983*, EPA-450/4-84-029 (EPA, 1985), p. 3-35.

a. The second highest daily maximum one-hour concentration of ozone.

where the severity of air pollution led the state government to adopt emissions standards more stringent than those imposed in the federal program. Measures of ozone and nitrogen dioxide concentrations at several monitoring stations show a decline in a station near Los Angeles, but an offsetting increase at a station in San Bernardino, downwind of Los Angeles. Apparently, the change in the supplies of ozone precursors over downtown Los Angeles is delaying the conversion process, so that more conversion occurs in downwind areas. The measures of nitrogen dioxide concentrations bear out this viewpoint.[24] Overall, the results from California are consistent with the national results in showing virtually constant ambient air quality for ozone.

The air quality picture is somewhat clearer for carbon monoxide than for ozone or nitrogen dioxide. Carbon monoxide is nonreactive, so that the relationship between emissions and ambient concentrations is nearly linear. Passenger cars are virtually the only carbon monoxide sources that have been controlled; hence credit for any air quality improvement may be

24. Thomas C. Austin, Robert A. Cross, and Patty Helnen, "The California Vehicle Emission Control Program—Past, Present and Future," Society of Automotive Engineers Technical Paper 81-1232 (Warrendale, Pa.: SAE, 1981), pp. 15, 16.

Figure 5-2. Ambient Concentrations of Carbon Monoxide at National Air Monitoring Stations, 1975–83[a]

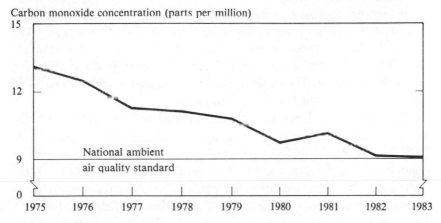

Carbon monoxide concentration (parts per million)

Source: EPA, *National Air Quality*, p. 3-22.
a. The second highest nonoverlapping eight-hour average concentration of carbon monoxide.

safely attributed to automotive emissions controls. Data drawn from forty-one sites show a 31 percent improvement over 1975–83 (figure 5-2).[25] In the same period, the EPA estimates that emissions fell by only 16 per-cent.[26] Thus ambient air quality appears to have improved at a faster rate than emissions have fallen. This outcome reflects the central city location of ambient air monitoring stations in a decade in which population and businesses were relocating from central cities into suburbia. The diffusion of emissions-producing activity has improved air quality at central city monitoring sites and degraded it at surrounding locations where no moni-toring occurs. For this reason, the EPA's ambient monitoring data over-state the air quality improvement experienced by the average American.

Potential Strategies to Reduce Emissions

Several means other than tighter new-source standards might be used to reduce emissions without incurring excessive costs. The phaseout of lead in gasoline—a 90 percent reduction in 1986, complete elimination in

25. EPA, *National Air Quality*, p. 3-22.
26. EPA, *National Air Pollutant Emission Estimates, 1940–83*, table 11.

1988—should narrow the performance shortfall by ending the misfueling of catalyst-equipped vehicles.[27]

A "two-car approach" would apply more stringent standards for cars sold in areas with air quality problems than for those sold elsewhere.[28] The current California standards are a crude version of the two-car strategy. Conceivably, these standards could be applied in other problem areas, but given the already stringent forty-nine-state standards, this would yield only a small incremental emissions reduction.

The costs of regulation can also be reduced without increasing emissions by permitting automakers to meet the standards on a companywide basis. In this way, manufacturers could exploit differences in the costs of controlling emissions from different engine families by producing some cars cleaner than the standards to compensate for others that would exceed the standards and could only be made to meet them at high cost. The EPA took a step in this direction by proposing to let GM compensate for excess emissions from some of their earlier models by producing an offsetting number of extra-clean cars.[29] The fuel economy standards program is already administered on a companywide basis.

Another approach to reducing emissions is to accelerate the retirement of old vehicles with high emissions rates. Retirement bounties or stiff registration fees for high-emission vintages could be used to promote retirement. Such policies would be particularly effective in 1985–95, when many pre-1975 cars with high emissions rates will be near the retirement margin. Unlike new-source standards, which tend to retard new car sales, a retirement-oriented policy would actually promote them. Furthermore, like the two-car strategy, accelerated retirement policies can be applied selectively, taking into account the air quality needs of each locality.

27. This represents an extra benefit of the lead phaseout, which was primarily motivated by concerns about lead pollution. The EPA currently estimates that 13 percent of catalyst-equipped vehicles are being misfueled at 50,000 miles, with a 2.6 percent increase for each additional 10,000 miles accumulated. See Economic Commission for Europe, Inland Transportation Committee, "Emissions of In-Use Vehicles: Update on the U.S. Experience," report transmitted from the United States for the 1984 annual meeting of the Group of Rapporteurs on Pollution and Energy, Geneva, pp. 7, 15.

28. David Harrison, Jr., "Controlling Automotive Emissions: How to Save More Than $1 Billion Per Year and Help the Poor Too," *Public Policy*, vol. 25 (Fall 1977), pp. 527–53.

29. This offset plan was overturned by a federal court decision that found the EPA lacking the statutory authority to negotiate offsets: *Center for Auto Safety* v. *Ruckelshaus*, 742 F. 2d 1 (1984).

Inspection and Maintenance

Compulsory inspection and maintenance of emissions control systems is another strategy that can be applied selectively. This approach seeks to close the gap between actual emissions performance and the standards by requiring cars to pass an emissions test. It operates both preventively, by discouraging tampering and misfueling, and correctively, through adjustments and repairs to restore emissions performance of cars that fail the test. Unlike the accelerated retirement strategy, inspection and maintenance has actually been adopted. The use of compulsory programs has grown dramatically in recent years—from four programs in 1981 to thirty in 1985.

The Clean Air Act Amendments of 1977 require states to implement compulsory inspection and maintenance programs in areas that could not demonstrate compliance with primary air quality standards for ozone and carbon monoxide by the end of 1982.

Table 5-6 summarizes the status of the inspection and maintenance effort. Despite the impressive sanctions specified by law for failure to institute inspection and maintenance in areas with ozone and carbon monoxide violations, states and localities have been very reluctant to begin their programs. Many areas missed the December 1982 target date by more than a full year. Several programs have not yet begun. Despite this recalcitrance, about one-third of the national fleet of cars and light trucks is now subject to inspection and maintenance, compared with only 6 percent at the start of the decade.[30]

In placing the burden of regulation directly on individual vehicle owners, the program represents a major shift in the thrust of the auto emissions control program, which had been focused entirely on regulating the manufacturers. In theory, inspection and maintenance programs make good sense. However, institutional and technical factors have an important role in determining the extent to which such programs will close the performance gap in emissions control.

In accord with the congressional mandate, states have considerable latitude in designing inspection and maintenance programs. All programs except one use an analysis of the hydrocarbons and carbon monoxide content of tailpipe emissions at idle as the primary inspection mecha-

---

30. Conversations with EPA officials at Ann Arbor, Michigan.

Table 5-6. Status of Inspection and Maintenance Programs, January 1985

Program location[a]	Starting date	Organization	Enforcement method
Operating			
Alaska: Anchorage, Fairbanks	7/85	Decentralized	Registration
Arizona: Phoenix, Tucson	1/77	Central contractor	Registration
California: South Coast, San Francisco, San Diego, Sacramento	3/84	Decentralized	Registration
Fresno	10/84	Decentralized	Registration
Colorado: Denver, Colorado Springs, Fort Collins	1/82	Decentralized	Sticker
Connecticut: statewide	1/83	Central contractor	Sticker
Delaware: Wilmington	1/83	Central, state run	Registration
District of Columbia	1/83	Central, locally run	Sticker
Georgia: Atlanta	4/82	Decentralized	Sticker
Idaho: Boise	8/84	Decentralized	Sticker
Indiana: Chicago, Louisville suburbs	6/84	Central contractor	Sticker
Kentucky: Louisville	1/84	Central contractor	Computer matching
Maryland: Baltimore, Washington suburbs	2/84	Central contractor	Registration
Massachusetts: statewide	4/83	Decentralized	Sticker
Missouri: St. Louis	1/84	Decentralized	Registration
Nevada: Las Vegas, Reno	10/83	Decentralized	Registration
New Jersey: statewide	2/74	Central/decentralized	Registration and sticker
New York: New York City area	1/82	Decentralized	Registration and sticker
North Carolina: Charlotte	12/82	Decentralized	Sticker
Oregon: Portland	7/75	Central, state run	Registration
Pennsylvania: Philadelphia, Pittsburgh, Allentown-Easton-Bethlehem	6/84	Decentralized	Sticker
Rhode Island: statewide	1/79	Decentralized	Sticker
Tennessee: Nashville	1/85	Central contractor	Registration
Memphis	2/83	Central, locally run	Sticker
Texas: Houston	7/84	Decentralized	Sticker
Utah: Salt Lake County	4/84	Decentralized	Registration
Davis County	4/84	Decentralized	Registration
Virginia: Washington suburbs	12/81	Decentralized	Registration and sticker
Washington: Seattle	1/82	Central contractor	Registration
Spokane	7/85	Central contractor	Registration
Wisconsin: Milwaukee	4/84	Central contractor	Registration
Planned			
Illinois: Chicago, St. Louis suburbs	10/85	Central contractor	Computer matching and sticker
Michigan: Detroit	12/85	Decentralized	Registration

Source: Environmental Protection Agency, Office of Mobile Sources, "Inspection/Maintenance Program Implementation Summary" (Ann Arbor, Mich.: EPA, January 1985).
a. Planned and operating only; several others are awaiting proposals.

nism.[31] This tailpipe test is designed to identify "gross" emitters while avoiding the time and expense required to apply the full federal test procedure.[32]

Test results are compared with a set of cutpoints that vary by model year to reflect the tightening of emissions standards over time. Cutpoints also vary across jurisdictions. In most areas, they are set at emissions rates far above the current federal standards, placing emphasis on the identification of gross, rather than marginal, violations.[33] In addition to testing idle emissions, many programs also include visual inspections for evidence of tampering. Newer vehicles are generally subject to a more elaborate tampering inspection. Inspection procedure varies widely across jurisdictions.

Early studies of the impact of inspection and maintenance programs in Portland, Oregon, and Phoenix, Arizona, using data collected before 1981, provided evidence that inspection and maintenance was effective. Emissions rates in these cities were found to be lower than in comparable control sites.[34] Moreover, because many failures of emissions control resulted from idle mixture and ignition problems that were relatively easy to diagnose and repair, the average cost of repairs to vehicles failing inspection in Portland was reported to be only $29.[35]

Two factors suggest caution in extrapolating from these early experiences to today's programs. First, beginning with the 1981 model year, the EPA adopted regulations requiring cars to meet the standards at any possible idle mixture setting. This led to manufacturers sealing the idle adjustment mechanism at the factory. Cars with the sealed idle mixture adjustment have markedly lower in-use emissions than those without it.[36] Thus, as these cars come to dominate the fleet, inspection and mainte-

31. The Houston program does not include an emissions test.

32. The full test procedure specifies the standardized driving cycle and ambient conditions at which emissions performance is certified.

33. For example, the EPA guidelines suggest cutpoints of 220 parts per million for hydrocarbons and 1.2 percent for carbon monoxide for 1981 and later cars. While there is no direct correspondence between the tailpipe test and the federal test procedure, a rough indicator of their stringency is provided by the observation that a well-maintained 1975 car will meet the 1981 cutpoints. 40 C.F.R. 85.2203 (1984).

34. James A. Rutherford and Rebecca L. Waring, "Update on EPA's Study of the Oregon Inspection/Maintenance Program," APCA 80-1.2, paper presented at the 1980 meeting of the Air Pollution Control Association, p. 4.

35. Jane A. Armstrong and Eugene Tierney, *Compilation of Inspection/Maintenance Facts and Figures*, EPA-AA-IMS/81-15, Environmental Protection Agency, Inspection and Maintenance Staff (Ann Arbor, Mich.: EPA, 1981).

36. Authors' analysis of data from the EPA Emissions Factor Test Program.

nance will no longer yield the cheap and easy emissions reductions obtained in the early programs.

Second, the adoption of three-way catalysts with closed-loop control of the fuel-air mixture, necessary to meet the stringent 1980 California and 1981 federal nitrogen oxide standards, represents a key technological change, the impact of which is not reflected in the early studies of inspection and maintenance. The emissions performance shortfall for cars equipped with these systems can be traced to the catastrophic failure of a relatively small proportion (approximately 5 percent) of these systems. The thirty highest hydrocarbon emitters in a sample of 993 vehicles subject to the 1981 standards contributed 21 percent of the fleet hydrocarbon emissions, and the thirty highest carbon monoxide emitters in the same sample contributed 27 percent of the fleet carbon monoxide emissions. There is nearly total overlap in the two "dirty thirty" groups, so that 3 percent of the vehicles are essentially contributing one-fifth to one-quarter of the total fleet emissions.[37] In-use failure rates for closed-loop systems are likely to be higher than for the EPA's sample fleets, since the accelerated rate of mileage accumulation in the test fleets provided fewer opportunities for malfunctions than in normal use.

Because systems incorporating closed-loop control of the fuel-air mixture vary their operating characteristics with changes in the operating mode, concern has been raised regarding the capability of the tailpipe exhaust tests used in most programs to identify failed systems yet avoid errors of commission—failing vehicles that actually meet the standards. A recent analysis shows that about one-third of 1981–82 model year cars that exceeded acceptable EPA levels on the two-speed idle test actually met the standards when subjected to the full federal test procedure.[38] The one-speed idle test used in the majority of programs performed better. For this test, there were no false failures for 1981 and 1982 cars equipped to meet forty-nine-state standards; however, one in five 1981 California vehicles that failed this test actually met the standards. Experience with operators and test equipment in the field is likely to be less favorable than these results, which reflect laboratory conditions. Errors of omission are also fairly widespread. Both the one- and two-speed idle tests identify 40 to 60 percent of the cars with excess emissions among 1981–82 federal vehicles

37. Authors' analysis of in-use emissions test data provided by EPA.
38. Philip A. Lorang, John T. White III, and David J. Brzezinski, "In-Use Emissions of 1980 and 1981 Passenger Cars: Results of EPA Testing," Society of Automotive Engineers Technical Paper 82-0975 (Warrendale, Pa.: SAE, August 1982), p. 16.

but only 14 to 31 percent of the cars with excess emissions among 1981 California cars.[39]

Even an ideal inspection system is of no value unless the failing systems identified in the inspection process are ultimately repaired. Our concerns over the adequacy of maintenance relate primarily to vehicles equipped with closed-loop systems—generally 1981 and newer cars. One potential problem is the questionable ability of nonspecialist mechanics to diagnose and repair those failing systems that are identified. Even if the necessary expertise becomes available, the cost of restorative maintenance on closed-loop systems will pose a significant barrier to the effective functioning of the program. The average cost of restorative maintenance performed by EPA contractor personnel on a group of nineteen closed-loop three-way catalyst vehicles that failed an emissions test was $105,[40] a figure that exceeds the $50–$75 repair cost liability ceiling incorporated in many inspection and maintenance programs.[41] Unless these repair cost liability ceilings are raised, most three-way catalyst vehicles will escape restorative maintenance entirely. If failure rates increase as these vehicles enter the second half of their lifetime (a phenomenon on which no evidence is yet available), cars with these systems could become a major pollution problem in the second half of the decade.

The effectiveness of inspection and maintenance depends to a significant extent on the manner in which it is administered. The majority of programs (seventeen of thirty) use decentralized, privately operated inspection facilities despite the difficulty of maintaining uniformity of inspection procedures and quality control under this arrangement. When decentralized emissions inspection is only one part of a larger business, there are also incentives for purposefully inaccurate inspection, either to generate repair business or avoid antagonizing valued customers. For example, a 1981 test program in which unmarked vehicles were submitted

39. Ibid.

40. Ibid., p. 20. This figure is biased downward by the exclusion of four vehicles that incurred very high repair costs from the average and the fact that the repairs were performed by EPA contractor personnel with unusual expertise in emissions control systems.

41. A recent study of repair cost reports for eighty 1981 closed-loop vehicles failing their initial emissions inspection showed values ranging from zero to $163. The twenty-nine reports of zero undoubtedly reflect repairs made under warranty at unspecified cost. Since the other reports may reflect partial warranty coverage, this data provides little insight into actual repair costs. See U.S. Department of Energy, Office of Policy, Planning and Analysis, *Analysis of Inspection/Maintenance Data from the Arizona Program: Final Report* (DOE, April 1983), app. H.

for emissions inspection at 211 Rhode Island garages found that 57 percent of the garages visited issued inspection stickers without performing the emissions test; of garages that did test, only 37 percent followed correct procedures. Controlling for differences in cutpoints and test procedures, decentralized programs have a significantly lower failure rate than centralized ones. Virginia and New York, decentralized program states with cutpoints that should result in failure rates of 20 percent and 10 percent, are experiencing failure rates of 3 percent and 5.5 percent, respectively.[42]

A system that denies registration to vehicles that fail to submit to emissions inspection provides a much greater inducement to comply than a sticker system, which is only effective to the extent that owners perceive a high risk of being stopped and fined for failure to display a sticker. Yet eleven of thirty operating programs rely on a window sticker system as the sole enforcement mechanism. Surveys of compliance in Georgia, Colorado, and Connecticut, three states with sticker enforcement, show compliance rates ranging from 50 percent to 80 percent, far below the 90 percent or better typical of registration-enforced programs.[43]

Recent data show that cars that fail inspection in any year are five times as likely to fail in the following year as cars of the same make and model year that pass the first inspection.[44] If this pattern persists in later years, strong enforcement measures will be needed to force owners of these "emissions lemons" to submit to inspection. Window stickers will not suffice.

Clearly the details of implementation determine the effectiveness of an inspection and maintenance program. The history of the Pennsylvania program illustrates the difficulty of implementing effective inspection and maintenance in a recalcitrant state. Only after Pennsylvania's refusal to honor a consent decree to begin inspection and maintenance led to the impoundment of federal highway funds did the state legislature vote to authorize a program. Emissions reduction was at best a secondary goal of this enabling legislation: the primary objective was to secure the release of highway funds while placing minimum burdens on those subject to the program. To this end, the legislature specified a $50 repair liability limit

42. General Accounting Office, *Vehicle Emissions Inspection and Maintenance Program Is Behind Schedule*, GAO/RCED-85-22 (GAO, 1985), pp. 22, 23.

43. Conversation with EPA officials, Ann Arbor, Michigan.

44. Energy and Environmental Analysis, *Investigations Relating to In-Use Emissions of 1980 and Later Vehicles*, prepared for Environmental Protection Agency, no. 68-01-6558 (Arlington, Va.: Energy and Environmental Analysis, September 1984), pp. 4-9–4-10.

($25 for pre-1974 vehicles). The liability limit does not include repairs covered under manufacturers' warranties or arising from tampering. Vehicles failing an idle test must undergo a low-emissions tune up or whatever part of it can be financed under the liability limit. After this tune-up procedure an emissions inspection certificate is automatically issued, regardless of emissions performance. The program is sticker enforced.[45]

At this juncture, there is no evidence on the effectiveness of inspection and maintenance in reducing total emissions or improving air quality in any area. Closed-loop catalyst system failures may be identified during an emissions inspection, but they are likely to go unrepaired under a cost waiver unless the vehicle is under warranty. Since these failures result in extremely high emissions rates, air quality may suffer if closed-loop system failures increase with age. Public resistance to regulating in-use vehicles, once directed against retrofit programs, is reappearing in the form of pressure for cost-waiver provisions that may permit high-emission cars with closed-loop systems to bypass restorative maintenance entirely.

In the short term, while pre-1981 vehicles dominate the fleet, compulsory inspection and maintenance, if diligently pursued, should be effective in reducing hydrocarbon and carbon monoxide emissions. However, the program's effectiveness may fall as vehicles with closed-loop systems become increasingly predominant. It is conceivable that in a regime with low repair cost liability limits, aggregate emissions of hydrocarbons and carbon monoxide would be lower if there was a return to open-loop oxidation catalyst emission control systems. This would require some rollback in the present nitrogen oxide standard.

The Benefits and Costs of Controlling Auto Emissions

The limited information on the effect of emissions controls on air quality, together with even more limited knowledge of the relationship between air quality and its effects, poses formidable barriers to precise estimation of the benefits of mobile-source emissions controls. The sketchy evidence that can be marshaled suggests that the costs of automobile emissions controls, as presently implemented, greatly exceed the value of their benefits. The discrepancy between costs and benefits is

45. *Pennsylvania Bulletin*, vol. 13 (November 5, 1983), pp. 3397–98. There is, however, no mechanism for identifying cases of tampering.

especially large at the margin of the program, where control costs are highest and benefits lowest. Indeed, the cost-benefit gap is so large that even the most extreme benefits estimates do not justify the present controls program in cost-benefit terms.[46]

The fact that the current mobile-source emissions standards cannot be justified on a cost-benefit basis does not mean that there are no interesting cost-benefit issues to consider. On the benefit side, future regulatory performance can be improved by an examination of how such a massive program was launched, given what appear in hindsight to be minimal benefits. On the cost side, without regard to the value of reducing emissions, one can consider whether the present program is achieving emissions reduction in a cost-effective manner. Although benefit uncertainties can lead to honest differences over the socially desirable level of regulation, whatever goals are set should be reached at the lowest possible cost.

Benefits

A survey by Freeman of the existing literature on the benefits of reducing concentrations of photochemical oxidants, nitrogen oxides, and carbon monoxide divides the benefits into categories: health benefits, reduction of damage to vegetation, reduction of damage to materials, and aesthetic benefits. For each category, the size of the benefit resulting from complete elimination of the relevant pollutant is estimated. Then this benefit is scaled to the pollution reduction that has actually occurred. A striking result of this analysis is that the current emissions control program for mobile sources is more costly than the value of the benefits associated with the complete elimination of ozone and carbon monoxide pollution.[47]

Health concerns provided the initial motivation for auto emissions controls. Primary ambient air quality standards are based upon prospective health risks to the most sensitive members of the group—such as cardiac patients—determined to be at risk from the pollutant. Since the entire group at risk includes only a fraction of the population, its most sensitive subset must be, in turn, an even smaller fraction of the overall population.

46. Cost-benefit analyses of stationary-source emission controls show a much more favorable outcome, with the present controls and even some additional ones justifiable on a cost-benefit basis. See Lester B. Lave and Eugene P. Seskin, *Air Pollution and Human Health* (Johns Hopkins University Press, 1977), chap. 10.

47. A. Myrick Freeman III, *Air and Water Pollution Control: A Benefit-Cost Assessment* (Wiley, 1982).

Only a part of this target population will reside in areas with air quality problems, further restricting the set of potential beneficiaries. Given the narrow base over which health benefits are distributed, their aggregate value must be small unless the benefits to the target individuals are very highly valued.

Consider first the case of nitrogen dioxide. In early studies, it was associated with increased susceptibility to viral infections, lung disease, and bronchitis. Because no short-term exposure effects were identified, a standard was set based upon an annual average. The statistical and epidemiological methods used in the early studies have been judged inadequate, and no additional evidence of health effects related to nitrogen dioxide exposure has been forthcoming. In any event, air quality monitoring data indicate that the current nitrogen dioxide standard is being attained throughout the country, providing protection against health effects that are very difficult to document, with the possible exception of some effects upon children.

For both carbon monoxide and ozone, the health effect that drives the current air quality standards is the impact of exposure on individuals with heart and respiratory diseases. Experiments find that some subjects engaging in vigorous exercise in the presence of elevated ozone or carbon monoxide concentrations feel unable to continue exercising or face pain and alarming symptoms.[48] The concentration at which these symptoms occur warrants caution against vigorous exercise on the smoggiest days in Los Angeles. These short-term exposure effects appear to be transitory and reversible, as does eye irritation, the other effect of short-term exposure to ozone.

In setting its air quality standards, the EPA interprets its mandate to protect the public health with "an adequate margin of safety" as requiring the selection of a standard at which 99 percent of the sensitive population (that is, cardiac patients) will not suffer health effects, including transitory discomfort. The EPA relaxed the ozone standard from 0.08 to 0.12 parts per million in its 1979 review, but many health experts felt that the evidence justified an even larger relaxation.

Most of the studies upon which the EPA has relied in setting its ozone ambient air quality standard are clinical studies or studies of hospital

48. Anthony J. DeLucia and William C. Adams, "Effects of Ozone Inhalation during Exercise on Pulmonary Function and Blood Biochemistry," *Journal of Applied Physiology*, vol. 43 (July 1977), pp. 75–81.

admissions under varying ozone concentrations. Few of these studies show much of an effect below 0.20 to 0.30 parts per million. A 1984 statistical epidemiological study shows that ozone concentrations are associated with increased "restricted activity days" among affected populations. However, the analysis projects very small beneficial effects from reducing ozone concentrations.[49] Since 1979 many other new studies have been performed, but the implications of the results of these studies have not yet been analyzed by the EPA.

Although the physiological mechanisms by which carbon monoxide affects health are well understood, the choice of a standard that is safe for 99 percent of the sensitive population has proven to be highly controversial. Such controversy is in part attributable to the EPA's interpretation of its health protection mandate. In contrast to most policy applications of experimental or statistical results, which emphasize the *average* result in the decision process, the EPA's decisions are largely driven by the results that show health effects at the *lowest* concentrations. Since averages are fairly insensitive to the inclusion or exclusion of a single result, the credibility of a particular investigator or experiment does not affect a policy process that focuses on the central tendency reported in the scientific literature. In the EPA's process, however, individual results matter a great deal. Moreover, the cost of experiments, time constraints, the problems of keeping a small human-subject pool at a remote laboratory or developing a comparable group of subjects, and the approval process for such human-subject experiments have discouraged independent efforts to replicate crucial experiments.

The narrow scientific basis of the EPA's regulatory process is well illustrated by the effort to reissue the ambient standard for carbon monoxide. Seven studies on the adverse health effects of carbon monoxide by a single investigator formed the basis of the EPA's August 1980 proposal to revise the standard. Subsequent questions regarding the adequacy of unrelated studies conducted by the same investigator for another government agency led the EPA to convene a peer review committee. The reviewers found that the validity of his results could not be substantiated. The EPA decided simply to retain the existing standard after five years of fruitless inquiry.[50]

49. Paul R. Portney and John Mullahy "Urban Air Quality and Acute Respiratory Illness," prepared for Environmental Protection Agency, Office of Air Quality Planning and Standards (Washington, D.C.: Resources for the Future, November 1984), pp. 24, 26.
50. See 50 Fed. Reg. 37484 (1985).

Freeman concludes from his survey of the health effects literature that the health benefits that would result from eliminating all automobile-related pollution would be no more than $2 billion (in 1978 dollars). Since he maintains that emissions control policies have not reduced ambient concentrations of nitrogen dioxide or oxidants and there is no conclusive evidence on adverse health effects from carbon monoxide, Freeman concludes that the most reasonable estimate of actual health benefits is zero.[51] If, as he concedes, air quality would have been worse without controls, the control program may have had some beneficial effects upon health, but he does not attempt to quantify them. Given the difficulty in modeling air quality and the very sketchy evidence on health effects, any estimate of the health benefits is suspect.

The other important benefits of reducing mobile-source pollution concern damage to vegetation and the aesthetic damage created by, among other things, a reduction in visibility. The damage to vegetation has been a source of increasing concern. It is likely that ozone reduces agricultural yields, damages ornamental shrubbery, and even harms forests. The total elimination of man-made oxidants could result in about $1 billion to $4 billion (1978 dollars) a year in vegetation benefits. However, because so little progress has been made in reducing oxidant concentrations, Freeman estimates the benefits to vegetation from reducing ozone concentrations are at best only $0.3 billion per year.[52] A more recent study also finds that vegetation damage due to ozone is likely to have a rather small economic cost. The authors estimate that a relaxation of the standard from 0.12 parts per million to 0.14 parts per million would reduce crop yields by less than $1 billion per year. Even this estimate may be too high since the ozone standard is more of a problem in dense urban areas than in rural agricultural areas.[53] For the value of aesthetic benefits, Freeman relies upon studies of property values and concludes that the elimination of photochemical smog and nitrogen oxides could yield aesthetic benefits valued at about $2 billion (1978 dollars) a year.[54]

---

51. Freeman, *Air and Water Pollution Control*, pp. 81–82.

52. Ibid., p. 91.

53. Raymond J. Kopp and others, "Implications of Environmental Policy for U.S. Agriculture: The Case of Ambient Ozone Standards" (Washington, D.C.: Resources for the Future, 1984), pp. 18–19.

54. Freeman, *Air and Water Pollution Control*, p. 120; and Jon P. Nelson, *The Effects of Mobile-Source Air and Noise Pollution on Residential Property Values*, U.S. Department of Transportation, Office of the Secretary (DOT, 1975).

Summing all the benefit categories, Freeman finds that the only realized benefit of automobile emissions controls is increased vegetation growth valued at $0.3 billion annually.[55] This value, which reflects the lack of discernible improvement in ambient air quality since 1970, is probably too low, since without the substantial reduction in automobile emissions from the baseline, air quality would have deteriorated from its 1970 level. Nonetheless, if the total damage attributable to actual smog levels is as limited as Freeman suggests—approximately $5.2 billion a year (in 1978 dollars)—it seems unlikely that the value of the benefits from automobile emissions controls could be very great.[56] Even the complete elimination of man-made smog through automobile emissions controls—an unlikely possibility—would be worth only $8.3 billion in 1984 dollars.

Costs

The calculation of the total costs of the mobile-source program is much more straightforward. The Council on Environmental Quality estimated the annual cost of the mobile-source program in 1979 at $8.1 billion and predicted that this would rise to $14.7 billion by 1988.[57] Had emissions standards been kept at their 1979 level, the present value of control costs would have been $800 a car in 1984 dollars, or about $8.4 billion a year for a steady state replacement rate of 10.5 million cars a year. But the more onerous current standards would raise this total to as much as $16.8 billion in 1984 dollars.[58] It is obviously possible that our cost estimates are too high or that technological progress will reduce them over the next few years. Nevertheless, the annual costs of the current automobile emissions program are certainly greater than $10 billion a year for a steady state output of 10.5 million cars a year.

Comparing Costs and Benefits

On the basis of current knowledge of the benefits of smog control, it is difficult to conclude that the expenditures on emissions control for automobiles are well spent. Even if current controls succeed in removing *all*

55. Freeman, *Air and Water Pollution Control,* p. 128.
56. Ibid., pp. 81, 91, 95, 119. This figure is calculated by summing over all benefit categories using the "most reasonable" point estimates.
57. Council on Environmental Quality, *Environmental Quality, 1980: The Eleventh Annual Report of the Council on Environmental Quality* (GPO, 1980), p. 394.
58. These data are based on the estimates in table 3-5.

perceptible vestiges of photochemical smog, Freeman's estimates and more recent studies would suggest that the benefits would still be less than the costs. At the margin, it is obvious that costs must greatly exceed benefits since incremental costs of control rise rapidly in the vicinity of current standards.

Of course, new information on benefits could change the program's cost-benefit ratio. It may be that individuals place a large value on improved visibility and a reduction in the general discomfort caused by photochemical smog. Alternatively, researchers may find that smog is associated with long-term chronic health effects, although this seems unlikely, given the long history of smog formation and human exposure to it. Finally, the relationship between exposure to nitrogen dioxide and children's health may be more serious than currently believed. At present, however, it would be difficult to justify the expenditure of more than $15 billion a year on controlling automobile pollutants. One can only conclude that our society is very cautious about potential undiscovered health effects or that the emissions control program for automobiles is too stringent.

Conclusion

The automobile emissions standards and dates for achieving them embodied in the 1970 Clean Air Act were a dramatic statement that Congress wanted something done to improve air quality. While a dramatic gesture may have been called for by public sentiment and by the slow progress in Detroit, the program was ill conceived. It resulted in a decade of confrontation between Congress and the auto makers, imposed large costs on automobile owners, and achieved at best only modest success in its two principal aims: improving air quality and reducing the adverse health effects from air pollution. To be sure, the immediate goal of reducing aggregate emissions of pollutants from automobiles appears to have been achieved. However, there is little evidence of improvement in ambient air quality, particularly for smog. Air quality would probably have been worse without an emissions program. Yet even if the program has improved air quality substantially compared with what it would have been, the marginal costs greatly exceed the marginal benefits.

Since pollution was a new issue in 1970, one should not have expected to find a large health effects literature to guide the EPA in setting initial ambient air quality standards. It is, however, somewhat surprising that fifteen years later the relevant health effects literature remains so limited that doubts concerning the work of a single investigator can severely disrupt the regulatory process. The lack of attention to the scientific basis for regulation is also apparent in the paucity of data to trace the improvements in air quality since 1970.

While the value of the auto emissions control program must ultimately be measured in terms of its impact on air quality and the resulting benefits, a narrower evaluation of the emissions-reducing impact of the program is also instructive. For a number of reasons actual emissions reduction has fallen short of the levels implicit in the standards. First, emissions of new cars do not meet the federal standards on average. Furthermore, these cars deteriorate faster than Congress anticipated: their emissions at 50,000 miles are two to four times larger than the standards (see table 5-3).

The second problem is that the poor performance and increased expense of new vehicles with emissions controls have combined with slow economic growth to dampen the sales of new cars. As a result, older cars stay in the fleet longer, giving rise to greater emissions levels both because they had greater emissions when new than cars produced today and because emissions controls degrade over time.

The third problem is the failure to ensure that vehicles that violate the standards are repaired and brought into compliance. Some states initiated inspection and maintenance requirements early and found the programs could be successful in detecting and correcting emissions problems at low cost. However, inspection and maintenance will be less successful in the future for two reasons: states forced to implement the system are not likely to enforce the provisions, and the post-1980 control technology is sufficiently complicated that failures are difficult to diagnose and expensive to repair.

Economic efficiency was never a congressional concern in designing air pollution policy. Congress perceived a need to act, but it did not have the information on which to base its decision. It did not know what was achievable nor what was worth achieving. Unfortunately, the costs of automobile emissions controls turned out to be higher than anyone expected and the benefits much smaller. If the enormous resources spent had been targeted better, air quality could have been improved significantly. This is not a matter of mere historical interest, for the emissions control program continues to have substantial costs without corresponding benefits. Surely, after fifteen years of crisis management, it is time to ask whether the goals of the program make sense and if the current policies are likely to achieve them.

CHAPTER SIX

Regulation of Fuel Economy

GOVERNMENT regulation of fuel economy takes two forms—the corporate average fuel economy standards (CAFE) and the "gas guzzler" tax. At the time both policies were enacted, the government was simultaneously encouraging gasoline consumption by imposing maximum price regulation on crude oil and refined products. This counterproductive strategy has since been abandoned as oil and gasoline prices have been allowed to reach market-clearing levels.

When safety regulation began in 1966, there were no other exogenous changes (with the possible exception of increased product liability exposure) that would have induced automobile producers to increase the safety of their vehicles dramatically. Indeed, we have argued that the improvement in vehicle safety must be attributed in large part to government regulation. Similarly, one would not have expected the dramatic reduction in vehicle emissions that has occurred since 1968 if there had been no government regulation of emissions.

In the case of fuel economy, however, the Arab oil embargo and the subsequent rise in the real price of motor fuel would surely have induced a response from the automobile companies and consumers in the absence of fuel economy regulation. Automobiles would be much more fuel efficient today even if the government had not chosen to regulate fuel efficiency. In fact, it is by no means clear that the CAFE standards imposed a binding constraint on automobile producers until real gasoline prices began falling in 1981. As we shall see, however, it is not easy to sort out the effects of regulation from those of the rise in gasoline prices.

Automobile Design and Fuel Economy

The diversity of consumer tastes and the proliferation of automobile designs to address these tastes always complicate attempts to model the automobile industry's product offerings. There are some people who want

117

heavy "road cruisers" while others desire sports cars with superior handling. Others simply opt for basic transportation. In each case, however, one may assume that rational consumers will pay for added fuel efficiency up to the point where the added cost of delivering fuel efficiency just equals the present value of gasoline saved.[1] Otherwise, one could not explain the penchant for diesel engines among U.S. owners of Mercedes (particularly in northern climates).[2]

Automobile manufacturers offer an array of vehicles with different efficiency-performance characteristics to appeal to various groups of consumers. In chapter 3, we provided a model of the response of manufacturers to changing regulatory demands, factor prices (including fuel), and tastes. In this chapter, we explore the reaction of the domestic automobile companies to higher fuel prices and government regulation of fuel economy.

Time plays a very important role in adjusting automobile purchases to changes in relative operating costs. A sudden increase in gasoline costs causes consumers to adjust their use of cars already on the road and their purchases of new automobiles. At first, the choice of new cars is from those models in current production, whose design reflects manufacturers' expectations as much as four or five years ago. For instance, a consumer choosing to allocate y dollars in annual expenditures on automobile travel may have the choice between performance—acceleration, ride, handling, and interior comfort—and annual mileage as shown by the convex line, y, in figure 6-1. If he wants to drive M_1 miles per year, at current gasoline prices, the best performance available is that of, say, a Chevette. If he chooses to buy a car and operate it only M_0 miles per year, he can buy a GM Cavalier—a car with better performance.

What if gasoline prices suddenly rise? The consumer's opportunities rotate around R' downward along y'. At each mileage, the consumer can afford less performance because of higher gasoline prices. But the locus, y', reflects automobile choices from a selection of models brought to the market by manufacturers when gasoline prices were lower. In time, manufacturers will reduce performance levels or improve engineering or both in an effort to improve fuel economy. As a result, the consumer's eventual

---

1. Roger Blair, David Kaserman, and Richard Tepel, "The Impact of Improved Mileage on Gasoline Consumption," *Economic Inquiry*, vol. 22 (April 1984), pp. 209–17.
2. Carl Nash reminds us that Mercedes need diesels to meet CAFE standards, but diesels antedate CAFE.

Figure 6-1. Trade-offs between Performance and Annual Vehicle Miles Traveled, before and after a Major Increase in Gasoline Prices

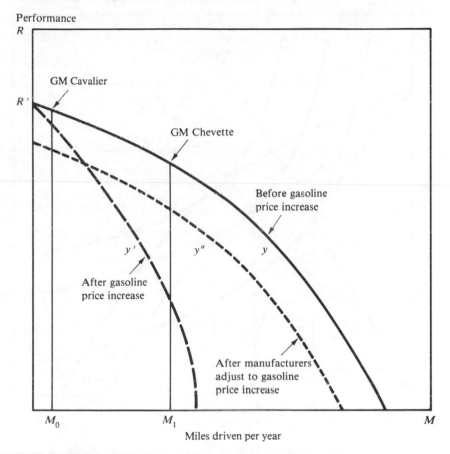

Performance

Miles driven per year

choices will be made along y'' for y dollars in annual outlays. This opportunity set will be inside the original locus, y, because at all performance levels the cost per mile of driving is higher with the new models than with the older models and lower gasoline prices.

After new models begin to appear, reflecting the improved fuel efficiency at each performance level, consumers begin to readjust their purchases toward higher-performance (and perhaps larger) cars. In addition, these more efficient cars permit greater annual mileage accumulation. This result is shown in figure 6-2, where a hypothetical consumer is shown to find his optimum at the tangency of an indifference (constant satisfaction)

Figure 6-2. The Response to Higher Gasoline Prices

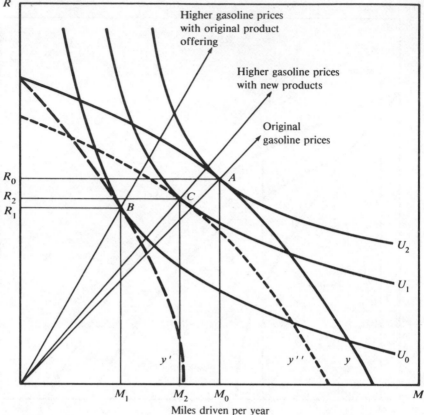

Performance

curve and the y opportunity locus—a point labeled A. When gasoline prices rise, his choice is changed temporarily to B, since he reduces both mileage and performance substantially when confronted with the same old choice of vehicles, reducing his satisfaction level from U_2 to U_0. When automobile producers adjust to the new gasoline prices, our hypothetical consumer would move to C, reflecting a choice of performance and mileage between A and B. His satisfaction level would be increased to U_1. When offered a more fuel-efficient set of vehicles, consumers move back toward their original equilibrium. This explains why one frequently hears the lament that automobile buyers are "returning" to the large cars, forgetting the "lessons" learned from a recent gasoline price shock.

The Fuel Economy Standards

Congress imposed corporate average fuel economy standards (CAFE) on automobile manufacturers in 1975. These standards set the harmonic-weighted fleet average for manufacturers, based upon EPA city-highway ratings, at 18 miles per gallon by the 1978 model year and 27.5 miles per gallon by the 1985 model year.[3] The Department of Transportation was empowered to set interim standards for 1981–84. Fines are imposed on a manufacturer failing to make the CAFE standard, but those who exceed the standards in previous or future years are allowed carryovers and carry-backs. These carryovers and carrybacks were extended from one to three model years by 1980 legislation.[4] In addition, gas guzzler taxes—manufacturers' excise taxes—are added to each car that fails to achieve a given fuel economy.[5]

According to EPA data, the fleet-average fuel efficiency of U.S. cars has nearly doubled over 1973–84 (table 6-1); however, much of this improvement would surely have occurred without regulation.[6] The sharp increase in the price of gasoline and declining real income growth would have led consumers to be much more cognizant of fuel efficiency. On the other hand, the erratic pace of real gasoline price increases may have slowed progress somewhat. For instance, the real CPI motor fuel index jumped by 22 percent in 1974 (table 6-1) but then receded by 7 percent in the next four years, in part because of federal price regulation. Between 1978 and 1981, it rose sharply once again—by 50 percent over this three-year period. Since 1981 gasoline prices have eased substantially, and the

3. Energy Policy and Conservation Act of 1975 (89 Stat. 902). This act amended the Motor Vehicle Information and Cost Savings Act (86 Stat. 947). The CAFE standard is a harmonic-weighted fleet average rather than an arithmetic average because the total mileage amassed by an individual manufacturer's model-year sales is $\Sigma M_i Q_i$ where M_i is the annual mileage accumulated by the ith model and Q_i is the number of ith models sold; the total gallons consumed by these cars is equal to $\Sigma(M_i Q_i / E_i)$, where E_i is the mpg rating of the ith model; and, assuming that all M_i are equal, the mpg for the manufacturer's total fleet is equal to $\Sigma Q_i / \Sigma(Q_i / E_i)$.

4. Automobile Fuel Efficiency Act of 1980 (94 Stat. 1821).

5. See Internal Revenue Code sec. 1016(d). The tax is set at $5 per 1/10 of a mile per gallon below the CAFE standard, per car.

6. For a discussion of fuel economy measures, see Karl H. Mellman and J. Dillard Murrell, "Why Vehicles Don't Achieve the EPA MPG on the Road and How That Shortfall Can Be Accounted For," Society of Automotive Engineers Technical Paper 820791 (Warrendale, Pa.: SAE, 1982).

Table 6-1. Estimates of Fuel Economy, Model Years 1968–84

Year	Mileage (miles per gallon)			Real price of motor fuel (1967=100)[b]
	City	Highway	Harmonic average[a]	
1968	12.59	18.42	14.69	97.3
1969	12.60	18.62	14.74	95.4
1970	12.59	19.01	14.85	90.8
1971	12.27	18.18	14.37	87.6
1972	12.15	18.90	14.48	85.9
1973	12.01	18.07	14.15	88.7
1974	12.03	18.23	14.21	108.3
1975	13.68	19.45	15.79	106.0
1976	15.23	21.27	17.46	104.3
1977	15.99	22.26	18.31	103.7
1978	17.24	24.48	19.89	100.5
1979	17.70	24.60	20.25	122.2
1980	20.35	29.02	23.51	149.6
1981	21.75	31.12	25.16	150.8
1982	22.32	32.76	26.06	134.7
1983[c]	22.21	32.90	26.01	126.1
1984[c]	22.67	33.69	26.59	119.2

Sources: R. M. Heavenrich and others, "Passenger Car Fuel Economy . . . Trends thru 1984," Environmental Protection Agency Paper 840499 (EPA, 1984), p. 4; and *Economic Report of the President, February 1985*, pp. 291, 293.

a. Based on 55 percent city driving and 45 percent highway driving.
b. Consumer price index for motor fuel divided by total CPI.
c. Based on estimated sales weights supplied by the manufacturers.

real price of motor fuel in 1984 was 21 percent lower than in 1981. Given this erratic behavior of fuel prices, it is possible that the CAFE regulations accelerated the adjustment to more fuel-efficient cars. Automobile manufacturers typically require long lead times to respond to changing technologies or consumer tastes. The CAFE standards may have forced a more rapid adjustment.

Manufacturers' Responses

The first CAFE standards applied to 1978 model cars that were introduced less than three years after the passage of the Energy Policy and Conservation Act in 1975. In this short period, automobile manufacturers could not have been expected to have completed their response to the required standards (if binding) or to the 1973–74 gasoline price increases. Designing, engineering, and producing a new automobile can require four years or more.[7] Adjusting a major manufacturer's entire product offering may require a decade or more.

General Motors provides a good example of the difficulties of adjusting an entire product offering to the new demand for fuel efficiency. In response to the sharp increase in the demand for small cars, GM introduced the Chevette in 1975. This was hardly a major product change since the Chevette was largely an amalgam of design features drawn from European cars. In the 1977 model year, GM introduced its first downsized standard cars, and the company downsized its intermediate cars in the 1978 model year. In 1979 the X-body was introduced, representing the first major design change by GM since the 1973–74 oil shock. The new front-wheel-drive J-body cars were introduced in 1981 to compete with the more expensive fuel-efficient imports from Japan. The J cars also represented a major design change, although at first they utilized a disappointing version of an existing GM engine. In 1982 GM introduced a new series of front-wheel-drive A-body cars—intermediate Chevrolets, Buicks, Pontiacs, and Oldsmobiles. The company downsized some of the larger cars in its fleet in 1984, but even by then it had not fully readjusted its fleet to 1984 gasoline prices, competitive offerings from imports and its domestic competitors, and the changes in consumer tastes.[8]

General Motors was preparing to reduce the weight of its cars two years before the Arab oil embargo.[9] This meant that product development decisions were being reexamined as early as 1971, but none of these decisions could have affected product offerings before 1974. In 1970–72 the model lines offered by the major U.S. producers were clearly designed for low gasoline prices. By 1975, fuel prices were substantially higher, but major changes in vehicle design or engines could not have been expected before 1977 or 1978. The Energy Policy and Conservation Act was also passed in 1975, mandating CAFE standards for 1978 through 1985. Any effects of this new set of government regulations on automobile design might have

7. See Energy and Environmental Analysis, *The Technology/Cost Segment Model for Post-1985 Automotive Fuel-Economy Analysis*, prepared for the Department of Energy (Arlington, Va.: Energy and Environmental Analysis, 1981), chap. 3.

8. GM's decisions to build subcompact cars in a joint venture with Toyota and to undertake a major new subcompact program (the Saturn) are evidence of a continuing attempt to adjust its product mix to the new realities of the market.

9. See John Z. DeLorean and J. Patrick Wright, *On a Clear Day You Can See General Motors: John Z. DeLorean's Look inside the Automotive Giant* (Avon Books, 1979), pp. 215–17, for John DeLorean's discussion of the proposal to downsize GM cars.

begun to appear by the 1978 model year, but the major impact would have been in evidence no earlier than the 1979 or 1980 model years.

To see how the vehicle manufacturers responded to changing fuel prices and CAFE standards, one might begin with a simple listing of the attributes of three different size classes of automobiles—full-size, low-price sedans; intermediate sedans; and subcompacts. The fuel economy, acceleration from 0 to 60 miles per hour, and weight of each of the Big Three's representative product offerings for various years in the 1970s are exhibited in table 6-2. To increase fuel economy, the manufacturers could reduce weight, reduce engine power, or improve the technology of existing engine-weight combinations. Clearly, all three major manufacturers chose to reduce both weight and acceleration in response to the increase in energy prices.

There was only marginal improvement in fuel economy through 1975–76, much of it obtained by sacrificing acceleration. In addition, emissions controls were exacting a fuel penalty during these years. Between 1975 and 1979, all three assemblers reduced the weight of their full-sized models by nearly 15 percent. The resulting fuel economy was about 15 percent above 1975 levels for the generally smaller V-8s reported in *Consumer Reports*. In the case of intermediate cars, Ford and General Motors increased fuel economy by reducing weight sharply between 1975 and 1978 without sacrificing acceleration. Only Chrysler failed to downsize its intermediate offerings, but it managed a 12 percent improvement in fuel economy between 1971 and 1978 with little loss in acceleration and even an increase in weight. The subcompact cars showed only minor improvements in fuel economy between 1971 and 1976. (Chrysler had no domestic car in this category.) Ford improved the performance and fuel economy of its Pinto while adding weight to it in 1971–76, but GM clearly sacrificed acceleration to gain fuel economy with its Chevette.

The foregoing analysis suggests that the major vehicle producers in the United States began to improve fuel economy in a minor way by 1975, but that the major improvement occurred with the reductions in vehicle weight in 1977–78, three years after the Arab oil embargo. This is somewhat less than the product-development lead time generally required by Detroit in recent years. Therefore it appears that the major changes in product offerings before the development of front-wheel-drive cars were driven by the sharp rise in fuel prices in 1973–74 and not by the enactment of the CAFE program in 1975.

Table 6-2. Weight, Acceleration, and Fuel Economy for New Passenger Cars, Selected Model Years, 1971–79

Year and automobile	Curb weight (pounds)	Acceleration from 0–60 (seconds)	Mileage (miles per gallon)[a]
Full-size, low-price sedans (V-8)			
General Motors			
1971 (Chevrolet Impala)	4,209	12.0	14.0
1975 (Chevrolet BelAir)	4,440	14.0	15.0
1979 (Chevrolet Caprice Classic)	3,840	15.4	17.0
Ford			
1971 (Galaxie 500)	4,154	13.5	14.0
1975 (LTD)	4,657	13.5	14.0
1979 (LTD)	3,725	13.4	17.6
Chrysler			
1971 (Plymouth Fury III)	4,096	13.0	14.0
1975 (Plymouth Fury)	4,498	14.5	16.0
1979 (Dodge St. Regis)	3,830	15.2	18.2
Intermediate sedans (six cylinders)			
General Motors			
1971 (Chevelle)	3,329	15.5	17.0
1975 (Chevelle)	3,897	18.5	16.0
1978 (Chevrolet Malibu)	3,155	18.2	20.5
Ford			
1971 (Torino)	3,302	16.5	19.0
1975 (Mercury Monarch)	3,432	21.0	15.0
1978 (Fairmont)	2,965	15.8	20.2
Chrysler			
1971 (Dodge Dart)	3,048	17.0	18.0
1975 (Plymouth Valiant)	3,264	16.0	19.0
1978 (Plymouth Volare)	3,430	17.2	20.5
Subcompact two-door (four cylinders)			
General Motors			
1971 (Chevrolet Vega)	2,264	15.5	28.0
1976 (Chevette)	2,035	22.2	29.0
Ford			
1971 (Pinto)	2,046	19.0	25.0
1976 (Pinto Pony)	2,565	13.6	26.5

Source: *Consumer Reports*, various issues.
a. Average trip.

Compliance with CAFE, 1978–85

The three major U.S. producers have very different records of confor-
mance to CAFE standards. In 1978 all three were safely over the standard,
but falling real gasoline prices found Ford and GM very close to the

Table 6-3. The Big Three's Compliance with Corporate Average Fuel Economy Standards for Cars Produced in the United States, Model Years 1978–85[a]
Miles per gallon

Year	Standard	General Motors	Ford	Chrysler
1978	18.0	19.0	18.4	18.4
1979	19.0	19.1	19.1	20.4
1980	20.0	22.4	22.6	22.1
1981	22.0	23.7	23.9	26.7
1982	24.0	24.6	25.0	27.6
1983	26.0	24.0	24.3	27.0
1984	27.0	24.9	25.3	27.1
1985	27.5	25.1[b]	25.9[b]	n.a.

Sources: National Highway Traffic Safety Administration, *Annual Fuel Economy Program*, various years; General counsel, U.S. Department of Commerce, to NHTSA, "Comments Concerning . . . Petitions by GM and Ford," April 30, 1985; and "EPA Grants Automakers Fuel Economy Credits to Compensate for Test Changes," *EPA News*, June 26, 1985.
n.a. Not available.
a. Based on 55 percent city driving and 45 percent highway driving. Manufacturers' estimates for 1980–84 reflect revisions by the EPA in 1985.
b. Predicted by the companies.

standard in the 1979 model year. The Iranian revolution led to a sharp increase in fuel prices and a resultant shift toward smaller cars in 1979–80, thereby raising the mpg ratings for all three manufacturers to more than 22. Beginning in 1981, however, Chrysler, with its small cars, began to exceed the CAFE standard by a substantial margin (table 6-3) while GM and Ford remained rather close to it. In 1983, as gasoline prices fell, the demand for the larger cars produced by GM and Ford began to rise sharply, and these two companies found themselves falling below the standard for the first time. This was not a problem in 1983 because both had substantial carryover credits from 1980 that would have expired at the end of the model year. By 1985, however, both companies admitted that their current model offerings and prices would put them so far below the standard that they would exhaust their previous carryforward credits and begin paying fines for noncompliance for the first time.[10] Chrysler, on the other hand, remained safely above the CAFE standard and was arguing for continuing the program without easing the standards. In October 1985, however, the Department of Transportation announced a reduction in the standard to 26 mpg for the 1986 model year.[11]

10. *Automotive News*, January 7, 1985, p. 1.
11. 50 Fed. Reg. 40528 (1985).

A Test of the Effect of Standards upon Fuel Economy

To estimate the temporal pattern of changes in fuel economy and the impact of CAFE standards, a more precise analysis is required. Since fuel economy should be a function of engine size, the weight moved by this engine, and the design of the car, the following relationship suggests itself:

(1) $MPG = f(DISP, WT, FWD)$,

where *MPG* is the miles per gallon for a specified driving mode, *DISP* is the interior volume of the engine in cubic inches, *WT* is curb weight, and *FWD* is a dummy variable for the new front-wheel vehicle designs. Equation 1 is estimated in loglinear form since the effect of weight and engine size should be multiplicative. Dummy variables are added for three of the four manufacturers to capture firm-specific differences (AMC is omitted). In addition, time dummies are included to capture the effect of other influences, such as technological change and regulation. The equation estimated is

(2) $\log MPG_i = a_0 + a_1 \log WT_i + a_2 \log DISP_i$

$$+ a_3 FWD_i + a_4 D71_i + \ldots + a_{17} D84_i$$

$$+ a_{18} GM_i + a_{19} FORD_i + a_{20} CHRYS_i + u_i.$$

To estimate equation 2, observations are drawn from all domestic U.S. sedans tested by Consumers Union during 1970–84. In all, 186 models qualify, reflecting a satisfactory mix of all size classes. This data base is especially useful because it provides estimates of fuel economy from actual road tests. The fuel economy estimates are reported for city and highway driving and for a specified test trip. Unfortunately, the nature of the test trip used by Consumers Union and the maximum speeds during such a trip have changed over the 1970–84 period. For this reason, we estimate equation 2 for mileage reported for city driving, for highway driving, and for a harmonic average (55 percent city, 45 percent highway) of the two as well as for the test trip. These estimates appear in table 6-4.

In each case, the estimated effect of weight on fuel economy is very large and statistically significant. *DISP* is also inversely correlated with fuel economy, as expected. Chrysler and General Motors appear to obtain

Table 6-4. Determinants of Fuel Economy as Measured by Mileage under Selected Conditions [a]

Independent variable	Measured trip	City	Highway	Harmonic average [b]
Constant	8.71*	9.72*	8.05*	9.28*
	(17.09)	(19.18)	(14.73)	(20.09)
Log WT	−0.63*	−0.83*	−0.51*	−0.73*
	(6.42)	(8.52)	(4.92)	(8.31)
Log $DISP$	−0.14*	−0.12*	−0.15*	−0.13*
	(2.53)	(2.24)	(2.60)	(2.64)
FWD	0.08*	0.02	0.07*	0.03
	(3.39)	(0.72)	(2.87)	(1.55)
Chrysler	0.02	0.03	0.03	0.03
	(1.02)	(1.21)	(1.18)	(1.36)
Ford	0.01	−0.01	−0.01	−0.01
	(0.55)	(0.41)	(0.30)	(0.42)
General Motors	0.03	−0.01	0.04*	0.01
	(1.44)	(0.35)	(2.00)	(0.40)
Time dummies				
D71	−0.03	−0.01	−0.02	−0.02
	(1.10)	(0.47)	(0.65)	(0.62)
D72	−0.10*	−0.01	−0.05	−0.02
	(2.78)	(0.16)	(1.36)	(0.61)
D73	−0.12*	0.01	−0.06*	−0.01
	(4.06)	(0.42)	(2.06)	(0.38)
D74	0.01	−0.01	−0.01	−0.01
	(0.20)	(0.33)	(0.26)	(0.32)
D75	0.01	0.06	−0.05	0.02
	(0.28)	(1.74)	(1.52)	(0.81)
D76	0.10*	0.16*	0.04	0.12*
	(3.14)	(4.77)	(1.05)	(4.04)
D77	0.08*	0.15*	0.04	0.12*
	(2.19)	(4.19)	(1.02)	(3.60)
D78	0.11*	0.13*	0.09*	0.12*
	(3.04)	(3.69)	(2.41)	(3.72)
D79	0.14*	0.14*	0.12*	0.13*
	(4.02)	(4.13)	(3.26)	(4.35)
D80	0.17*	0.11*	0.16*	0.13*
	(3.71)	(2.55)	(3.30)	(3.12)
D81	0.10*	0.18*	0.13*	0.17*
	(2.39)	(4.52)	(2.94)	(4.52)
D82	0.15*	0.18*	0.19*	0.18*
	(3.63)	(4.53)	(4.50)	(5.08)
D83	0.20*	0.27*	0.28*	0.27*
	(5.52)	(7.38)	(7.24)	(8.23)
D84	0.12*	0.22*	0.19*	0.21*
	(2.87)	(5.44)	(4.36)	(5.74)
Summary statistic				
$\bar{R}^2$	0.919	0.926	0.902	0.934

* Statistically significant at the 95 percent confidence level.
a. Dependent variable is logarithm of *MPG*. Numbers in parentheses are *t*-statistics.
b. Based on 55 percent city driving and 45 percent highway driving.

better fuel economy than Ford or AMC, other things being equal. Finally, the front-wheel-drive sedans appear to get between 2 and 8 percent better fuel economy than their rear-wheel-drive counterparts. This may be due to a number of design changes, including the shape of the outer body, facilitated by a complete redesign of the vehicle.

For our purposes, we are particularly interested in the coefficients of the time dummies, for these estimates give us an estimate of the technological improvement in vehicle design, not just the reduction in weight and horsepower. These suggest no fuel economy improvements until 1975 or 1976, but steady improvement thereafter. There is some sign of a flattening of this improvement in 1980–81, but a resumed increase in fuel economy in 1983. Before drawing any conclusions from these coefficients, however, we must attempt to correct for the penalties incurred because of emissions regulation in order to obtain estimates of temporal improvement in fuel economy generated by design changes. For this purpose, we use White's estimates of the emissions control penalties in each year. These are added to the harmonic averages of city and highway mileage of the time dummies from table 6-4 (see table 6-5). For instance, the fuel economy penalty of 8 percent in 1973 and 1974 is added to the coefficients of $D73$ and $D74$, each of which is -0.01, to obtain an estimated "total" increase of 7 percent over 1970 fuel economy for both years. By 1977 it appears that cars were 15 percent more fuel efficient, holding weight, engine size, and emissions control constant. By 1981 this had risen to 24 percent above 1970 levels, and by 1983 the improvement was 34 percent.

The estimated progress in fuel economy reflected in table 6-5 has one sharp discontinuity in 1975, the year in which the major assemblers shifted to the catalyst technology for controlling emissions. One would expect the coefficient of $D75$ in table 6-4 to be substantially larger than the coefficient of $D74$, but this obviously is not the case. It is possible that some manufacturers had difficulty in adjusting to the new technology. General Motors developed it and might be expected to have had better experience with it. To test for significant differences between GM and the other companies, we reestimate equation 2 for each of the three major firms in the industry. As the results in table 6-6 clearly indicate, GM's progress in fuel economy was much steadier than that of its rivals. In the watershed year of 1975, it realized a 6 percent improvement—very close to White's estimate of the reduction in the emissions control penalty—while the other firms showed no significant improvement. Moreover, GM evidenced an improvement of approximately 45 percent from 1970 through 1983 while Ford showed an improvement of 37 percent and Chrysler may have

Table 6-5. Fuel Economy Improvement over 1970 Model Cars, Model Years 1971–84
Percent

Year	Estimated improvement[a]	Estimated emissions control penalty[b]	Total improvement
1971	−2	0	−2
1972	−2	0	−2
1973	−1	8	7
1974	−1	8	7
1975	2	1	3
1976	12	1	13
1977	12	3	15
1978	12	3	15
1979	13	3	16
1980	13	6	19
1981	17	7	24
1982	18	7	25
1983	27	7	34
1984	21	7	28

a. From table 6-4.
b. Estimates by Lawrence J. White, *The Regulation of Air Pollutant Emissions from Motor Vehicles* (Washington, D.C.: American Enterprise Institute, 1982), p. 21.

improved its fuel economy by perhaps 11 percent, after adjusting for the fuel penalty from emissions control. Surprisingly, front-wheel drive seems to do little for fuel economy for any of the firms. Given the difficulties GM has had with reliability and performance of its early front-wheel-drive cars, it may be wondering if the transformation of its fleet has been worthwhile.

The surprising result from this analysis is that the companies responded to the demand for fuel efficiency at quite different rates. General Motors showed substantial improvement in efficiency by 1974. This is consistent with reported observations that GM had begun to develop more fuel-efficient cars two years before the 1973 oil shock. Ford, on the other hand, evidenced substantial progress in its 1976 and 1983 models—two years after the first oil shock and four years after the second. Finally, Chrysler seemed to make little progress until about 1979, when the second oil shock was occurring. Apparently, Chrysler simply relied upon the strategy of eliminating its large cars, making itself vulnerable to the small car competition from Japan that began in earnest in the late 1970s.

Despite its difficulties with the CAFE standards since 1982, it is clear that GM has made the greatest progress in improving fuel efficiency since 1970, given the weight of its cars. Its progress has been more than double

Table 6-6. Determinants of Fuel Economy for General Motors, Ford, and Chrysler Cars, Model Years 1970–84[a]

Independent variable	General Motors (N=72)	Ford (N=47)	Chrysler (N=42)
Constant	10.07*	9.14*	9.16*
	(12.38)	(9.39)	(6.97)
Log WT	−0.91*	−0.74*	−0.62*
	(5.64)	(3.99)	(2.51)
Log DISP	−0.02	0.09	−0.26
	(0.23)	(0.92)	(1.85)
FWD	0.02	0.04	0.07
	(0.60)	(0.70)	(1.11)
Time dummies			
D71	0.02	0.01	−0.12
	(0.47)	(0.20)	(1.88)
D72	0.00	−0.06	0.02
	(0.08)	(0.82)	(0.28)
D73	0.01	−0.08	−0.01
	(0.30)	(1.29)	(0.23)
D74	0.08	−0.04	−0.03
	(1.51)	(0.61)	(0.38)
D75	0.14*	−0.08	−0.04
	(2.74)	(1.20)	(0.58)
D76	0.20*	0.12	0.06
	(3.89)	(1.90)	(0.93)
D77	0.18*	0.12	0.01
	(3.66)	(1.56)	(0.15)
D78	0.20*	0.07	0.03
	(3.91)	(0.90)	(0.55)
D79	0.20*	0.09	0.09
	(4.17)	(1.35)	(1.40)
D80	0.22*	0.08	−0.07
	(3.80)	(0.77)	(0.79)
D81	0.29*	0.15	0.00
	(5.26)	(1.83)	(0.02)
D82	0.30*	0.14*	0.07
	(4.69)	(2.00)	(0.97)
D83	0.38*	0.30*	0.04
	(7.61)	(4.36)	(0.59)
D84	0.27*	0.25*	0.00
	(4.89)	(3.40)	(0.01)
Summary statistic			
$\bar{R}^2$	0.956	0.925	0.950

* Statistically significant at the 95 percent confidence level.

a. Dependent variable is logarithm of harmonic average of city and highway driving. Numbers in parentheses are *t*-statistics.

Chrysler's even though Chrysler has had greater success in meeting the CAFE standards. The explanation for this apparent anomaly, of course, is that Chrysler has virtually abandoned large cars while GM continues to produce very successful big cars.

A further statistical analysis shows that the average annual rate of progress for GM in increasing fuel economy for vehicles of a given weight and engine displacement was approximately 3 percent through 1983. Ford's trend rate of improvement was 2 percent and Chrysler's a bare 1 percent. In 1970–73, before the oil crisis, Chrysler's automobiles were approximately 6 percent more fuel efficient than those of Ford and 8 percent more fuel efficient than those of GM, holding weight and displacement constant. Thus it would appear that by 1983 GM cars were substantially more fuel efficient than Chrysler cars and marginally more fuel efficient than Ford cars for a given weight and displacement.

A Test of Fuel Economy without Standards

All three major domestic assemblers improved the fuel economy of their vehicles in 1970–83, with most of the improvement coming after 1975. Nevertheless, Ford and GM had made substantial progress by 1976—before the prospective requirements of the Energy Policy Conservation Act of 1975 could have been anticipated. This fact alone suggests that the market price of gasoline and the growing competition from imports was impelling the assemblers along a path of improving fuel economy.

Had there been no CAFE standards, the vehicle producers could have been expected to increase fuel economy as long as the gain in operating costs of a car was at least as great as the increase in the costs of producing and distributing the car. Improving aerodynamic design and drive trains and even substituting low-weight materials for iron and steel require increases in costs. The cost-minimizing choice of fuel efficiency (E) and vehicle price (P) is easily stated as[12]

$$(3) \qquad\qquad c = \frac{p_g M/E}{rP},$$

12. This follows from the assumption of rational consumer choice in fuel price-efficiency trade-offs. If vehicle manufacturers can obtain higher fuel efficiency through

where c is the elasticity of the cost of producing a vehicle with respect to fuel efficiency, p_g is the price of gasoline, M is annual vehicle miles traveled by the consumer, and r is the cost of capital to the consumer for holding a durable good such as an automobile.

Equation 3 simply states that vehicle manufacturers should offer fuel economy on each model line up to the point where the elasticity of the cost of production with respect to fuel economy is equal to the ratio of annual gasoline costs to the annual capital costs of holding the car. Unfortunately, we have no data on production costs from which to estimate c directly, but we can proceed along a somewhat less elegant route.

First, it is possible to assemble data on the cost of operating and holding a new automobile. According to estimates published by the Department of Transportation, the ratio of the present value of gasoline costs to that of capital costs for a car held for four years was 0.31 for 1972 model automobiles and 0.42 for 1981 model cars.[13] The 1981 figure reflects the sharp rise in gasoline prices in 1979–81 after the fall of the Shah of Iran. Further improvements in fuel economy and lower gasoline prices in 1982–84 would surely lower this ratio. A reasonable approach would be to average the 1972 and 1981 estimates and suggest that the implicit estimate of c, the elasticity of costs with respect to fuel economy, is about 0.365.

Further corroboration of this estimate may be found in a 1980 Congressional Budget Office study that analyzed potential fuel efficiency improvements over 1985–95.[14] This study estimated that potential improvements

---

additional engineering expense and if these costs are passed on to buyers, the manufacturers should increase fuel economy until the additional cost of holding a car for a year is just equal to the annual savings in gasoline costs: $\partial[P_g M/E]/\partial E$. This simplifies into equation 3.

13. Authors' calculations based on Department of Transportation, Federal Highway Administration, *Cost of Operating an Automobile* (DOT, 1972), and *The Cost of Owning and Operating Automobiles and Vans* (DOT, 1982).

14. Congressional Budget Office, *Fuel Economy Standards for New Passenger Cars after 1985* (Government Printing Office, 1980), pp. 30–31, 38. Earlier estimates of the costs of achieving 1978–85 standards vary considerably. *The Final Impact Assessment of the Automotive Fuel Economy Standards for Model Year 1981–84 Passenger Cars*, prepared by the National Highway Traffic Safety Administration in 1977, estimated the total unit cost of raising mpg from 20 to 27 at $195 per car. The average cost per car in 1977 was $4,788, based upon a Bureau of Economic Analysis estimate of an average 1977 transaction price of $5,985 and a 25 percent markup. Therefore the elasticity of fuel economy with respect to cost would be 0.116 from these data. This estimate is very low because most of the prospective improvements derive from downsizing and diesel engines.

A more recent study by Energy and Environmental Analysis, *The Technology/Cost Segment Model*, estimates a 40 percent improvement in fuel economy from eleven techno-

in fuel economy of 26.9 percent would cost $562 per new vehicle (in 1980 dollars). Given an average new car price of $7,578 in 1980, this translates into a 7.4 percent increase in car prices to obtain a 26.9 percent savings in fuel. The implicit value of c from this exercise would be 0.28. A more pessimistic CBO scenario sees a 17.6 percent fuel economy improvement for $624 in increased new car prices, or an implicit value of c equal to 0.47. The midpoint of these estimates is very close to our estimate of 0.365.

If the estimated elasticity of the price of a new automobile with respect to fuel economy is about 0.36, the effect of increased gasoline prices upon the engineering of fuel efficiency may be deduced quite simply. We know that in equilibrium manufacturers will satisfy equation 3. The differential of this expression (assuming constant M) is

$$(4) \qquad dc = \frac{-p_g M}{rPE^2} \, dE + \frac{M}{rPE} \, dp_g - \frac{p_g M}{rP^2 E} \, dP - \frac{p_g M}{r^2 PE} \, dr.$$

If the elasticity is constant in the relevant range of costs, $dc = 0$ for all changes in fuel prices or other variables. Equation 4 may therefore be rewritten and simplified into

$$(5) \qquad dp_g/p_g = dE/E + dP/P + dr/r.$$

This simply says that the sum of the proportional changes in vehicle price, fuel efficiency, and the user cost of capital must equal the proportional change in gasoline prices. But if $c = 0.365$, then $dP/P = 0.365(dE/E)$. Thus, if dr/r is zero,

$$(6) \qquad dp_g/p_g = 1.365 \, (dE/E).$$

Since the real price of gasoline rose by 40 percent from 1970 through mid-1983, vehicle manufacturers might have been expected to increase

---

logical changes that result in an increase in the average car price of $1,031. This translates into an estimate of the elasticity of costs with respect to fuel economy of 0.373.

Finally, GM has estimated that during the 1974–81 period it has invested $1 billion for each 0.5 mpg improvement. At a 10 percent cost of capital and a five-year life of this capital, this translates into an elasticity of 0.412 for a 1977 midpoint. William G. Agnew, *Automotive Fuel Economy Improvement*, General Motors Research Laboratories, GM-3493 (Warren, Mich.: GM, 1980).

fuel economy (for given other attributes) by about 29 percent. Since the annual capital charge has also risen slightly, the expected increase is even smaller. The sum of interest plus depreciation has risen by about 1 percentage point, from 37 percent to 38 percent of the initial car price. Thus dr/r is approximately 0.03. This suggests that manufacturers should have increased fuel efficiency by about 26 percent from 1970 through 1983.

Our estimates in tables 6-5 and 6-6 are surprisingly close to this prediction. General Motors and Ford appear to have exceeded the 26 percent prediction, but Chrysler has fallen somewhat short of it. Overall, it appears that the improvement in fuel economy for the industry was very close to what would have been expected without the CAFE standards.

Sources of Improvement in Fuel Economy

At this point, we might attempt to summarize the sources of fuel economy improvements realized since the 1973 Arab oil embargo. Manufacturers have reduced engine size and acceleration and downsized their vehicles. In addition, consumers have gravitated toward the smaller size classes. Finally, technology and aerodynamic design have changed, increasing fuel economy for any given weight-displacement combination. How much has each of these changes contributed to improved fuel efficiency?

The improvement has been considerable, if one is to believe EPA mileage estimates. Both city and average (55 percent city/45 percent highway) mileage have nearly doubled from their 1973 lows (table 6-1). These EPA estimates are known to overstate actual fuel economy obtained from road tests such as those conducted by Consumers Union.

The sources of mileage improvement between the 1974 and 1984 model years can be summarized as follows. The average new passenger-car weight fell by approximately 22 percent in this period, from 3,968 pounds to 3,103 pounds. This was due to downsizing and to a shift away from larger cars. The average displacement of engines in U.S. automobiles declined by 38 percent, from 289 cubic inches to 179 cubic inches. Finally, the share of front-wheel-drive passenger cars rose from virtually zero in 1974 to 52 percent in 1984.[15]

The results in table 6-4 suggest that the elasticity of the average city-

---

15. R. M. Heavenrich and others, "Passenger Car Fuel Economy . . . Trends thru 1984," Environmental Protection Agency Paper 840499 (EPA, 1984).

highway mileage with respect to weight is approximately −0.8, the elasticity with respect to displacement is about −0.13, and the effect of front-wheel drive is to raise mileage by about 5 percent.[16] Using the 1984 weights (and excluding luxury vehicles), this suggests an 18 percent improvement due to weight reductions, a 5 percent increase in fuel efficiency due to smaller engines, and a 3-percent improvement due to the shift to front-wheel-drive cars. Our estimate of other design technology influences between 1974 and 1984 (from table 6-5) is a 21 percent improvement in average mileage. Multiplying these four components together, we get a total improvement of 54 percent, of which design changes and reductions in engine size and weight are each approximately equally responsible. This is substantially less than the 87 percent improvement in the EPA's estimates,[17] but the divergence of EPA estimates, obtained from test cars operated on a dynamometer, and actual road performance is widely recognized.

Pricing to Induce Small Car Purchase

It is possible that the CAFE standards have had another impact—on the relative prices of large and small cars.[18] While the standards may not have affected the pace of fuel efficiency improvement for cars in each size class, they may have forced the vehicle producers to raise large car prices relative to the price of smaller, more fuel-efficient ones in order to meet year-to-year CAFE requirements.

To analyze the 1978–84 pricing decisions by the domestic producers, we estimate a hedonic list-price equation for comparably equipped cars over the 1970–77 period to predict 1978–84 prices. The hedonic equation estimated includes variables for vehicle weight (*WEIGHT*), acceleration from 0 to 60 mph (*ACCEL*), the real cost per mile of gasoline consumption for a 55 percent-45 percent mix of city and highway driving (*GASCOST*), indexes of the quality of ride (*RIDE*) and handling (*HAND*), a set of dummy variables for size class (*COMPACT*, *INTERMEDIATE*, *FULLSIZE*, and *LUXURY*), and dummy variables for model years. The sample is all cars tested by Consumers Union (112 between 1970 and

16. The results in tables 6-4 and 6-6 diverge on displacement and front-wheel drive. This calculation is for illustrative purposes, but its uncertain nature should be noted.

17. Heavenrich and others, "Passenger Car Fuel Economy," p. 4.

18. See John E. Kwoka, Jr., "Behavior of an Auto Firm under the Fuel Economy Constraint," Bureau of Economics Working Paper 28 (Federal Trade Commission, 1980).

Table 6-7. Estimates of Equation Used to Predict 1978–84 Model Year Prices[a]

Independent variable	Estimate	Independent variable	Estimate
Constant	7.028	FULLSIZE	0.149
	(64.47)		(2.58)
WEIGHT	0.00016	LUXURY	1.092
	(3.90)		(11.72)
ACCEL	0.0022	D71	−0.041
	(0.51)		(1.30)
GASCOST	−0.961	D72	−0.028
	(0.61)		(0.78)
RIDE	0.064	D73	−0.066
	(2.78)		(2.19)
HAND	0.008	D74	−0.155
	(0.52)		(3.98)
COMPACT	0.053	D75	−0.106
	(1.75)		(2.56)
INTERMEDIATE	0.109	D76	−0.121
	(2.50)		(3.34)
		D77	−0.067
Summary statistic			(1.78)
$\bar{R}^2$	0.899		

a. Dependent variable is logarithm of the list price deflated by the consumer price index. Numbers in parentheses are *t*-statistics.

1977) for which complete data are available. *ACCEL, GASCOST, RIDE,* and *HAND* are based upon Consumers Union test results.

The results of the hedonic estimation are reproduced in table 6-7 for small (compact and subcompact) and large (intermediate and full-size) cars. When the estimated equation is used to project 1978–84 model prices, deflated for changes in the consumer price index, it generally underpredicts actual prices. In part, this is because regulatory costs are not netted out of our new car price series, but it also reflects the sharp increase in new car prices after 1980, probably because of the Japanese import restraints.

It is difficult to see any effect upon relative prices of the CAFE standards through 1981. The table below shows the average prediction error as a share of the forecast values for the 1978–84 model years. In 1979 GM and Ford were very close to their CAFE minimum, but there does not seem to be any noticeable difference between small- and large-car prediction errors in that year. For the next two years, the soaring price of gasoline alleviated the CAFE pressure while greatly exacerbating the industry's problems with Japanese imports. From 1982 through 1984, the prediction errors rise substantially, partly in response to increased emissions control costs, but also because of the Japanese import quotas. By 1984, it is clear that the large car residual is substantially larger than the prediction error for smaller cars. This is quite consistent with the fact that Ford and GM fell substantially short of the CAFE requirement in 1982–84 as gasoline prices fell. By 1984, it appears that this deficiency led to substantial upward pressure on large car prices.

	1978	1979	1980	1981	1982	1983	1984
Small cars	−0.020	−0.055	−0.006	0.110	0.125	0.154	0.117
Large cars	−0.003	−0.029	−0.112	0.004	0.197	0.117	0.235

The Gas Guzzler Tax

The gas guzzler tax, imposed in 1980, is designed to penalize manufacturers for producing individual model lines that fall below a given mileage (city/highway) in each model year. As the table below shows, this standard rises to 22.5 mpg for the 1986 model year, and the tax can become quite severe.[19] For example, manufacturers will have to pay $1,050 per car for any automobile achieving only 19 mpg, and a staggering $3,850 for a 12 mpg car. By fiscal 1983 these manufacturers' excise taxes had generated only $4 million a year in revenues,[20] but they could become much larger in a world of falling gasoline prices.

Mileage (miles per gallon)	Tax (dollars)
22.5 or more	0
21.5–22.5	500
20.5–21.5	650
19.5–20.5	850
18.5–19.5	1,050
17.5–18.5	1,300
16.5–17.5	1,500
15.5–16.5	1,850
14.5–15.5	2,250
13.5–14.5	2,700
12.5–13.5	3,200
Less than 12.5	3,850

19. 26 U.S.C. 4064.
20. Internal Revenue Service, *News Release*, IR-84-38, March 6, 1984.

Conclusions

This chapter has reviewed in some detail the progress that the three major U.S. automobile producers have made in improving fuel economy since 1970. The results show that General Motors started earliest and achieved the greatest improvement in fuel efficiency for a given weight and engine size, followed by Ford and Chrysler, in that order. Chrysler began with the most fuel efficient cars for a given weight and displacement, but Ford and GM succeeded in achieving the greatest improvement through design changes and technological advances in drive trains. Nevertheless, Chrysler emerged in 1985 as the only company without a CAFE problem because it had virtually abandoned the larger-car market. The Department of Transportation's 1985 decision to reduce the CAFE standard for 1986 cars to 26.0 mpg may alleviate much of the pressure on GM and Ford.

The principal conclusion of this chapter is that the automobile producers' increase in fuel economy is about what one should have expected given the rise in gasoline prices since 1973. The CAFE standards appear to have provided little but nuisance value until recently. As gasoline prices have fallen in real terms, the standards have become a binding constraint upon producers attempting to satisfy the demand for larger cars. They have also made it very difficult for Ford and GM to produce or purchase their smaller cars in Japan or Korea, where production costs are much lower at the 1984–85 value of the dollar. Thus CAFE has become an issue of trade protection as much as one of energy conservation.[21]

Should the CAFE program be continued? At present, there seems to be little reason for suggesting that automobile drivers should not be allowed to respond to market prices of energy in the same fashion as commercial, industrial, or residential users of fossil fuels. If there is a societal case for increasing conservation efforts—and it appears rather weak in 1985—the appropriate mechanism would appear to be a federal tax on all liquid and gaseous hydrocarbons, not a set of technological standards applied to new cars.[22] The CAFE standards only encourage higher large car prices and the postponement of replacement decisions. This postponement is counterproductive with respect to the policy of reducing emissions, vehicle deaths,

21. This point is made by David R. Henderson in "The Economics of Fuel Economy Standards," *Regulation*, vol. 9 (January–February 1985), p. 46.
22. See Blair and others, "The Impact of Improved Mileage on Gasoline Consumption," for an estimate of the effectiveness of regulatory and gasoline-price options for reducing gasoline consumption.

and fuel consumption. Since the Japanese import restraints were lifted in March 1985, the CAFE standards have become an even greater problem for Ford and GM because the Japanese imports will take small car sales away from these companies, leaving them with an even greater CAFE deficiency. In 1985 there were suggestions that a decision to eliminate Japanese export quotas could be combined with the elimination of CAFE standards.

CHAPTER SEVEN

The Conflicting Goals of Regulation

THE individual regulatory programs affecting the automobile industry have a mixed track record. Safety regulation appears to have worked tolerably well, emissions regulation has served to reduce air pollution (at a very high marginal cost since 1981), and fuel economy regulation appears to have been largely an irrelevancy until the recent decrease in gasoline prices. But how well have these regulatory programs been coordinated to achieve the maximum impact for the lowest cost? The simple answer is "not at all," since each program is administered separately. Moreover, different pieces of legislation have set different regulatory goals and different specific standards with little regard to conflicts with other goals. Unfortunately, the full story is even more complicated, for the very structure of these programs has been counterproductive to the rapid achievement of clean air, safe highways, and reduced gasoline consumption. By reducing the replacement rate for automobiles, Congress and the regulators have served to exacerbate the very problems they thought they were curing.

Static Conflicts

An automobile is a complex product, designed to perform a number of functions. When an additional regulatory requirement is imposed to enhance safety, emissions control, or fuel efficiency, it will have ramifications for a number of different aspects of vehicle design. For example, requiring a bumper that can withstand a five-mile-per-hour collision adds weight that immediately diminishes fuel economy. It also indirectly affects design because the chassis must be strengthened and the balance and handling of the vehicle corrected. Thus any single regulation will eventu-

141

ally lead to myriad changes in design, with an increase in price and some compromises in performance.

The adjustments to a single regulation are made somewhat differently by each manufacturer; each sees the necessity for implementing the regulation at a low cost with little performance penalty. However, the regulatory programs for safety, emissions, and fuel economy are administered by three agencies with little concern for the other legislated goals. Safety equipment, such as strengthening the doors, adds to weight and thus lowers fuel efficiency. Yet nothing in its legislation instructs the National Highway Traffic Safety Administration to worry about the effect on fuel consumption. Similarly, emissions control reduces fuel efficiency, but emissions standards were set by Congress and are administered by the Environmental Protection Agency, which is not given the authority to modify them. Furthermore, Congress set the standards in 1970, long before the energy crisis. There are other, less important conflicts among auto regulations.

Some analyses have shown these contradictions to be important.[1] In some cases the magnitude of these "secondary" effects is as large as or larger than the primary costs of the regulations. For current purposes, we focus on the effects that vehicle weight and emissions control have on fuel economy.

The estimates of the fuel economy penalty incurred by emissions control are somewhat controversial. White based his measure of the fuel penalty on comparisons across political jurisdictions with different standards. He found that Canadian versions of U.S. automobiles obtain 6 percent better fuel economy. However, these cars are optimized for the larger U.S. market and are not likely to reflect fully the fuel economy available under less onerous standards. Hence White argued that the 1981 emissions standards are exacting about a 7 percent fuel penalty.[2] Even though the differences between U.S. and Canadian cars have now virtually disappeared,[3] our analysis in chapter 3 supports White's estimate of a 7 percent fuel penalty.

1. See Lester B. Lave, "Conflicting Objectives in Regulating the Automobile," *Science,* vol. 212 (May 22, 1981), pp. 893–99.

2. Lawrence J. White, *The Regulation of Air Pollutant Emissions from Motor Vehicles* (Washington, D.C.: American Enterprise Institute, 1982), pp. 63–64.

3. Jeffrey Dowell and others, "U.S. and Canadian Comparison of Passenger Car Fuel Economy and Technological Trends, 1974 to 1984" (Ottawa: Energy, Mines and Resources Canada, Coal and Alternative Energy Branch, December 1984).

The conflict between safety and fuel efficiency in the choice of vehicle weight is both obvious and controversial. Clearly, light vehicles—such as bicycles and motorcycles—fare poorly in collisions with trucks, buses, or limousines. But is it clear that, all else being equal, any reduction in vehicle weight makes cars inherently less safe? As we have shown in the time-series estimates of the highway death rate, the average weight of vehicles on the road is inversely related to highway deaths (chapter 4). This is a plausible result for vehicle occupants, but it also appears to hold for pedestrians and bicyclists. Why lighter cars should be a threat to pedestrians and cyclists is not clear unless one believes that smaller cars are operated in a more risky fashion, particularly for innocent bystanders.

The relationship between weight and fuel efficiency is uncontroversial. Our results suggest that the elasticity of gasoline consumption with respect to weight is approximately 0.8. Safety standards from 1968 to 1982 are estimated to have added 136 pounds to a 1980–82 model year vehicle, or 4.4 percent of the average weight of a 1982 car, thus increasing fuel consumption by 3.5 percent.[4]

In summary, emissions controls and safety regulation are in conflict with attempts to improve fuel economy, but these policies together penalize current fuel efficiency by no more than 10.5 percent. A slight relaxation in emissions standards and weakening or abolishing the bumper standard could reduce this fuel economy penalty by 50 percent. The penalty for the 1977–79 emissions standards was only 3 percent, rather than the 7 percent for the standards since 1981. Had the emissions standards been held at the 1979 levels, total vehicle emissions of carbon monoxide and hydrocarbons would have been lower for several years into the 1980s and the fuel efficiency of new cars would have been 4 percent higher. Before the bumper standard was relaxed in 1982, at least 40 percent of the fuel efficiency loss from safety regulation came from the bumper standard. If this standard had not been imposed, there would have been no measurable loss of safety, but there would have been about a 2 percent improvement in the fuel efficiency of new cars. Thus relaxation of these two standards alone could have made the new cars of the early 1980s approximately 6 percent more fuel efficient.

4. Authors' calculations based on NHTSA contractor studies on federal motor vehicle safety standards; and NHTSA, *The Cost of Automobile Safety Regulations* (DOT, 1982). See chap. 3.

Dynamic Conflicts

A second, but often neglected, source of conflict and inefficiency in automobile regulation has been overall energy policy. The decision to control the price of crude oil and to use entitlements policy to keep refined products prices low through 1979 was obviously in conflict with the goal of reducing gasoline consumption. Kalt has estimated that the entitlements policy may have kept gasoline prices as much as 8 percent below world market-clearing levels.[5] Surely this encouraged inefficient use of fuel in transportation, including personal automobiles.

Effects upon Vehicle Purchases

In the 1960s Congress decreed that U.S. automobiles were unsafe and generated too much pollution. But there were 75 million automobiles on the road with these attributes. Unless Congress was willing to consider mandating a massive retrofitting of the stock of vehicles on the road, it could only achieve improved air quality and highway safety by encouraging rapid substitution of new, safer, and cleaner vehicles for existing automobiles.

Similarly, when in 1975 Congress announced the seemingly ambitious goal of doubling fleet-average fuel efficiency for automobiles, it should have been concerned with replacing the older, less efficient cars on the road. Yet it acted to keep gasoline prices from rising, thereby discouraging replacement of the older "gas guzzlers." It also refused to reconsider those emissions and safety policies that had raised vehicle prices and reduced the performance of new cars. Had it done so, it might have come to the conclusion that less costly safety and emissions regulation and more costly gasoline would have accelerated the pace of adjustment toward improved air quality, safety, and fuel efficiency by increasing the rate of replacement of the older cars.[6]

Feedback on Other Policies

The effect of government regulation of the automobile industry is even

5. Joseph P. Kalt, *The Economics and Politics of Oil Price Regulation: Federal Policy in the Post-Embargo Era* (MIT Press, 1981), p. 158.

6. See Howard K. Gruenspecht, "Differential Regulation: The Case of Auto Emission Standards," *American Economic Review,* vol. 72 (May 1982, *Papers and Proceedings, 1981*), pp. 328–31; and chap. 5 for a discussion of the effect of reduced new car purchases on emissions.

more contorted and counterproductive than the above discussion suggests. The 1970s witnessed the growth of a dynamic new automobile industry in Japan. The Japanese producers began to introduce one new attractive model after another, offering improved performance and more reliable quality at an attractive price. These automobiles were generally smaller than U.S. automobiles, but they met U.S. emissions standards while delivering excellent fuel efficiency. Although the U.S. safety standards imposed additional costs upon Japanese manufacturers, there is little evidence that this created a competitive handicap for imported Japanese cars.

The combination of unstable macroeconomic policies and rising (and uncertain) regulatory costs placed Detroit automobile manufacturers under great strain. They recovered well enough from the 1974–75 recession, but the twin recessions of 1980 and 1981–82 sharply reduced demand. Had regulatory costs been lower, the sales of new automobiles would have been greater, thus obviating at least some of the problems of the industry. Employment and output would have been higher, and the Carter and Reagan administrations might have felt less inclined to worry about Japanese imports.

The import restrictions imposed on the Japanese from 1981 to 1985 have had the predictable effect of raising U.S. vehicle prices, thereby reducing new car purchases. Moreover, the stimulus to improve production efficiency and search for new fuel-efficient technologies has been reduced. U.S. producers have been far less imaginative in offering new power plant designs and attractive performance-efficiency options than the Japanese.

The trade protection of 1981–85 removed an important contemporary source of product quality rivalry for U.S. automobile makers. Had regulation been more farsighted, it might have been possible for the U.S. industry to fight through the 1980–83 period with higher sales and profits and with a less compelling case for trade protection. It is ironic that the regulatory-consumer movement begun in part by Ralph Nader has culminated in monopolistic trade protection for the intended targets.

Relaxing Emissions Standards and Repealing the Bumper Standard

Had Congress stopped with the 1979 automobile emissions standards and instructed NHTSA not to pursue the exterior crash protection (bumper) standard, direct regulatory costs might have been reduced by as much as $621 per new car delivered in 1981 (table 7-1). Moreover, annual

Table 7-1. Savings Achievable through Deletion of Bumper Standard and Post-1979 Emissions Standards, Model Years 1973-81
Current dollars per car unless otherwise indicated

Year	Cost of safety equipment (with learning)	Cost of emissions equipment	Total	Total without bumper standard and 1980-81 emissions standards	Saving	Price of new cars	Saving as a percent of new car price
1973	245	44	289	219	70	4,180	1.7
1974	381	49	430	298	132	4,523	2.9
1975	361	119	480	343	137	5,083	2.7
1976	377	126	503	361	142	5,504	2.6
1977	390	123	513	368	145	5,985	2.4
1978	400	133	533	385	148	6,481	2.3
1979	431	148	579	423	156	6,706	2.3
1980	481	222	703	461	242	7,630	3.2
1981	512	600	1,112	491	621	8,940	6.9

Source: Table 3-5. Price of new cars is from Motor Vehicle Manufacturers Association, *MVMA Facts and Figures '84*, p. 42.

fuel costs for new cars might have been 1.6 to 5.8 percent lower in 1973–81 (table 7-2). Since the bumper standard has had no apparent effects upon motor vehicle fatalities, consumers could have been offered the choice of energy-absorbing bumpers if they wanted them, with no implications for highway safety. Given the range of estimates from cost-benefit analyses of the bumper standard, it is likely that the failure to install crash-resistant bumpers would not increase net operating costs very much (if at all) for the average automobile owner.

Congress could have kept emissions standards at their 1979 levels without sacrificing air quality for some time, if at all. As we have shown, the benefits of reducing automobile emissions beyond the 1979 levels will be small even after the tighter standards have permeated the entire fleet, and the possibility of catastrophic failure in post-1980 emissions systems may actually lead to a deterioration in air quality.

The savings available from relaxation of just these two standards would have been substantial, as tables 7-1 and 7-2 demonstrate. The bumper standard was phased in between the 1973 and 1977 model years. Assuming 5 percent learning, the standard added $156 to the cost of the average new car by 1979. By 1981 the post-1979 emissions standards and the bumper standard may have added as much as $621 to the cost of a new car, or 6.9 percent of new car prices.

Assuming that capital costs are 2.5 times as important as gasoline costs

Table 7-2. Effects of Deletion of Bumper Standard and Post-1979 Emissions Standards on New Car Sales, Model Years 1973-81

Year	Percentage reductions			New car sales (millions)	Increase in new car sales under three elasticity demands (thousands)		
	Capital costs	Gasoline costs	User costs[a]		−1.0	−1.5	−2.0
1973	1.7	1.7	1.7	11.4	194	291	388
1974	2.9	2.5	2.8	8.7	244	365	488
1975	2.7	2.2	2.6	8.3	216	324	432
1976	2.6	2.0	2.4	9.8	235	353	470
1977	2.4	1.8	2.2	10.8	238	357	476
1978	2.3	1.8	2.2	10.9	240	360	480
1979	2.3	1.6	2.1	10.4	218	327	436
1980	3.2	4.8	3.7	8.8	326	488	652
1981	6.9	5.8	6.6	8.4	554	831	1,109

Source: Authors' calculations. Numbers are rounded.
a. Weights: 0.714 for capital costs; 0.286 for gasoline costs.

in the operation of a new car, the weighted average of cost savings that could have been available from avoiding the bumper standard and the post-1979 emissions standards rose from 1.7 percent in 1973 to 6.6 percent in 1981. Since lower automobile prices reduce other costs and less onerous emissions standards are likely to generate lower maintenance costs, we assume that this weighted average represents the reduction in all automobile user costs.[7]

There are no fully satisfactory studies of the demand for automobiles that include appropriately measured user costs as explanatory variables. However, most studies of automobile demand suggest that the price elasticity of (flow) demand is between −1.0 and −2.0.[8] Given actual new car sales, we use this range of elasticities and our estimates of the savings in user costs to generate predicted increases in new car sales from 1973–81 had the two standards not been in effect. These estimates, reproduced in table 7-2, show that suppressed new car sales were substantial. Assuming a demand elasticity of −1.5 with respect to user costs, the bumper standard appears to have reduced new car sales by an average of about 340,000 per year in the 1970s, and the addition of the tighter emissions standards since 1979 has resulted in an annual average reduction of about

7. We are ignoring the effects of the bumpers upon repair costs. This undoubtedly biases our estimate upward somewhat, but note that the larger share of the 1980–81 savings derives from emissions standards. We are indebted to Philip J. Cook for this suggestion.

8. Alan C. Hess, "A Comparison of Automobile Demand Equations," *Econometrica*, vol. 45 (April 1977), pp. 683–701.

Table 7-3. Effects of Deletion of Bumper Standard and Post-1979 Emissions Standards on Selected Indicators, 1981[a]
Percentage change

Indicator	No change in total vehicle miles	Increased total vehicle miles[b]
Highway deaths	−0.05	−0.04
Gasoline consumption	−2.72	−0.32
Emissions		
Hydrocarbons	−3.52	1.68
Carbon monoxide	−1.28	2.53
Nitrogen oxides	−3.84	1.58

a. Assumes price elasticity of demand for new cars is −1.5.
b. Assumes 2 percent increase with no change in miles driven per year for each vintage.

500,000. By 1981 the combined effect of these standards was to reduce new car sales by over 830,000 per year, and by over 1.1 million per year if the user cost elasticity is −2.0.[9]

The effect of these lost sales on Detroit, the automobile companies, and their workers is obvious. But they also contributed mightily to the aging of the vehicle fleet. Had these sales been made, the average car would have been newer, safer, cleaner, and more fuel efficient. For example, if the age distribution of cars on the road had been the same in 1981 as in 1973, we estimate that emissions would have been from 5 to 13 percent lower, and gasoline consumption 6 percent lower, for the same number of total vehicle miles. Even if the average number of miles driven by vintage year had remained constant, and total vehicle miles had risen by 5.8 percent, hydrocarbon and nitrogen oxide emissions would have been 3 to 4 percent lower and gasoline consumption would have been lower, but carbon monoxide emissions would have been somewhat greater. In either case, highway deaths would have been reduced by about 0.3 percent, or 150 people per year.

If the bumper standard and post-1979 emissions standards had not been imposed, by 1981 the cumulative savings (in 1981 dollars) in regulatory compliance costs for those vehicles sold would have been $22.1 billion. If vehicle miles had not increased in response to lower user costs and the lower average age of cars on the road, gasoline consumption and emissions would have been an average of nearly 3 percent lower in 1981 than actually recorded (table 7-3). If the average miles driven for each vintage

9. Once again, we ignore any possible increase in repair costs due to deletion of the bumper standard.

**Table 7-4. Effects of Deletion of Bumper Standard and Post-1979 Emissions
Standards on U.S. Auto Industry Employment and Profits, Model Years 1973–81[a]**

Year	Additional new passenger-car sales (thousands)	Increase in U.S. auto industry employment (percent)[b]	Additional cash flow for U.S. producers[b]	
			Millions of dollars	Percent increase
1973	291	1.3	380.5	4.6
1974	365	2.0	361.5	11.7
1975	324	2.0	357.2	7.4
1976	353	1.7	568.9	5.3
1977	357	1.5	652.4	5.0
1978	360	1.5	685.2	5.2
1979	327	1.6	572.3	6.1
1980	488	3.3	549.9	29.7
1981	831	5.7	1,393.3	22.9

a. Assuming a user cost elasticity of demand of −1.5.
b. Assumes 75 percent U.S. market share of additional car sales and 0.73 elasticity of employment with respect to output (derived from a simple regression of production worker-hours on vehicle output, 1970–81). Based upon a regression of real cash flow per vehicle on capacity utilization and a time trend.

had remained constant, resulting in a 2 percent increase in total miles, gasoline consumption would still have been reduced by almost 0.3 percent, but emissions would have increased by about 2 percent. In either case, a reduction in the regulatory burden would have reduced highway deaths by a small amount.

These simulations suggest that recent changes in emissions standards and certain safety regulations have had substantial deleterious feedback effects upon the health, safety, and conservation goals themselves, not to mention the extremely adverse effects upon the private costs of producing U.S. automobiles. Ironically, a slower pace of regulation could have reduced the unwanted side effects of automobile use more rapidly and at a lower cost.

To demonstrate the impact of regulation upon industry employment and profits, we continue to use the example of safety regulation without the bumper standard and with emissions standards no more stringent than those in place for 1980 model cars. If these regulations had never been imposed, car sales would have been between 291,000 and 831,000 greater in each year from 1973 through 1981, assuming a user cost elasticity of demand of −1.5. Given an elasticity of employee hours with respect to vehicle production of 0.73, this would have generated from 1 to 6 percent more labor hours in these years, alleviating some of the industry's unemployment problems (table 7-4). More dramatically, before-tax cash flow would have been from $357 million to $1,393 million higher in each year.

In 1980 industry cash flow would have been 30 percent higher in the absence of just these two regulations. We cannot say that this improvement in sales, profits, and employment would have sufficed to fend off protection, but it surely would have helped.

Product Quality and Regulation

Most of our discussion thus far has centered on the trade-offs between emissions control, safety, weight, and fuel economy. But regulation may create other problems in designing and building automobiles. By requiring new technologies for meeting ever more stringent emissions standards, regulation may create reliability problems. Moreover, the sheer complexity of the design problem coupled with the constraints imposed by tight compliance deadlines may make it difficult to achieve the same quality of engineering as was obtained in more tranquil times.

If regulation has reduced product quality and reliability, it should be most noticeable in the models produced during 1972–74, when the rapid rise in both safety and emissions control costs occurred, and 1979–81, when another tightening of emissions standards occurred. The uncertainty surrounding emissions controls standards in the former period certainly made product planning difficult. Moreover, the introduction of the energy-absorbing bumper and seat belt interlocks added to the engineering and design problems, albeit modestly.

Evidence on product reliability for different makes of automobiles is understandably difficult to obtain. Producers are not eager to allow publication of their warranty adjustments for fear that it might harm future sales. Fortunately, *Consumer Reports* tabulates responses from its readers for seventeen categories of repairs on recent models of U.S.-produced and imported cars. These responses are received from between 100,000 and 360,000 readers each year, but there is a distinct possibility that responses are biased. Uncommonly good or disastrously bad experiences may well motivate a higher frequency of responses than the average experience. In addition, the responses are subjective, rather than a precise detailing of actual repair expense. But because these data are the only relatively consistent data on reliability of passenger cars over the past fifteen years, we use them.

Figure 7-1 shows the simple, unweighted average repair records of cars produced by each of the three major domestic companies and Japanese

Figure 7-1. Relative Repair Frequency for Domestic Cars and Japanese Imports, Model Years 1968–84

Repair frequency (1 = best; 3 = average; 5 = worst)

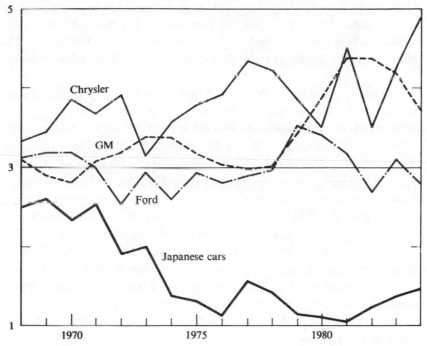

Sources: *Consumer Reports*, various issues.

imports. A rating of 3.00 is average, while smaller values are better than average and larger numbers are worse than average. Each car is assigned a value of between 1.00 and 5.00 reflecting the ordinal rankings in *Consumer Reports*. Ratings are not comparable over time; therefore we concentrate on the temporal pattern of the intrayear differences.

It is quite clear from figure 7-1 that the repair frequency of imported Japanese cars has improved dramatically relative to their U.S. counterparts. In 1968 and 1969 Ford and General Motors were fairly close to the Japanese in reliability, according to the *Consumer Reports* ratings, but since that time the U.S.-built cars have suffered a substantial decline relative to the Japanese models. The figure also shows that the sharp rise in relative repair frequency occurred in 1970 for Chrysler, in 1972 for GM, and in 1974–76 and 1978–81 for all of the Big Three. This corresponds almost exactly to the periods of increasing regulation identified earlier. However, there are troubling aspects to this correlation that cannot be explained away very easily.

First, why did Ford vehicles show better reliability than Chrysler or GM cars in the mid-1970s? Second, why did the second major surge in relative repair frequency begin for Ford and GM with the 1978 or 1979 models, when there was little change in regulatory requirements? The 1981 surge for Chrysler is more obviously correlated with rising emissions control requirements.

One possible answer to the 1978–81 puzzle is that the Big Three began to downsize their models in 1978, turning increasingly to front-wheel drive with transverse-mounted drive lines; but GM and Ford waited until 1979–1980 to introduce their first front-wheel-drive models—one to two years after their relative repair performance began to deteriorate. A simple regression analysis reveals that front-wheel-drive cars do not have significantly worse repair records than their rear-wheel-drive counterparts of the same model year. The deterioration at GM and Chrysler occurred across their entire product line, not just in their new front-wheel-drive cars. The 1978–81 deterioration relative to the Japanese cars may simply reflect the difficulties inherent in quickly transforming entire product lines to meet the new demand for fuel efficiency, tight emissions control, and performance. It is notable that Ford, which did not introduce major changes in its automobiles until 1980, suffered the least relative to the Japanese in terms of reliability in 1978–81.

A more precise test of the effects of increased regulatory costs is available. We know that the reliability of U.S. cars declined secularly over 1968–82 relative to Japanese cars, but we might expect that this decline was related to the erratic increases in real regulatory costs. In short, we might hypothesize that the relative repair frequency is a function of time and the *change* in real regulatory costs:

$$REPFREQ_i = f(TIME, DREGR),$$

where $REPFREQ_i$ is the difference between the ith firm's repair frequency and the Japanese import average, $DREGR$ is the change in real regulatory costs per car (without learning, in hundreds of dollars deflated by the CPI), and $TIME$ is a variable measuring the number of model years between the given year and 1967.

The results for each of the three major companies are reproduced in table 7-5. From these results, we find a large and significant relationship

Table 7-5. The Effects of Changes in Real Regulatory Costs on the Relative Repair Frequency of U.S. Automobile Models, 1968–82[a]

Independent variable	General Motors	Chrysler	Ford
Constant	−1.697	0.397	−0.546
	(5.33)	(0.83)	(1.09)
TIME	0.200	0.152	0.111
	(10.62)	(5.36)	(3.75)
DREGR	0.587	0.161	0.221
	(2.96)	(0.49)	(0.99)
Summary statistic			
$\bar{R}^2$	0.908	0.658	0.704
Rho	0.094	0.000	0.375

a. Dependent variable is *REPFREQ*. Numbers in parentheses are *t*-statistics.

between the decrease in product reliability and the change in regulatory costs for GM, but neither large nor significant relationships for Ford or Chrysler. Since Ford was the slowest to introduce new models, perhaps the regulatory effect is due to the combination of rapid model changes and changes in regulatory requirements.

From this evidence, one can at least conclude that mounting regulatory requirements and uncertainty about deadlines for emissions standards in particular added to the reliability problems suffered in Detroit in 1972–74 and 1978–81. The recent surge in reliability problems must, however, be attributed in part to the perceived need to redesign cars dramatically to obtain fuel economy improvements desired by motorists. This push for greater fuel economy is more related to changes in consumer tastes than regulation.

Conclusion

It is obvious that there are simple, static conflicts between the policy goals of emissions reduction, vehicle safety, and fuel efficiency, but these conflicts are to some extent unavoidable. Large cars are inherently safer and less fuel efficient than smaller cars. Emissions control must, at some point, compromise fuel efficiency.

The conflicts that should concern policymakers are those that arise because of dynamic feedbacks upon vehicle purchases and trade protection. Forcing rapid improvements in emissions, fuel efficiency, or safety upon car producers increases costs so much that it postpones consumer replacements of older, less socially desirable vehicles. This delay, in turn, reduces fuel efficiency and increases emissions. More important, the timing of these regulatory programs with both the cyclical turbulence in the U.S. (and world) economy and the need for massive retooling by the automobile companies has added to the quality problems of the U.S. companies, further reducing domestic new car demand.

These dual sources of downward pressure on sales and profits have led to the imposition of trade restrictions against clean, fuel-efficient Japanese cars and a reduction of the pressure upon Detroit to retool and innovate. In the last analysis, this protectionism may prove far more costly than the direct compliance costs associated with the three programs analyzed in this volume.

CHAPTER EIGHT

Conclusion

THE AUTOMOBILE is such an important, pervasive part of modern life that every problem associated with its use becomes a major national issue demanding immediate attention. For example, in 1974, when petroleum consumption became a national concern, the focus was on the automobile since half of petroleum consumption was associated with transportation. Despite the fact that the increased demand for fuel efficiency would have led auto manufacturers to provide more fuel-efficient cars anyway, there was a political consensus that the government had to respond immediately.

The decision to impose federal safety and emissions regulation in the 1960s was more understandable. Although individual manufacturer and consumer decisions would serve to prevent the worst safety outcomes, one can make a case for government policies to correct the remaining externalities. Obviously, the automobile's contributions to rising highway death rates and increasingly noticeable urban smog simply could not be ignored by the government. One might argue that the externalities created by the automobile could be handled by state governments. Unfortunately, there are important economies of scale in automobile design and production. Fifty different state laws, or even half a dozen different laws, could have caused chaos in the market. By the mid-1960s, it was generally agreed that the federal government would have to assume the responsibility for regulating automobile emissions and even safety.

Safety Regulation

The first federal automobile regulatory program attempted to deal with safety issues. This program has been the best planned and administered and the most successful in achieving its goals. Our estimates indicate that highway fatalities would be about 40 percent greater were it not for the safety features adopted since the beginning of this program.

The primary reason for the success of safety regulation is that the program did not impose extremely tight deadlines for new technologies, but rather proceeded with an incremental approach to the problems and proposed solutions. Moreover, there was a good base of data and well-known technologies for increasing safety.

None of this is to say that there have not been problems in regulating safety. The goals for the program were not carefully specified, and endless battles have resulted concerning how much safety is sufficient. The battle over passive restraints is almost as old as the National Highway Traffic Safety Administration, and after almost twenty years there still does not appear to be agreement on this issue.

Emissions Regulation

Emissions regulation became effective at about the same time as the General Services Administration's initial federal safety requirements. While both the safety and emissions programs eventually added hundreds of dollars to the cost of a new car, emissions control has been much more controversial with both manufacturers and the public because of its high costs and effects upon vehicle performance. If the measure of success is the reduction of emissions, federal emissions regulation has been successful, although not as successful as required by Congress. If the measure of success is improvements in health, the program has apparently accomplished little. With a thin base of data and little theory on the effects of automobile pollutants on human health, Congress acted precipitately in constructing a program with tight deadlines and extremely ambitious goals. Congress and the auto manufacturers were in continual direct confrontation, and the public was the loser.

The combination of stringent standards and tight deadlines led to jerry-built technologies, especially for the 1974 model year. The results were unreliable cars, high costs, and significant fuel consumption penalties. Since the law prohibits the sale of automobiles that do not pass the emissions certification test, the combination of stringent controls and deadlines also led to some leniency in certifying vehicles that simply did not meet the standards. Furthermore, the exclusive focus on new vehicles has meant that vehicles are relatively clean when new, but deteriorate with use. Clearly, more robust technologies that give low emissions over the entire lifetime of vehicles are needed.

Of the three regulatory programs, emissions regulation provides the greatest challenge. It is the one program that is clearly needed because of a market failure. The absence of a price mechanism to ration pollution creates a distinct need for regulation. Yet this program is the most inefficient and poorly designed of the three regulatory programs analyzed in this book.

The current standards cannot withstand a cost-benefit analysis. Ironically, to meet these standards manufacturers have been forced to adopt sensitive control technologies that fail during use. In theory, mandatory inspection and maintenance programs should correct these failures, but there is enormous political pressure to dilute these programs and sharply reduce their effectiveness. Many state inspection programs are actually designed to allow the worst control system failures to escape repair.

There is a need for clarifying the goals of the emissions control program. What is society trying to protect and how much protection does it desire in view of the regulatory costs? Enough is now understood about the diffusion of pollutants in the atmosphere and their chemical transformation that a careful specification of goals could be translated into emissions requirements for individual vehicles. It seems certain that the emissions standards could be somewhat more relaxed than the current standards if they were met over the lifetime of the vehicle. Moreover, it is quite clear that some form of a two-car strategy—applying more stringent standards in areas with air quality problems—is needed if smog is to be reduced in the most polluted areas without imposing unreasonable costs on the rest of the country.

Reform of emissions control appears to be a situation where everyone can win. The cost of purchasing and operating a car could be reduced. Annual inspection could probably be ended. Lifetime emissions could be reduced. In general, both environmentalists and car owners would gain by reform, with the additional benefits of increased new car sales.

Fuel Economy Regulation

The fuel economy of the average new car reached its nadir precisely when the Arab oil embargo and greater prices made it clear that much greater fuel economy was needed. Government's initial reaction in holding down the price of gasoline was dysfunctional; hence a fuel economy program was created to compel the desired behavior.

Our analysis shows that the fuel economy regulations have been largely irrelevant until recently. Consumers reacted to gasoline shortages and higher prices by demanding fuel-efficient cars. Manufacturers anticipated this shift in demand and spent tens of billions of dollars to increase the fuel efficiency of vehicles. The result has been a 54 percent increase in the fuel efficiency of new cars over the average 1973 level. (EPA data suggest an even higher estimate.)

Even though real gasoline prices have been declining since 1981, there is the possibility that fuel prices will be higher five to ten years from now. Despite this possibility, we see no need to compel further improvements in fuel efficiency. Car buyers can be left to choose their own fuel efficiency. If future improvements in fuel efficiency were desired, the most direct way to obtain them would be to raise gasoline prices by increasing the federal tax. Unlike new car standards, an increase in gasoline prices would raise the turnover in the automobile fleet, ridding society of gas-guzzling, polluting, and less safe vehicles.

The current regulations tend to increase the price of large cars that have less fuel efficiency and to decrease or even subsidize the price of small cars that are more efficient. This type of distortion reduces social welfare, and in the long run it creates a constituency for the program's continuation.

The penalty on the least fuel-efficient cars, the gas guzzler tax, is really a luxury tax on expensive cars. This tax is unlikely to raise an appreciable amount of revenue, and it is somewhat difficult to collect. Since we do not see a huge demand for gas-guzzling cars in the near future, we see this tax as more of a nuisance than a benefit. If it is desirable either to raise revenue or to enact a luxury tax on cars, it would be simpler to have a graduated federal sales tax on new cars, with the rate increasing with each additional $10,000 of price. The gas guzzler tax should be eliminated.

Conflicting Regulations

The social problems created by the automobile have been addressed one at a time without worrying about possible contradictions. It is now evident that there are contradictions between, for example, weight-increasing safety regulation and fuel economy requirements, as well as between emissions control standards and fuel economy regulations. Each regulatory agency should be instructed to estimate the effect of any proposed action on other statutory goals. Congress must either address these contradictions or designate some agency to address them. Although it certainly makes sense to have an Environmental Protection Agency, it also makes sense to examine all motor vehicle regulation in an integrated manner. In both the Federal Republic of Germany and Japan, a single agency has the primary administrative responsibility for all motor vehicle regulation, including emissions, safety, fuel economy, and noise.[1]

New versus Old Vehicles

No federal regulations have attempted to retrofit existing vehicles for safety, emissions, or fuel economy. Instead, the focus has been exclusively on new vehicles, leading to much tighter new car standards than would otherwise be required. These stringent new car standards have generated substantial increases in new car prices and large performance penalties in certain years, particularly for emissions controls in the 1970s.

Replacing a twelve-year-old vehicle with a new one has two desirable effects. First, the new vehicle is designed to be safer, less polluting, and more fuel efficient. Second, all three of these characteristics tend to deteriorate over time in a vehicle; use erodes safety, increases emissions, and decreases fuel efficiency. Not only are the desired improvements brought in through new vehicles, but limiting the period that older vehicles are kept in the fleet improves overall safety, emissions, and fuel consumption. The high prices of new cars required by strict new car standards provide a major disincentive for this desirable turnover in the vehicle stock.

Steps need to be taken to reduce the penalties associated with new cars. Requiring that existing cars continue to meet reasonable standards for safety, emissions, and fuel economy is one way to promote turnover to satisfy social goals. More generally, there needs to be recognition that extremely stringent new car standards have the opposite effect from that intended because they delay the replacement of older vehicles.

U.S. Competitiveness

For reasons we could only begin to explore, U.S. auto producers have had greater difficulty in adapting to fuel economy and emissions regulation

1. Massachusetts Institute of Technology. *Environmental Regulation of the Automobile* (MIT, Center for Policy Alternatives, January 1982), pp. 4–19.

than their Japanese competitors. It was to be expected that the increase in demand for fuel-efficient cars would help foreign companies since their vehicles were designed for higher gasoline prices than the United States had faced. However, it is not evident why the U.S. firms should have had such difficulty in making the transition to more fuel-efficient, less polluting cars.

Safety standards are unlikely to result in major new requirements in the future, with the exception of passive restraints. The 1970 emissions goals have essentially been achieved, at least for initial certification. Thus fuel economy is the one area of continuing pressure—and this is an area that will favor Japanese companies. If the fuel economy standards are eliminated and this decision is left to the marketplace, U.S. assemblers may close some of their domestic assembly lines for subcompacts and import their smaller cars. Removing fuel economy regulation may not be a panacea for the domestic industry, but at least it would no longer be a disruptive factor in the product planning of the U.S. industry.

Some Lessons for the Future

Society awoke in the mid-1960s to many of the problems created by more than 75 million motor vehicles on the road. Although safety regulators took some care to gather data and analyze what should be done, Congress arbitrarily set the standards for emissions control and fuel economy. This has proved to be a major mistake.

Throughout the 1970s, most automobile regulation, particularly that dealing with emissions control and fuel economy, has been characterized by confrontation and charges of bad faith. Most of the new wave of regulation took place in a crisis atmosphere characterized by the feeling that steps had to be taken immediately.

From the perspective of 1985, none of the problems were crises requiring immediate action. All would have benefited from a more leisurely pace and detailed analysis such as that which has characterized safety regulation. The problems created by the arbitrary goal of reducing emissions by 95 percent and of achieving 27.5 miles per gallon persist. We have not examined all of the issues involved in technology forcing. We did, however, show the large costs that are associated with it.

At this stage, it is evident that better regulation depends on clarifying goals, collecting relevant data, and performing a wide range of analyses. The era of confrontation and heroic actions has given way to one of deliberation and analysis. The agencies recognize this change; there is no evidence that Congress does. The underlying legislation needs to be changed and the agencies given the time and the budget for the data collection and analysis required to complete the task.

APPENDIX A

The Effects of Regulation on the Costs of Owning and Operating a Car

THIS APPENDIX provides a theoretical model for analyzing the effects of regulation on the costs of owning and operating a car, and it presents some empirical estimates of the model from 1956–81 data. The problem is more complicated than it might seem because the costs of operating a car are generally incurred by the owner, whereas the costs of manufacturing the car are determined by the manufacturer. If in fact the manufacturer minimizes the combined costs of manufacturing and operating the car (for a given product quality), there is a determinate and meaningful framework in which to analyze the effects of regulation. Our theoretical model shows that an auto manufacturer, whether competitive or monopolistic, does indeed have a strong economic incentive to produce a car that minimizes the sum of manufacturing and operating costs.[1] (If this assumption had not been met, the analysis would have been much more complicated.) Our model suggests some important considerations in formulating a functional relationship between auto ownership and operating costs on the one hand and regulatory constraints on the other.

Automotive services are produced by a combination of capital, gasoline, repairs, highway services, and insurance. Many of these inputs are partial substitutes—for example, greater expenditures on engineering can

---

1. Some similar points are made by Jack Hirshleifer, *Price Theory and Applications* (Prentice-Hall, 1980), chap. 12. However, Hirshleifer's analysis differs from that of the present study in several respects. First, he is concerned with fuel efficiency built into gasoline, rather than autos, so that he fails to take account of some of the needed elements analyzed here. Second, his analysis has not taken account of some of the assumptions needed to get his results, such as the need for substitution between fuel and other inputs in producing auto services (as described below). Third, Hirshleifer has not taken account of regulatory constraints, which is necessary for the present analysis. The arguments made here also parallel in some ways the arguments made regarding monopoly and other product quality attributes. See, for example, Peter L. Swan, "The Durability of Goods and the Regulation of Monopoly," *Bell Journal of Economics*, vol. 2 (Spring 1971), pp. 347–57.

reduce fuel consumption or repair frequency. This substitution casts doubt on the validity of measuring regulatory costs by simply totaling the reported increases in production costs due to individual regulations.

Consumers may choose various combinations of size and such performance attributes as ride, handling, acceleration, braking, and fit and finish. Other things being equal, decreasing emission of pollutants or increasing size, performance, safety, or fuel efficiency entails greater production and engineering costs. The extent to which the consumer pays for this depends upon the ability of the manufacturer to pass on these costs in higher prices.

Safety and emissions regulations have three effects: alteration of the ratios of fuel, capital inputs, repair services, and other inputs for each vehicle; a change in the mix of vehicles actually purchased; and a change in the quantity of auto services demanded. Even without regulation the sharp rise in gasoline costs during the 1970s should have led to smaller, more expensive cars. Indeed, regulation, the customers' budget constraints, foreign competition, and technological change have interacted to complicate the measurement of regulatory compliance costs.

Some Models of Auto Costs, Firm Behavior, and Regulation

To obtain useful estimates of the cost of regulation, we must attempt to measure the change in the full costs of owning and operating a car that are *not* due to changes in fuel and repair costs, the rental price of capital, or technological change. To begin, we assume that a representative firm produces cars that generate auto services (assumed to be vehicle miles, *VM*) according to the following relationship:

(1) $VM = f(X_1, \ldots, X_k, Q_1, \ldots, Q_m),$

where X represents factor inputs, such as fuel, capital, and mechanic's labor, and Q represents size and quality attributes. (For the time being, we ignore regulatory constraints, but we shall return to them.)

A Model Based on Competitive Markets

It is our ultimate intention to estimate a cost function for the ownership and operation of autos and to use it as a basis for our analysis of the costs of regulation. Such a cost function is most clearly defined if the markets for all factor inputs provided auto users (including the autos themselves) are competitive, and if these markets are all in long-run equilibrium. Before estimating such a cost function, we shall relax the assumption of perfect competition in the market for new cars, but, as in the case of many other exercises in economic modeling, it will help to clarify our arguments and methods if we first analyze the problem based on the assumption of perfect competition (with no externalities) in all markets.

Under these assumptions, the consumer or firm faces horizontal supply curves for all factors and seeks to minimize costs for owning and operating a car, based on the production function (equation 1) and the prices of the various factors. For the most part, it is reasonable to assume that the variable factor proportions shown in equation 1 can be achieved only before the car is built. It is also reasonable to assume that factor proportions will be fixed after the car is built; that is, the fuel economy must for the most part be engineered and built into the car.

In this case, the user of the car is not in a position to alter factor proportions. Nevertheless, competition among auto producers will produce cost-minimizing factor proportions for consumers because, under the assumption given above, it will be possible for a new auto producer to enter the market and earn a profit as long as the factor proportions are different from the cost-minimizing ones or as long as the price of a car is above its marginal cost once optimal proportions have been built in.

Assuming that this competitive process occurs, an auto user will then face a long-run average cost function of the following type:

(2) $$C_u = C_u(C_m, w_2, w_3, \ldots, w_n, Q_1, \ldots, Q_m, VM),$$

where the w's are factor prices, the Q's are qualitative attributes, and C_m is the first factor price, the long-run marginal cost of manufacturing a car with a standardized set of attributes, which will be equivalent to the price of such a car if the auto market is competitive.

Now suppose that government agencies impose various regulatory constraints on auto manufacturers and users, that each regulatory constraint can somehow be measured (grams of various types of pollutants per unit of time), and that these constraints vary over time. These constraints affect the user cost function defined above in two ways: first, they cause the cost of manufacturing a vehicle to rise. Thus the minimum cost of manufacturing a given vehicle is a function of the regulatory constraints:

(3) $C_m = C_m(R_1, \ldots, R_k)$,

where the R's represent measures of the regulatory constraints. Note that if all markets are competitive and if auto manufacturing is a constant cost industry, then in the long run the full costs of regulation in manufacturing are passed on to consumers.

The second way in which regulation affects the cost of owning and operating cars is directly, through reduced fuel economy or increased maintenance costs. Thus the vector of R variables enters directly as parameters in equation 2, as well as indirectly through the C_m variable. If for simplicity we were to redefine C_m as the cost of manufacturing a vehicle of standardized attributes without any regulatory constraints, we could then subsume both effects into a single reduced-form equation:

(4) $C_u = C_u(C_m, w_{21}, \ldots, w_n, Q_1, \ldots, Q_m, R_1, \ldots, R_k, VM)$.

It would be possible to estimate equation 4 econometrically if the assumptions given above were met, pooled cross-sectional and time-series data were available for a sample of auto users, regulatory constraints could be measured, the marginal costs of manufacturing autos of different combinations of attributes in a given year without regulatory constraints could be estimated, changes in technology over time could be adequately controlled for, and all adjustments observed over motorists and time were long run in nature. Such an equation could then be used to analyze consumers' full costs of regulation (for both ownership and operations) under varying regimes of factor prices. It is our goal to estimate such an equation and to use it to analyze the costs of regulation. However, most observers of the U.S. automobile industry would question whether the stringent assumptions necessary to make the above model appropriate are at all valid. For that reason, we now discuss a model relaxing one of the most stringent assumptions, that of perfectly competitive markets for new autos in the United States.

A Model Allowing for Monopoly Power

It is possible that by the late 1970s the U.S. auto industry had become nearly a competitive one in the face of Japanese rivalry. Even if this were true, however, the period of time needed to analyze the effects of regulatory policies goes back into the 1960s, when it is much more likely that the

U.S. producers had substantial market power. It is therefore necessary and appropriate to develop a model of the costs of owning and operating a car that assumes the manufacturer has some monopoly power, allowing as well for possible changes in the degree of monopoly power.

Mainly for the sake of exposition, we introduce some further simplifying assumptions relative to the competitive model mentioned above. First, we assume that the consumer's ownership and operating costs of autos is independent of fleet size, so that the production function (equation 1) has constant returns to scale in *VM*. Second, we reduce the number of factor inputs to the consumer to three: fuel, maintenance and repair services, and the auto itself. Third, we hold quality attributes constant, analyzing firm and consumer behavior for a vehicle of specified quality. We demonstrate that under very plausible assumptions a monopolist has every bit as much an incentive to produce fuel-efficient (or price-efficient in use of all factors) cars as a competitive auto industry would have — a less than obvious result and one seemingly ignored by some policymakers.

To start, we assume that our auto producer is a monopolist with a market demand dependent not simply on the price charged for the car, but on the full user cost of owning and operating the car for a given (fixed) utilization rate of, say, 15,000 miles per year. (For the time being, assume that a car lasts only one period, so that interest and depreciation need not be considered.) Thus the number of autos demanded per unit of time is:

$$(5) \qquad\qquad D = D(C_u),$$

where C_u is the user cost as defined above. Temporarily holding the factor prices for fuel and maintenance constant, we then define the user cost function as:

$$(6) \qquad\qquad C_u = C_u(P, F, M, R),$$

where P is the price charged for an auto by the manufacturer, F is the fuel intensity of the car (it can be viewed as fuel efficiency conventionally measured, in miles per gallon), M is the maintenance and repair intensity of the car (it could be measured in man-hours per year), and R is a vector of regulatory constraints (to be viewed as parameters, beyond the control of consumers and producers).

It is worth noting that whereas equation 4 represents an ex ante cost function, with substitution among the factors, equation 6 represents an ex post cost function, with no possible substitution of the factors once intensities have been built in.

Thus, when factor prices increase, costs will rise proportionately, depending on the intensities built into the car for each type of factor. Moreover, since we are (for the moment) assuming away any conceptual questions associated with the car's durability, it is worth noting that an increase of $1 in the purchase price of the car will increase user costs by $1. Once again, the reason is that once factor intensities have been built into the car there is no opportunity to reduce costs by substituting other factors for the cost of the car itself.

Incorporating the fact that cars are durable would complicate the analysis somewhat, but would leave the basic conclusion unchanged: under those circumstances, we can view the price of the car as an annualized stream of interest and amortization costs, depending on the price charged for the new car and the interest rate. Once again, it could not be changed once factor intensities were built into the car. This point regarding fixed factor intensities after the car is built is an important one to our subsequent results, as we shall see, but we believe it is basically a realistic assumption.

We assume that the manufacturer is beyond minimum-efficient scale in production, so that marginal and average costs are equal.[2] The average cost of production for a vehicle of given attributes is:

$$(7) \qquad\qquad C_m = C_m(F, M, R),$$

where the variables are as defined before, and R is once again a vector representing parametric constraints. Holding auto size and other attributes

2. In the context of a multiproduct firm (which the large auto manufacturers indeed are), the concepts of average and marginal costs need further clarification. The concept of long-run marginal cost (which C_m is) still exists in a multiproduct context: it is simply the extra cost of producing an extra unit of a product, holding all other product quantities constant. Although the concept of average cost does not exist in a multiproduct context, nevertheless there is an equivalent concept of constant overall returns to scale, which occurs when marginal cost pricing on all products will recover total costs. The most recent study of automobile manufacturing costs, by Friedlaender, Winston, and Wang, indicates that for a typical U.S. firm over the time period studied (1955–79), total costs are in fact about 105 percent of the amount marginal cost pricing would recover, and the amount does not differ significantly from 100 percent. In a multiproduct context, this is equivalent to saying that marginal and average costs are equal, as we have assumed. For the statistical result cited, and a discussion of multiproduct cost theory as applied to the auto industry, see Ann F. Friedlaender, Clifford Winston, and Kung Wang, "Costs, Technology, and Productivity in the U.S. Automobile Industry," *Bell Journal of Economics*, vol. 14 (Spring 1983), pp. 1–20.

constant, an increase in fuel economy reduces operating costs, all other costs being equal, but raises manufacturing costs. Similarly, a reduction in required maintenance and repairs reduces operating costs, but raises manufacturing costs.

The monopolist attempts to maximize profits, which, given our assumptions, can be expressed as follows:

$$(8) \qquad \pi = D[C_u(P, F, M, R)] \, P - C_m(F, M, R) \, D \, [C_u(P, F, M, R)].$$

Conditions for maximum profits are as follows:

$$(9) \qquad \frac{\partial \pi}{\partial P} = D + \left(\frac{\partial D}{\partial C_u} \cdot \frac{\partial C_u}{\partial P} \right) P - C_m \left(\frac{\partial D}{\partial C_u} \cdot \frac{\partial C_u}{\partial P} \right) = 0;$$

$$(10) \qquad \frac{\partial \pi}{\partial F} = P \frac{\partial D}{\partial C_u} \frac{\partial C_u}{\partial F} - \frac{\partial C_m}{\partial F} D - C_m \left(\frac{\partial D}{\partial C_u} \frac{\partial C_u}{\partial F} \right) = 0;$$

$$(11) \qquad \frac{\partial \pi}{\partial M} = P \frac{\partial D}{\partial C_u} \frac{\partial C_u}{\partial M} - \frac{\partial C_m}{\partial M} D - C_m \left(\frac{\partial D}{\partial C_u} \frac{\partial C_u}{\partial M} \right) = 0.$$

These can be rewritten as:

$$(12) \qquad - D = (P - C_m) \frac{\partial D}{\partial C_u} \frac{\partial C_u}{\partial P};$$

$$(13) \qquad \frac{\partial C_m}{\partial F} D = (P - C_m) \frac{\partial D}{\partial C_u} \frac{\partial C_u}{\partial F};$$

$$(14) \qquad \frac{\partial C_m}{\partial M} D = (P - C_m) \frac{\partial D}{\partial C_u} \frac{\partial C_u}{\partial M}.$$

Dividing equation 12 by equation 13 and equation 13 by equation 14, and then simplifying, we have

$$(15) \qquad \frac{\partial C_m}{\partial F} \bigg/ \frac{\partial C_m}{\partial M} = \frac{\partial C_u}{\partial F} \bigg/ \frac{\partial C_u}{\partial M};$$

$$(16) \qquad \frac{-\partial C_m}{\partial F} = \frac{\partial C_u}{\partial F} \bigg/ \frac{\partial C_u}{\partial P}.$$

These results are important, because they indicate that even under our assumptions of monopoly, a producer has an incentive to build factor proportions into its cars that minimize total social (that is, consumer plus manufacturing) costs. Equation 15 states this clearly in that it indicates that the ratio of benefits that comes from increasing fuel efficiency and maintenance efficiency by one unit each (respectively) should be equal to the ratio of incremental manufacturing costs for increasing each type of efficiency.

To interpret equation 16, it is useful to recall our result from above that the partial derivative of C_u with respect to P must be 1: that is, given our assumptions, an increase in the price of a new car increases our ex post cost function by $1. As a result, equation 16 can be rewritten as:

(17) $$\frac{-\partial C_m}{\partial F} = \frac{\partial C_u}{\partial F} .$$

In this form, it states that the extra cost of adding a unit of fuel efficiency should equal the amount by which operating costs can be reduced from that increased efficiency. (This is equivalent to the amount by which the price for a car can be increased from that higher efficiency, holding total quantity demanded constant.)

These conditions, taken together, indicate that given our assumptions, a monopolist will indeed provide cost-minimizing factor proportions. The reader can readily show that if the goal were simply to minimize costs, equations 15 and 17 would be the necessary first-order conditions, given our assumptions.

This result depends on two critical but realistic assumptions. First, the user cannot vary factor proportions in response to factor prices once the car is built. Second, for given qualitative attributes, it is only the user cost of the auto that affects the demand for it: neither the price of the car nor its level of fuel economy has an independent effect on demand. But both assumptions are consistent with known technology and rational behavior.[3]

What we have shown so far establishes that even with monopoly behav-

---

3. It might be argued that a third necessary assumption for our results is that the discount rate applied by the monopolist (or the private sector in general) be the same as the socially optimal discount rate, because some economists believe that these differ. Without getting into this debate, we would argue that if those discount rates do differ, the best public policy is to use macroeconomic (fiscal and monetary) policies to equalize them. In any event, no one has used this possible difference in interest rates as a justification for regulating or subsidizing autos.

ior on the part of auto producers, it is possible to define a cost function for auto services based on the assumption that the consumer and producer jointly select cost-minimizing inputs for the provision of automotive services. That being so, if we knew the cost of manufacturing the autos in our sample, we could then estimate the cost function shown in equation 4. Manufacturing cost for models of each attribute would be used to calculate the left-hand variable, and the right-hand C_m variable could be an estimated index of what it would cost to manufacture a vehicle of a standardized type in the absence of regulatory constraints.

Detailed data (by make and model for each year) for long-run auto manufacturing costs are not available for calculating the left hand side of equation 4. The only data available at that level of disaggregation are the list prices paid by consumers (or possibly dealers) for each make and model. In the case of the competitive model, this would not be a problem, for in long-run competitive equilibrium the price of an auto would be equal to the long-run average cost of manufacturing it.

Suppose that manufacturers' prices, rather than costs, are used to calculate the left-hand side equation of 4, and suppose auto manufacturers nevertheless have some degree of market power. Under those circumstances, the markup of the price of the car (P) above the manufacturer's costs (C_m) could reasonably be expected to depend upon a vector of demand parameters, e, the most important of which would be the price elasticity of demand faced by each automobile producer. Therefore:

$$(18) \qquad P = C_m \cdot h(e),$$

where h is an unknown function.

Therefore, if the automobile producers have some degree of market power, the total user cost of owning and operating a car (including the monopoly profits) should be most reasonably related to the price elasticity of demand (and perhaps other demand parameters as well), in addition to the cost of manufacture, other factor prices, quality attributes, and the regulation parameters previously mentioned.

The relationship can be summarized as follows:

$$(19) \quad C_u = G\,[C_m \cdot h(e),\, w_2,\, \ldots,\, w_n,\, Q_1,\, \ldots,\, Q_m,\, R_1 \ldots,\, R_k],$$

or, combining G and h into a single function, H, we have:

$$(20) \qquad C_u = H\,(C_m,\, e,\, w_2,\, \ldots,\, w_n,\, Q_1,\, \ldots,\, Q_m,\, R_1,\, \ldots,\, R_k).$$

This is the form desired for estimation. On the left-hand side is total ownership and operating cost, based upon manufacturers' prices as a factor cost. On the right-hand side is C_m, an index of the costs of a standardized vehicle in the absence of regulation; e, some functional measure of demand conditions (such as the price elasticity of demand facing a typical automobile producer); and the other variables as defined before.

Some Problems of Data, Specification, and Estimation

Equation 20 suggests some variables that should be included in the estimation of an automobile ownership and operating cost function, but it does not suggest the form of the function. One of the more workable specifications of a generalized cost function of the sort mentioned above is the transcendental-logarithmic (translog) cost function. We have estimated our cost equation based on the translog specification, but we have also tested the extent to which our results are consistent with the Cobb-Douglas form, which is a restricted case of the translog.

The Potential for Estimation Bias

All factor prices and attributes must be exogenous to the model if ordinary least squares estimates of the coefficients are to be unbiased. For some variables, such as fuel prices and interest rates, this is plausible, for the portion of the markets of these goods accounted for by American auto users is arguably small enough that they have little influence on factor prices. In the case of the cost of new cars to users, the price should not generally be thought to be exogenous: it will be determined by market conditions, degree of monopoly power, and, among other things, various shocks in supply and demand. Our reduced-form specification, however, is designed to minimize these problems of simultaneous-equations bias, because the independent variables contain three sets of components that could be reasonably expected to be exogenous. The first is an estimate of what autos of standardized characteristics would cost to manufacture in the absence of regulation. The second is a measure of degree of monopoly power (that is, demand elasticity) facing domestic auto producers. The third is a vector of variables representing regulatory constraints. Thus the reduced-form specification, as derived above, is designed to avoid simultaneous-equations bias stemming from the nonexogeneity of the auto price variable. It can also be similarly argued that the qualitative-attribute variables and the regulatory-constraint variables themselves are exogenous to the process, so that consistent estimates of the coefficients should be possible.

The Data Sample

The data sample comes from two studies. Since the 1950s the Runzheimer Corporation has estimated for the American Automobile Association the ownership and operating costs for subcompact, compact, intermediate, and full-sized models.[4] The Baltimore study (based on typical operating costs in that area) was begun in 1960 by the U.S. Department of Transportation.[5] We used retail list prices for the relevant cars in calculating capital costs.[6] This may impart some upward bias to our cost estimates, but the effect is unlikely to be important unless discounts vary enormously among cars. To obtain consistent estimates of interest and depreciation from year to year, we calculated costs assuming that the consumer buys a car new, keeps it for four years and 49,000 miles, then sells it at the used car price for the relevant car size class.[7]

Factor Prices

Initially we used three different factor-price variables: fuel, repairs, and a durable capital equipment series. However, collinearity, plus the fact

4. The American Automobile Association publishes these figures in an annual pamphlet called "The Costs of Operating Your Car." The Runzheimer Corporation's numbers are derived from a large sample of autos in private corporate fleets. They are based on real-world experience, as opposed to hypothetical estimates.

5. The Department of Transportation releases these figures from time to time in a publication, *The Cost of Owning and Operating Automobiles and Vans*. Most of these figures are also reprinted in the Bureau of the Census, *Statistical Abstract of the United States*.

6. These retail list prices are taken from the annual automobile issue of *Consumer Reports* for the relevant years.

7. This utilization rate over four years is consistent with the assumptions in the American Automobile Association figures. We constructed consistent figures from the Department of Transportation data by basing costs on the first four years and 49,000 miles only. Capital costs were calculated over the four-year period by estimating wholesale trade-in values for some of the cars in the sample and using those values to estimate depreciation over the four-year period for different types of cars. These estimated depreciation rates were used as the basis for four-year-old trade-in values. Interest costs were calculated based on unpublished data on auto loan rates from the General Motors Acceptance Corporation.

that repairs account for a relatively small portion of total auto ownership and operating costs, forced us to subsume repair costs into a single category of current direct operating costs, including fuel, oil, repairs, and parts (P_k). As a factor-price variable, the average price per gallon of fuel (P_f) was both readily available and worked well. Use of it, however, leads to an understatement of the cost of regulation because the fuel cost increase due to the use of unleaded gasoline is treated as exogenous, rather than as a cost of regulation.

We used a durable price index—the price of household appliances such as refrigerators, washers, and ranges—to capture the increase in auto prices that would have occurred in the absence of regulation.[8] These are mass-produced consumer goods, generally with moving parts, motors, and enameled stampings. Unlike autos, these household durables have been subject to relatively little direct regulation. The Bureau of Labor Statistics price index for these appliances is multiplied by a measure of the user cost of holding a dollar's worth of consumer durables (interest and depreciation), and it has been adjusted to reflect the higher wages paid in the auto industry.

Qualitative Attributes

For automotive attributes, measures of size are the most important. In many previous hedonic studies of auto prices and costs, weight has most often been used. However, our study covers a period (1956–81) when the relationship between vehicle weight and various other attributes relevant to consumers (such as interior volume and quietness) shifted substantially, due both to technological change and to increased fuel prices. After some experimentation, we found that the wheelbase (W) seemed to capture size effects best: it measures the length of the passenger compartment, the best and most consistent measure of the comfort of a car.[9] Some studies have managed to find significant relationships between costs and other attributes, such as acceleration and interior noise. However, preliminary explorations suggest that such structural relationships have not persisted or at least are rather weak.

8. The price indexes for fuel, oil, repairs, and household appliances all come from the Bureau of Labor Statistics Consumer Price Index series. They were obtained directly from the BLS.

9. Wheelbase data (and weight data for experimental estimation as well) came from the annual *Consumer Reports* automobile issue.

Market Conditions Facing Auto Producers

For market-condition variables, we needed measures of the degree of competition existing at any one time for the U.S. auto industry. It can be argued that domestic competition did not change much over 1947–81, with four domestic producers maintaining roughly the same market positions. Thus measures of the importance of international competition are the most important candidates for inclusion in our equations to account for shifting market conditions.

Perhaps the most obvious candidate is a measure of import market share, which would measure directly the amount of competition faced. The problem with this variable is that it is not exogenous: import share is to some extent determined by domestic pricing policies.

To represent import competition, two types of variables would be appropriate. The first would measure the relative tastes of American and foreign motorists: historically, the combination of lower fuel prices, long driving distances, higher living standards, and good highways made the car that typical American motorists wanted to buy quite different from the car preferred by their European or Japanese counterparts. The typical American car tended to be substantially larger than its foreign counterpart, with a more powerful engine, and with convenience items that were less preferred abroad because of their tendency to use fuel (such as automatic transmission and air conditioning). This difference in American preferences gave producers of larger American cars market power they might not have had if Americans had preferred smaller cars. It can be argued that the dramatic fuel price increases of the 1970s made the car demanded by typical American motorists much more like that desired by Europeans and Japanese, thereby eliminating some of Detroit's market power.

The second set of variables relates to the comparative costs of producing cars here and abroad. Several studies have found that the increase in American auto manufacturing costs (especially relative to Japanese costs) occurred rather recently: in 1974 the cost differential between the two countries was small (especially considering the U.S. import tariff on autos), whereas by 1980 the cost differential may have been fairly substantial.[10]

10. José A. Goméz-Ibañéz and David Harrison, Jr., "Imports and the Future of the U.S. Automobile Industry," *American Economic Review,* vol. 72 (May 1982, *Papers and Proceedings, 1981*), pp. 319–23; and Eric J. Toder, *Trade Policy and the U.S. Automobile Industry* (Praeger, 1978), chap. 6.

Perhaps coincidentally, two changes reducing the market power of U.S. producers seem to have occurred simultaneously in the late 1970s. First, the dramatic fuel price increase of 1979 appears to have altered American car-buying habits permanently. (The 1974 fuel price increase may have altered tastes in the shorter run, but lower real U.S. fuel costs in 1975–79, induced partially by domestic gasoline price regulation, may have caused U.S. motorists to shift back to larger cars during this period.) Second, it appears that during 1975–79, U.S. auto manufacturers suffered an increase in their production costs for a given car size relative to those of the Japanese.

For want of a more precise variable to reflect the deterioration of Detroit's market fortunes around 1979, we include a binary variable valued at 0 before 1979 and 1 thereafter. Since our data were collected near the beginning of each model year and the dramatic 1979 fuel price increase occurred in the spring and summer, our variable will be 0 from 1956–79, and 1 for 1980–81. If Detroit's market fortunes did decline around 1979, we should expect this variable to have a negative sign in the ownership and operating cost equation.

Regulatory Constraints

Regulatory constraints are among the most difficult variables to measure in our equations. Ideally, we would like to measure them in physical terms, but most physical measures seem somewhat arbitrary. Rather, we measured regulatory constraints by the estimated engineering costs developed earlier (R in equation 3).[11] Inclusion of these variables is not circular, because we are regressing them against very independent estimates of the costs of owning and operating a car. Analysis of the coefficients of these variables should help us determine whether the costs of regulation faced by consumers are less than, equal to, or greater than costs as estimated by engineering means. Consistent with the analysis in the first section of this appendix, we include in our equation values for both current regulatory constraints (R) and constraints lagged one year [$R(-1)$].

11. R, then, is the estimated engineering cost of regulation, including both emissions controls as estimated by White and safety costs as estimated by us earlier in this book. We also attempted to estimate separate coefficients for each type of regulation, but collinearity produced unreliable estimates of the separate effects. Furthermore, the coefficient of dollar values for safety regulation did not differ significantly from the coefficient for emissions regulation, making aggregation of the two an appropriate procedure.

Technological Change

The consumer durables price index provides a direct measure of inflation-adjusted productivity increase in producing consumer durables. Inclusion of a time trend simply reduces the level and significance of the durables index; it appears that they are both capturing the same effect. We conclude that the time trend adds nothing to the explanatory power of the model. (Tests for which we got these negative results included both Hicks-neutral and biased technological progress.)

Specification, Estimation, and Results

We have specified our translog cost function to be translog in factor prices, as previous cost studies have done, and loglinear in other variables, including wheelbase, regulatory constraints, and binary variables. Specification for translog estimation takes the following form:

$$(21) \quad \ln C = a_0 + \sum_i a_i \ln P_i + \tfrac{1}{2} \sum_j \sum_i c_{ij} \ln P_i P_j$$
$$+ b_1 \ln W + b_2 \ln R + b_3 \ln R(-1) + b_4 D + b_5 D8081,$$

where all variables are as previously defined, save for the binary variable D, which reflects consistent differences in the data between the two sources we used for ownership and operating cost estimates. (It is set to 0 for sample points from the Runzheimer study and 1 for the Baltimore study.)

For the translog cost function to represent consistent, cost-minimizing behavior, certain constraints on the coefficients of equation 21 are necessary.[12] They include the following:

$$(22) \qquad\qquad a_1 + a_2 = 1;$$

$$(23) \qquad\qquad c_{11} + c_{22} = 0;$$

$$(24) \qquad\qquad c_{1j} + c_{2j} = 0, \text{ for } j = 1, 2;$$

12. For a discussion of the rationale behind these constraints, see, for example, Lauritis R. Christensen and William H. Greene, "Economies of Scale in U.S. Electric Power Generation," *Journal of Political Economy*, vol. 84 (August 1976), pp. 655–76.

(25) $c_{ij} = c_{ji}$, for all i, j.

Incorporating these constraints into the translog cost function, equation 21 can be rewritten as follows:

(26) $\ln C - \ln P_f = a_0 + a_1 (\ln P_k - \ln P_f) + k_1 Z_1$

$$+ b_1 \ln W + b_2 \ln R + b_3 \ln R(-1)$$

$$+ b_4 D + b_5 D8081,$$

where

$$Z_1 = \ln P_f \ln P_k - \tfrac{1}{2} (\ln P_f)^2 - \tfrac{1}{2} (\ln P_k)^2$$

and

$$k_1 - c_{12} = c_{21}.$$

For the estimation of the translog cost function, both the cost function and a factor-share equation were estimated jointly, using Zellner's method of seemingly unrelated coefficients, essentially doubling the available degrees of freedom. (The factor-share equation estimated was for fuel and maintenance costs; since factor shares must add up to 1, the two factor shares must add to 1.)[13]

Our estimation, then, is based on a sample of various auto types over 1956–81. (Model types include subcompact, compact, intermediate, and full size; in some cases, we have more than one observation for a given model type in a given year, one from the Baltimore study, and one from Runzheimer; in other years, we do not have all four model types; and in some years, we have no observations at all.)

When both current and lagged regulation variables are used, the results indicate a negative and insignificant coefficient for the lagged regulation variable (see table A-1). On the other hand, results for the current-period regulation variable are positive and of plausible value. The results in the equation without the lagged regulation variable suggest plausible values

---

13. For a description of this procedure and its theoretical rationale, see ibid. and Ann F. Friedlaender and Richard C. Spady, *Freight Transport Regulation: Equity, Efficiency, and Competition in the Rail and Trucking Industries* (MIT Press, 1981), apps. A–C.

Table A-1. Estimates of the Determinants of the Costs of Operating an Automobile[a]

Variable	Coefficient with lagged regulation variable	Coefficient without lagged regulation variable
Constant	−9.733	−9.666
	(−13.351)	(−13.632)
$\ln P_k - \ln P_f$	0.6072	0.6055
	(19.733)	(19.775)
Z_1	0.0694	0.0662
	(1.191)	(1.141)
$\ln W$	1.614	1.608
	(11.159)	(11.220)
$\ln R$	0.0262	0.0171
	(1.398)	(1.755)
$\ln R(-1)$	−0.0035	. . .
	(−0.592)	. . .
$D8081$	−0.0608	−0.0626
	(−2.320)	(−2.231)
D	0.0590	0.0563
	(3.124)	(2.999)

a. Numbers in parentheses are t-statistics.

and significance for just about every coefficient, except perhaps the translog interactive term Z_1. (The t-statistic of just over 1 for that coefficient in both equations suggests that the evidence supporting the translog specification over the Cobb-Douglas is not strong, although inclusion of it adds modestly to the equation's goodness of fit.)

For present purposes, we shall base our calculations of the effects of regulation on the translog coefficients with only the current regulation variable included in the equation. (Perhaps the seeming inconsistency between these results and those found with aggregate time-series data stem from the different alignments of calendar years and model years.)

The results for the other coefficients are of some interest. The large and significant value of the wheelbase variable indicates the continuing importance of size in determining the cost of owning and operating a car. And the negative value of the 1980–81 dummy suggests that Detroit may indeed have been forced to charge lower prices for its cars because of import competition during this period, suggesting in turn that the need to charge lower auto prices in the recent past probably contributed to Detroit's deteriorating financial fortunes before the import quotas.

Of most interest for the present study are the results regarding the impact of regulation. To analyze the effects of regulation, we have calculated two sets of figures: the costs (as predicted by our estimated equation) of owning and operating a car without the regulatory constraints of a given year, and the costs (similarly predicted) with regulatory constraints. The difference between the two should give an estimate of the effects of the regulatory constraints on the costs of owning and operating a car.

To make these estimates from the coefficients shown in table A-1 requires several more assumptions. First, because of its good fit and plausible coefficients, we have selected the equation without the lagged regulation variable for these simulations. Second, for the sake of conservatism in our estimate, we shall assume that even in the absence of regulation, certain basic safety devices (such as three-point front seat belts and simple rear seat belts) would have been installed by the manufacturers. The results of these simulations are shown in table 3-6 and discussed in chapter 3.

Estimating the Effects of Emissions and Safety Regulation on Prices and Profits

IN CHAPTER 3 we report the results of a simple recursive two-equation model of automobile prices and profits. In the first equation, the price of a new automobile is related to production costs and demand. In the second equation, industry cash flow per vehicle is related to the new car price and costs. In each equation, costs include labor, capital, and purchased components as well as regulatory costs.

The price equation is a reduced-form equation of a supply-demand model. Specifically, price is marked up over incremental cost to a level determined by overall consumer demand and the strength of import demand:

(1) $$P_v = MC(wL/Q, rK/Q, P_i) \cdot \lambda D(CAPUTIL),$$

where P_v is the average new vehicle price, wL/Q is equal to labor costs (wL) per vehicle (Q), rK/Q is unit capital costs, P_i is unit costs of purchased inputs, and λD is a markup that depends upon capacity utilization in the domestic automobile industry $(CAPUTIL)$.

Regulation is introduced into equation 1 by including the annual costs per vehicle of meeting emissions and safety standards. These costs are in addition to the costs of producing an unregulated vehicle; hence we attempt to standardize the labor inputs at their preregulatory level $(L/Q)_0$ and allow them to decline at an annual rate of g due to productivity growth. Regulatory costs are then simply entered into the costs function as REG:

(2) $$P_v = MC \left[w(L/Q)_0 e^{gt}, rK/Q, P_i, REG \right] \cdot \lambda D(CAPUTIL).$$

The stochastic form of equation 2 estimated for 1960–80 is:

(3) $P_{vt} = [a_0 + a_1 LABOR_t + a_2 CAPITAL_t + a_3 STEEL_t$

$+ a_4 REG_{t-x}] \cdot a_5 CAPUTIL_t + a_6 D72_t$

$+ a_7 D73_t + a_8 D74_t + u_t,$

where

$$P_{vt} = \text{the average price of a new car in year } t;$$

$$LABOR_t = \text{production-worker wages per motor vehicle (factory sales) in year } t;$$

$$CAPITAL_t = \text{unit capital costs in year } t, \text{ excluding depreciation and the cost of equity (Moody's Aaa bond rate times the capital stock in SIC 371 divided by factory sales of motor vehicles);}$$

$$STEEL_t = \text{the producer price index for steel mill products in year } t;$$

$$REG_{t-x} = \text{the estimated direct cost of equipment installed to comply with safety and emissions regulation in year } t-x;$$

$$CAPUTIL_t = \text{capacity utilization in the motor vehicle industry as measured by } 1 + \text{ the proportional deviation from the 1960–80 trend in vehicle production;}$$

$$D72_t, D73_t, \text{ and } D74_t = \text{dummy variables for the years of price controls;}$$

$$u_t = \text{random error term.}$$

In estimating equation 3, the use of a productivity growth factor for labor costs proved unsuccessful. Rather, contemporaneous actual production labor costs per vehicle were much more directly related to the price of new vehicles. The price of purchased inputs is captured by the use of the producer price index for steel mill products (*STEEL*). *STEEL* was lagged one year since this lag provided greater explanatory power than the contemporary value of this variable. This may reflect the fact that steel purchase prices are set at the beginning of the year.

To estimate equation 3, we use two different measures of the cost of emissions and safety equipment from table 3-5. The first assumes no learning economies in safety costs, and the second assumes a 5 percent annual learning rate. Both estimates are in current dollars and include none of the user costs of maintenance, additional fuel consumption, or other operating cost penalties. In both cases, regulatory costs were entered with lags of from zero to two years.

The results in table B-1 reflect estimates of both the multiplicative specification (equation 3) and a specification in which *CAPUTIL* is entered in additive form. The multiplicative form is estimated by using alternative values of a_5 and searching for the lowest residual of squares. The reported estimates use a value of a_5 equal to 0.1.

In every case, the effects of regulation appear to be registered in vehicle prices after about one year's lag. The coefficients of $REG(-1)$ in table B-1 are not significantly different from unity, but they are generally significantly different from zero. This is consistent with the hypothesis that, after a lag, all regulatory costs are passed forward in prices, but it is not resounding evidence that precisely all of the costs are shifted to consumers. There is little to choose between the regulatory cost variable that assumes no learning and one that assumes a 5 percent annual learning curve.

The coefficients of *LABOR, CAPITAL,* and $STEEL(-1)$ in table B-1 reflect the estimated contribution of labor and capital costs to the price of new automobiles at the point of means in our sample.[1] The average price of a car is $4,300; hence the estimates of labor's contribution are between 47 and 51 percent. The price of steel, reflecting purchased steel and component costs, appears to contribute another 18 to 21 percent to the price. Finally, capital charges are much less important, suggesting that prices do not respond as directly to the costs of capital services; but our measure does not capture the full user costs of capital services.

The remaining coefficients in table B-1 are reasonably satisfactory. The strength of capacity utilization is always associated directly with new car prices. The estimates of *LABOR*'s contribution to vehicle prices is consistent with labor's share of the retail price of an automobile of 40 percent. Similarly, the coefficient of *STEEL* suggests that purchased inputs contribute 20 percent of the retail price of a car, exclusive of regulatory costs. The capital cost component, reflecting only debt service, has a very small and statistically insignificant coefficient. This is not surprising, given the likely role of capital costs in a pricing decision.

1. The value of the cost of labor (*LABOR*), the cost of capital (*CAPITAL*), and the cost of steel [$STEEL(-1)$] are normalized to have a mean value of 1 so that the value of the coefficients of these variables can be interpreted as the contribution of each to the total cost at the point of means.

Table B-1. Regression Estimates of the Effects of Regulation on Prices and Profits, 1960–80[a]

	Price equation (1961–80)		
Independent variable	Equation 1[b]	Equation 2[c]	Equation 3[d]
Constant	. . .	674.9	. . .
	. . .	(3.79)	. . .
LABOR	2,094	2,189	2,040
	(6.76)	(7.07)	(6.12)
CAPITAL	117.4	48.42	93.01
	(2.88)	(0.87)	(2.57)
STEEL(−1)	842.6	768.6	884.8
	(4.15)	(3.93)	(4.38)
REG(−1)	0.6223	0.7354	0.6330
	(2.04)	(2.48)	(1.98)
CAPUTIL	1,131	473.4	1,139
	(7.86)	(3.24)	(7.52)
D72	−46.93	−61.23	−40.37
	(0.77)	(1.03)	(0.65)
D73	−135.0	−163.6	−178.3
	(2.08)	(2.56)	(2.78)
D74	−132.2	−136.9	−192.1
	(1.79)	(1.88)	(2.43)
Summary statistics			
Standard error	55.85	54.01	56.24
$\bar{R}^2$	0.999	0.999	0.998

	Profit equation (1960–80)	
	Equation 1[e]	Equation 2[f]
Constant	−866.9	−720.8
	(4.29)	(4.32)
P_v	0.944	0.9262
	(7.16)	(6.82)
LABOR	−1,135	−1,195
	(2.54)	(2.63)
CAPITAL	−348.6	−354.9
	(10.02)	(9.72)
STEEL	−771.8	−852.9
	(2.77)	(3.01)
REG	−0.790	−0.648
	(2.22)	(1.99)
Summary statistics		
Standard error	56.21	57.74
$\bar{R}^2$	0.923	0.919

a. Numbers in parentheses are t-statistics.
b. Assumes no learning economies in safety costs, using multiplicative specification.
c. Assumes no learning economies, using additive specification.
d. Assumes 5 percent annual learning rate, using multiplicative specification.
e. Assumes no learning economies.
f. Assumes 5 percent annual learning rate.

The profit equation utilizes the domestic price of a new automobile and *current* costs as regressors. Profits are total motor vehicle industry cash flow as reported by the Department of Commerce. These profits are adjusted for inventory valuation but include capital consumption allowances. The profit equation is derived as follows:

(4) $$\pi = (P_v - C)\,Q,$$

where π is cash flow, P_v is the new car price, C is current costs (excluding capital consumption), and Q is industry output. There are two possibilities for measuring Q: vehicle sales or total SIC 371 output. In fact, both give very similar results when equation 4 is transformed for estimation:

(5)
$$\pi_t/Q_t = b_0 + b_1 P_v - b_2 LABOR_t - b_3 CAPITAL_t$$
$$- b_4 STEEL - b_5 REG + v_t.$$

The results of estimating equation 5 with Q equal to factory sales of all motor vehicles are shown in table B-1 for both measures of *REG*. Once again the measure of *REG* without learning performs better than the one with learning. Both assume coefficients that are insignificantly different from -1, suggesting that the industry absorbs all of the estimated regulatory costs in the year they are imposed. This absorption is in addition to the effects of *REG* on the price of cars in equation 3, of course. Therefore our results suggest that costs are fully recorded in industry cash flows in the year incurred and that they are passed on fully after one year's lag. In the first year, however, these regulatory costs are not passed on by the manufacturers.

Further Statistical Analysis
of Motor Vehicle Deaths

THE RESULTS in chapter 4 (tables 4-5 and 4-6) are reported for the entire 1947–81 period, using one variant of the *SAFETY* variable based upon Graham's pooled cross-sectional/time-series estimates.[1] In this appendix, we report estimates using a slightly different *SAFETY* variable and some analysis of the 1947–65 period used by Peltzman to predict post-1965 fatalities.[2]

The results reported in chapter 4 use a *SAFETY* variable that weights vehicle miles by the safety of each vintage of automobile, according to Graham's results. Graham's results show greater safety gains than the 1976 General Accounting Office report, which was based upon intensive investigation of actual crashes, and, unlike the GAO report, they extend through the 1974 model year.[3] The GAO model weights for each vintage are 1.0 for pre-1966 cars, 0.87 for 1966–68 cars, 0.78 for 1960–70 cars, and 0.77 for 1971 and later models. Graham's results provide a value of 0.66 for 1974 and later models.

As a check on the robustness of our results, we use the GAO weights in constructing *SAFETY* and reestimate the equations reported in tables 4-5 and 4-6. The results are reported in tables C-1 and C-2. The specifications are identical to those in tables 4-5 and 4-6 with the exception of the *SAFETY* variable.

The results using the GAO results for the safety index, *SAFETY(GAO)*, are very similar to those using Graham's weights. The improvement in the

1. John D. Graham, "Automobile Safety: An Investigation of Occupant Protection Policies" (Ph.D. dissertation, Carnegie-Mellon University, 1983), chap. 3.
2. Sam Peltzman, "The Effects of Automobile Safety Regulation," *Journal of Political Economy*, vol. 83 (August–December 1975), pp. 677–725.
3. General Accounting Office, *Effectiveness, Benefits, and Costs of Federal Safety Standards for Protection of Passenger Car Occupants, National Highway Traffic Safety Administration, Department of Transportation*, CED-76-121 (GAO, 1976).

Table C-1. Estimates of the Determinants of Highway Fatalities, 1947–81, with Speed as Endogenous, Using GAO Safety Index[a]

Independent variable	Total deaths	Passenger-car-occupant deaths	Nonoccupant deaths	Pedestrian and bicyclist deaths
SAFETY (GAO)	1.18*	2.35*	−0.69*	−0.72*
	(4.68)	(6.16)	(2.37)	(2.91)
WEIGHT	−1.93*	−0.52	−2.40*	−1.70
	(2.23)	(0.49)	(2.40)	(1.99)
VINTAGE	−0.23*	−0.53*	0.21*	0.13
	(2.78)	(4.29)	(2.16)	(1.55)
INCOME	0.88*	0.39	1.53*	1.06*
	(4.26)	(1.33)	(6.37)	(5.20)
YOUTH	0.41	0.81*	−0.33	0.49*
	(1.91)	(2.52)	(1.36)	(2.32)
ALCOHOL	0.34	0.58	0.53	0.48
	(1.16)	(1.66)	(1.57)	(1.69)
COST	0.06	0.05	0.06	−0.05
	(1.42)	(1.01)	(1.42)	(1.43)
EMBARGO	−0.07	−0.13*	−0.02	−0.17*
	(2.01)	(2.91)	(0.44)	(4.91)
PFUEL	−0.09	0.02	−0.21*	−0.03
	(1.29)	(0.26)	(2.68)	(0.44)
LIMITED ACCESS	−0.03	−0.08*	0.05*	−0.005
	(1.47)	(2.41)	(2.31)	(0.25)
TRUCK	0.42*	0.29*	0.71*	0.16
	(4.72)	(2.19)	(6.90)	(1.79)
MILES	0.33*	0.61*	−0.38*	−0.35*
	(2.23)	(2.90)	(2.24)	(2.44)
Summary statistics				
$\bar{R}^2$	0.988	0.987	0.988	0.968
Rho	−0.690	−0.080	−0.612	−0.660

* Statistically significant at the 95 percent confidence level.
a. All variables except *EMBARGO* are in natural logarithms; numbers in parentheses are *t*-statistics.

passenger-car-occupant fatality rate remains more than double that expected from the engineering estimates. The offsetting effect of safety on deaths other than passenger-car occupants does not appear in tables C-1 and C-2. However, the offsetting effect does emerge in the pedestrian-bicyclist equations. In this version, *VINTAGE* assumes a statistically significant coefficient, perhaps capturing the improvement in post-1971 cars that is missing from *SAFETY(GAO)*. *VINTAGE* increases throughout the 1970s and 1980s due to sluggish new car demand. Otherwise the results are very similar to those obtained using Graham's weights.

Table C-2. Estimates of the Determinants of Highway Fatalities, 1947–81, with Speed as Exogenous, Using GAO Safety Index[a]

Independent variable	Total deaths	Passenger-car-occupant deaths	Nonoccupant deaths	Pedestrian and bicyclist deaths
SAFETY (GAO)	1.05*	2.20*	−0.46	−0.88*
	(4.24)	(5.01)	(0.85)	(3.03)
WEIGHT	1.16*	0.13	0.19	1.80*
	(2.43)	(0.55)	(0.50)	(3.22)
VINTAGE	−0.15	−0.42*	0.19	0.22*
	(1.84)	(2.97)	(1.07)	(2.28)
INCOME	0.91*	0.39	1.11*	1.15*
	(4.61)	(1.32)	(3.06)	(4.95)
YOUTH	0.71	0.12	−0.27	−0.16
	(0.37)	(0.36)	(0.66)	(0.71)
ALCOHOL	0.50	0.73*	1.29*	0.59*
	(2.04)	(2.25)	(3.26)	(2.07)
COST	0.04	0.05	0.03	−0.10*
	(1.15)	(0.90)	(0.47)	(2.31)
SPEED	1.06*	1.38*	0.75	1.62*
	(4.82)	(3.97)	(1.76)	(6.32)
LIMITED ACCESS	−0.04*	−0.08*	0.02	−0.02
	(2.14)	(2.22)	(0.48)	(0.74)
TRUCK	0.42*	0.28	0.57*	0.08
	(5.31)	(1.92)	(3.17)	(0.82)
MILES	0.06	0.36	−0.62*	−0.65*
	(0.52)	(1.58)	(2.21)	(4.57)
Summary statistics				
$\bar{R}^2$	0.987	0.987	0.980	0.951
Rho	−0.820	0.196	0.191	−0.825

* Statistically significant at the 95 percent confidence level.
a. All variables are in natural logarithms; numbers in parentheses are *t*-statistics.

Our analysis of the 1947–65 preregulatory period produced results analogous to those obtained by Cantu and Peltzman in their work.[4] Peltzman has used his results to project fatality rates over the post-1965 period in order to compare them with actual rates. The difference between projected and actual rates is then taken to be the measure of the impact of regulation.

Peltzman rejects the use of time-series analysis over the entire pre- and postregulatory period (in his case, 1947–72) because he believes that the effect of regulation is to change the underlying structural relationships

4. Oscar R. Cantu, "An Updated Regression Analysis on the Effects of the Regulation of Auto Safety," Working Paper 15 (Yale School of Management, 1980).

Table C-3. **Stability of the Preregulation Coefficients of Total Highway Death Rate Regressions, 1947–61 through 1947–65**

Independent variable	1947–61		1947–62		1947–63		1947–64		1947–65	
	Equation 1[a]	Equation 2[b]	Equation 1[a]	Equation 2[b]	Equation 1[a]	Equation 2[b]	Equation 1[a]	Equation 2[b]	Equation 1[a]	Equation 2[b]
YOUTH	0.186	−0.205	0.488	0.047	0.463	0.049	0.352	0.073	−0.097	−0.059
ALCOHOL	1.248*	1.359*	1.447*	1.919*	1.429*	1.847*	1.418*	1.767*	1.162*	1.766*
INCOME	0.874	1.184*	0.621	0.626	0.651	0.528	0.583	0.495	1.004*	0.391
PERMANENT INCOME	0.113	. . .	−0.326	. . .	−0.307	. . .	−0.365	. . .	−1.495*	. . .
COST	−0.296	−0.527*	−0.247	−0.261	0.248	−0.261	−0.236	−0.256	−0.300	−0.270*
SPEED	−0.483	−0.888	0.579	1.896	0.468	1.846	0.660	1.675	1.789*	1.809*
LIMITED ACCESS	0.037	0.039	−0.042	−0.024	−0.036	−0.030	−0.039	−0.031	−0.123*	−0.026
TREND	−0.063	−0.069*	−0.042	−0.066*	−0.043	−0.063*	−0.042	−0.060*	−0.025	−0.061*

* Statistically significant at the 95 percent confidence level.
a. Includes permanent income.
b. Excludes permanent income.

among speed, income, price, drinking, and risk taking. Therefore, he suggests, it is necessary to estimate the underlying structural model before regulation and to use that model to project the fatality rates that would have existed in the absence of regulation. Peltzman's argument may have some validity, but there are a number of problems with his empirical approach.

First, Peltzman's results are based upon the 1947–65 period, but these results are extremely sensitive to this choice of period if our results are any indication (see table C-3). The 1947–65 results change dramatically when the period is shortened by one or more years. Results for two formulations of the total highway death rate regressions, one with permanent income and one with only a time trend, are shown. With only fifteen to eighteen observations, addition or deletion of an observation can make a major difference in the coefficient of speed or in the trend estimate. In both cases, a shortening of the period of estimation by as little as one year makes a major difference in many of the coefficients.

Our 1947–81 regression results for total highway deaths are not as sensitive to minor changes in the period of estimation, in part because of the greater number of observations available (see table C-4). There are small changes in the coefficients when the period of estimation is shortened by one or two years, but the changes are generally less than 10 percent of the value of the coefficient. Therefore these results appear much more stable than those derived from the 1947–65 period.

Second, Peltzman's model incorporates a trend term that he believes captures the effect of rising permanent income. Our results (table C-3) only partially confirm his result, for the addition of a permanent-income term contributes significantly to the explanatory power of the equations in only one of the five periods and reduces the value of the trend term.[5] Peltzman does not introduce permanent income explicitly; thus he obtains a very large (negative) trend in his estimates. He then uses these large negative trend values to predict future death rates. But if this trend represents the growth in permanent income, using the same value for the period since 1965 and for the 1947–65 period would be extremely misleading. The growth rate in permanent earned income since 1965 has been about one-third of the growth rate in 1947–65. Even in Peltzman's 1965–72

5. The permanent-income variable is constructed as a weighted sum of lagged real earned income with the weights reported in Hal R. Varian, "Friedman's Permanent Income Estimate," in Thomas Mayer, ed., *Permanent Income Wealth and Consumption* (University of California Press, 1972), app. 2. We use his results for B = 0.4.

Table C-4. Stability of the Coefficient for Total Highway Deaths, 1947–71 through 1947–81[a]

Independent variable	1947-71	1947-72	1947-73	1947-74	1947-75	1947-76	1947-77	1947-78	1947-79	1947-80	1947-81
SAFETY	0.735	0.755*	0.876*	0.949*	0.961*	0.979*	0.987*	0.978*	0.981*	1.027*	0.803*
	(1.80)	(2.08)	(3.57)	(3.91)	(3.99)	(4.37)	(4.39)	(4.14)	(4.27)	(5.28)	(4.67)
WEIGHT	-2.229*	-2.279*	-2.441*	-2.357*	-2.496*	-2.512*	-2.510*	-2.596*	-2.636*	-2.736*	-2.102*
	(2.42)	(2.55)	(3.18)	(3.00)	(3.27)	(3.55)	(3.53)	(3.50)	(3.79)	(4.73)	(4.05)
INCOME	1.343*	1.340*	1.275*	1.163*	1.153*	1.141*	1.115*	1.125*	1.127*	1.111*	1.266*
	(4.80)	(4.91)	(5.54)	(5.50)	(5.51)	(5.94)	(5.85)	(5.59)	(5.68)	(6.26)	(7.40)
SPEED	-0.366	0.357	0.422	0.785	0.644	0.608	0.586	0.540	0.522	0.468	0.670*
	(0.60)	(0.60)	(0.75)	(1.86)	(1.70)	(1.74)	(1.67)	(1.49)	(1.57)	(1.60)	(2.29)
LIMITED ACCESS	-0.029	-0.030	-0.038	-0.051*	-0.049*	-0.050*	-0.051*	-0.050*	-0.050*	-0.052*	-0.040*
	(0.99)	(1.04)	(1.66)	(2.65)	(2.60)	(2.84)	(2.90)	(2.71)	(2.72)	(3.07)	(2.36)
TRUCK	0.506*	0.500*	0.479*	0.445*	0.449*	0.463*	0.484*	0.475*	0.473*	0.486*	0.478*
	(4.01)	(4.28)	(4.66)	(4.26)	(4.34)	(4.84)	(5.13)	(4.75)	(4.76)	(5.26)	(4.85)
MILES	0.235	0.246	0.305	0.308	0.350	0.368	0.387	0.399	0.405	0.440*	0.224
	(0.85)	(0.91)	(1.35)	(1.31)	(1.54)	(1.77)	(1.86)	(1.82)	(1.91)	(2.50)	(1.49)
Summary statistic											
$\bar{R}^2$	0.983	0.985	0.987	0.986	0.986	0.986	0.986	0.986	0.986	0.987	0.985

* Statistically significant at the 95 percent confidence level.
a. Numbers in parentheses are t-statistics.

Table C-5. The Ratio of Actual to Predicted Death Rates for Three Alternative Trend Specifications in the 1947–65 Time-Series Regressions, 1966–81[a]

Year	Total death rate			Passenger-car-occupant death rate			Nonoccupant death rate		
	Permanent income and trend	Permanent income only	Trend only	Permanent income and trend	Permanent income only	Trend only	Permanent income and trend	Permanent income only	Trend only
1966	1.086	1.119	1.043	1.020	1.026	1.010	1.135	1.147	1.097
1967	1.098	1.137	1.044	1.001	0.994	0.987	1.193	1.182	1.148
1968	1.041	1.079	0.991	0.949	0.939	0.924	1.182	1.161	1.100
1969	0.984	1.016	0.946	0.895	0.875	0.870	1.157	1.113	1.066
1970	0.917	0.929	0.892	0.808	0.768	0.801	1.115	1.024	1.067
1971	0.771	0.773	0.766	0.705	0.670	0.697	0.964	0.885	0.892
1972	0.807	0.789	0.829	0.740	0.677	0.743	1.063	0.921	1.063
1973	0.758	0.729	0.798	0.676	0.608	0.683	1.083	0.907	1.116
1974	0.756	0.668	0.853	0.669	0.541	0.751	1.006	0.707	1.338
1975	0.772	0.672	0.901	0.683	0.529	0.775	1.064	0.696	1.464
1976	0.691	0.579	0.847	0.657	0.497	0.757	0.955	0.601	1.375
1977	0.741	0.622	0.914	0.652	0.482	0.746	1.167	0.704	1.697
1978	0.734	0.611	0.915	0.618	0.451	0.707	1.245	0.737	1.841
1979	0.756	0.612	0.978	0.665	0.469	0.780	1.264	0.705	1.971
1980	0.777	0.606	1.059	0.713	0.482	0.858	1.334	0.694	2.177
1981	0.729	0.551	1.037	0.696	0.455	0.857	1.265	0.621	2.167

a. All equations include ALCOHOL, LIMITED ACCESS, YOUTH, COST, INCOME, and SPEED as independent variables.

period, the growth rate in permanent earned income had declined by about 25 percent relative to 1947–65. Therefore, if one is to project fatality rates after 1965, one should take this reduction in the potential trend term into account.

The differences in projections between those equations containing a permanent-income term and those that do not are striking. The ratios of actual fatality rates to the predictions for the 1966–81 regulatory period from various 1947–65 regression results are displayed in table C-5. In each case, *SPEED, COST, INCOME, ALCOHOL, YOUTH,* and *LIMITED ACCESS* are included as independent variables. The trend component is captured by either permanent income or an exponential trend or both. The ratios of actual to predicted death rates are reported for each of the three equations for the three death rates—the total highway death rate, the ratio of passenger-car-occupant deaths to total vehicle miles, and the ratio of nonoccupant deaths to total vehicle miles. It is clear that the use of *TREND* alone leads to the Peltzman result—a reduction in occupant deaths relative to predictions, but an increase in nonoccupant deaths. On the other hand, using permanent income alone as the trend variable leads to a reduction in *all* death rates relative to predictions. Finally, including both variables generates predictions that are between the two extremes, with the total death rate actually somewhat below predictions for 1969–81. Use of an explicit permanent-income variable therefore appears to negate Peltzman's most important conclusion—that the increase in the nonoccupant death rate fully offsets the improvements in the occupant death rate generated by safety regulation.

Automobile Scrapping Rates

REGULATION that raises the cost of buying and operating new cars affects both the sales of new cars and the scrapping of old ones. Our modeling approach focuses on scrapping effects, using the implied effect on new car sales as a check on the reasonableness of the estimated scrapping effects.

The scrapping decision for an individual car is based on a comparison of its "dead" and "alive" values. Specifically, a car in need of repair is scrapped only if its market value in operable condition minus its scrap value is less than the cost of the required repair. Therefore the scrapping rate for any model of car is inversely related to its market value and directly related to the price of repairs and scrap values. It also depends on the repair incidence distribution, which is a function of design, manufacturing quality, and age.

New cars and used cars are substitutes. Any increase in the price or operating cost of new cars, including those attributable to regulation, causes substitution toward old ones. Starting from an initial equilibrium in all vehicle markets, such an increase would result in excess demand for used cars. As the supply of used cars is perfectly inelastic at any point in time, prices must rise to clear used car markets, which results in lower scrappage rates.

According to the mechanism outlined above, new car price developments affect scrappage rates solely through their impact on used car prices. However, the poor quality and limited coverage of the available used car price data forced us to adopt a reduced-form approach in which we used new car prices and other structural determinants of used car prices to explain scrappage rates directly. Estimates of the reduced-form regression model for scrappage rates are reported in table D-1. The coefficients *PAGED5-PAGED14* are used to adjust the vintage mix in the Environmental Protection Agency's MOBILE 2 model to account for the impact of higher new car prices resulting from regulation.

The reasonableness of the scrappage impact estimates can be tested

Table D-1. Reduced-Form Scrapping Rate Regression[a]

Independent variable [b]	Estimate	Independent variable [b]	Estimate
PR	3.415 (5.451)	PAGED10	−0.873 (−3.605)
ESM1	0.016 (12.065)	PAGED11	−1.139 (−4.520)
VMTPC	−0.202 (−1.261)	PAGED12	−1.338 (−4.932)
UMALE	−0.108 (−10.320)	PAGED13	−1.688 (−5.578)
YD72	−0.528 (−3.383)	PAGED14	−2.162 (−6.352)
RCP	−0.043 (−6.531)	AGED5	−2.963 (−9.389)
GASR	−0.896 (1.685)	AGED6	−2.672 (−10.211)
GASSY	−1.768 (−3.136)	AGED7	−2.540 (−11.287)
PSS	0.115 (5.844)	AGED8	−2.668 (−13.753)
PAGED5	−1.406 (−4.263)	AGED9	−2.443 (−14.219)
PAGED6	−1.632 (−5.509)	AGED10	−2.115 (−13.824)
PAGED7	−1.565 (−5.691)	AGED11	−1.669 (−11.481)
PAGED8	−1.077 (−4.220)	AGED12	−1.118 (−9.312)
PAGED9	−0.915 (−3.737)	AGED13	−0.597 (−5.519)
		Summary statistic $\bar{R}^2$	0.9657

Source: Howard K. Gruenspecht, "Differentiated Regulation: A Theory with Applications to Automobile Emissions Control" (Ph.D. dissertation, Yale University, 1982), p. 118.

a. Dependent variable is $\log(PS/(1-PS))$, where PS is the scrappage rate; numbers in parentheses are t-statistics. Results reported are for weighted least squares regression.

b. Definition of variables: PR = real repair price index; $ESM1$ = effective stock of vehicles in last period; $VMTPC$ = per capita vehicle miles traveled; $UMALE$ = male unemployment rate; $YD72$ = real disposable income per capita; RCP = commercial paper rate; $GASR$ = ratio of observation year to model year real gas prices; $GASSY$ = observation year real gas price; PSS = real steel scrap price index; $PAGED5-14 = PN \times AGED5-14$, real new car price index stratified by age (PN = BLS new car price index deflated by personal consumption deflator); and $AGED5-14$ = age dummies.

under the maintained hypothesis that the desired size of the vehicle stock is not sensitive to new car prices. Under this assumption, the reduction in scrappage is exactly matched by reductions in new car sales, so the scrappage impact estimates imply an estimate of the price elasticity of new car sales that can be compared with the numerous direct estimates. The fact that the implied price elasticity of 1.0 falls near the midpoint of the range of published direct estimates corroborates the validity of the estimation procedure.

MOBILE 2 incorporates a mapping between age and annual vehicle miles traveled to reflect the fact that new vehicles have a higher average annual mileage accumulation than old ones. If this relationship is held constant as the composition of the vehicle stock shifts in favor of old vehicles, the implied value of aggregate vehicle miles traveled will fall. In fact, it is unlikely that the aggregate demand for travel will fall as used cars are substituted for new ones. Therefore, as the composition of the vehicle stock shifts, the correspondence between vehicle miles traveled and age also shifts to allow for an unchanged aggregate level of vehicle miles traveled.

Since the model includes twenty vintage groups—with all vehicles twenty years old and up placed in the last category—it takes twenty years for scrapping rate changes to be reflected in a new steady state vintage mix.

Index

Regulating the Automobile

ROBERT W. CRANDALL,
HOWARD K. GRUENSPECHT,
THEODORE E. KEELER,
AND LESTER B. LAVE

Automobiles are subject to three major types of federal regulation: safety and emissions standards, which both began in the mid-1960s, and fuel economy, which began after the oil shock of the early 1970s. This provocative volume examines the costs and effectiveness of all three.

The authors point out that each of the regulatory programs operates independently of the others and that they have conflicting goals: for example, both emissions and safety standards contribute to decreased fuel economy. More significantly, because safety and emissions regulations have greatly increased the price of new American cars — an estimated additional $1,300–$2,200 per car by 1981 — people have put off replacing their old, less safe, less fuel-efficient, and more polluting cars. This has exacerbated the very problems the regulations were supposed to cure. Also, the regulations have created problems of reliability in American cars and have added to the pressure for trade protectionism against Japanese competitors because of their effects upon sales and employment. The authors recommend removing the fuel economy standards, relaxing the emissions standards, and attempting to coordinate the goals of all three forms of regulation.

Robert W. Crandall is a senior fellow in the Economic Studies program at Brookings. Howard K. Gruenspecht is assistant professor of economics in the Graduate School of Industrial Administration at Carnegie-Mellon University. Theodore E. Keeler is professor of economics at the University of California at Berkeley. Lester B. Lave, a former senior fellow in the Brookings Economic Studies program, is now James H. Higgins Professor of Economics at the Carnegie-Mellon Graduate School of Industrial Administration.